Cardiff a

Cardiff and The Vale Records 1

Shopkeepers and Tradesmen in Cardiff and The Vale 1633-1857

What could you buy from local shops and tradesmen 350, 250 or 150 years ago?

The Evidence from Old Documents

Introduction and transcription
of original documents by

PETER BOWEN

Published by Peter Bowen

Copyright © 2004 Peter Bowen

Published by
Peter Bowen
146 Llandaff Road, Canton, Cardiff, CF11 9PW
Telephone: (02920) 216519

The right of Peter Bowen to be identified as the
Author of the Work has been asserted by him in
accordance with the Copyright, Designs
and Patents Act 1988.

*All rights reserved. No part of this publication may be
reproduced, stored in a retrieval system or transmitted, in
any form or by any means without the prior permission of
the publisher, nor be otherwise circulated in any form of
binding or cover other than that in which it is published
and without similar condition being imposed
on the subsequent purchaser.*

A CIP catalogue record for this book is
available from the British Library.

ISBN 0-9548794-0-6

Printed and bound in Wales by
Dinefwr Press Ltd.
Rawlings Road, Llandybie
Carmarthenshire, SA18 3YD

Acknowledgements

During the early 1990s, the Education Advisory Service of the County of South Glamorgan bought a considerable number of Probate Wills and Inventories from the National Library of Wales as part of its resource material for the local history component of the National Curriculum. It is these documents to which I have been given access by Alan Geach, Humanities Adviser for the City and County of Cardiff, and Richard Evans of the Vale of Glamorgan County Council, the Authorities that replaced South Glamorgan. Thanks are due to both gentlemen and to the new Councils. Small sections of some of the documents are in Latin. I am most grateful to Michael Wilcox of the Glamorgan Record Office for aid in translation. Finally, I thank the National Library of Wales for permission to include photocopies of small sections of original wills and inventories – two of the mid-seventeenth century, two of the mid-eighteenth, and two of the mid-nineteenth century. Those not familiar with these sources will, thus, be able to see examples of these documents in their raw state.

Peter Bowen
May 2004

Contents

Introduction	9
Copies of Original Inventories and Wills	29
The Documents: Probate Inventories of Shopkeepers and Tradesmen:	
Village Shopkeepers	32
Pedlars	47
Keepers of General Shops/Provisions Stores in 'Towns'	49
Hardware Trades: Hardware Shop Owners; Chandler; Blacksmiths	75
Fabric Trades: Weavers; Tailor; Mercers; Feltmakers/Hatter; Hoziers	85
Leather Trades: Tanners; Cordwainers; Sadlers; Glovers	131
Wood Trades: Carpenters; Cooper; Sawyer; Ship Builder; Builder	155
Farmers with Commercial Interests; Gardener	167
Salters	183
Gentlemen with Commercial Interests; Parson with Bookbinders' Press	189
Mariners	191
Innkeepers/Maltsters; Vintner	205
Appendices – Summary	239
Appendix 1 – The Inventory of James Harries of Usk, mercer/chandler etc.	240
Appendix 2 – The Inventory, List of Debts and Administration Bond of Jennet John of the parish of Llancarvan, widow	250
Appendix 3 – A Tabular Record of Information from every Inventory relating to the seven major categories of wealth, converted to a cash value and a percentage of the total wealth of each individual	252
Appendix 4 – Charts Relating Value of Estate to Value of Clothing, Value of Household Goods and amount of Debt Owing	252
Glossary	261

List of Illustrations

The opening section of the Inventory of Richard Sheeres
of Cardiff, mercer, dated 19th January, 1659/60 29

The opening section of the Will of Richard Sheeres
of Cardiff, mercer, dated 30th December, 1659 29

Selected sections of the Inventory of Edward Evans
of Cardiff, carpenter, dated 12th November, 1751 30

The opening section of the Will of Edward Evans
of Cardiff, carpenter, dated 10th October, 1751 30

Selected sections of the Inventory of Nathaniel Young
of Cowbridge, sadler, dated 12th May, 1842 31

Opening section of the Will of Nathaniel Young
of Cowbridge, sadler, dated 29th May, 1838 31

Introduction

What could people buy from shops or tradesmen in Cardiff and the Vale 350, 250, or 150 years ago? Most people might well think that such information was never recorded, and for the most part this is probably true. However, excellent information still survives in documents called probate inventories, and it is these documents that forms the main body of this book. One probate inventory, that of an eighteenth century Cowbridge grocer, Richard John, has been selected to provide an introduction to the documents. Richard John's wife, Joan, obtained a grant of administration from the local probate court – the Consistory Court of the Diocese of Llandaff – in November, 1715, and a condition of the grant was that an inventory of her late husband's estate be made. Richard John's inventory is short, but it still contains information about almost all the major categories of personal wealth that are described in probate inventories. These categories are: (1) clothing; (2) household goods; (3) livestock/crops/farm machinery; (4) shop/trade goods; (5) debts owed or owing; and (6) leases held. The only important missing element is (7) 'ready money,' – cash in hand. For the purposes of this Introduction, each of these categories of wealth is identified in the Richard John inventory, and this information is then viewed alongside related information from the other inventories in the book. Each 'item' in the John inventory has been numbered (not present in the original), to make its identification simpler in the discussion which follows.

A true & perfect Inventory of all & singular the Goods, Chattles & Creditts of Richard John of Cowbridge in the County of Glamorgan & Diocess of Landaffe Grocer Lately dece[ase]d, taken, valued & appraised the 24th day of November An[n]o D[omi]ni 1715 by the persons undernamed appointed appraisors

	li s d
1 Imp[ri]mis His wearing apparel at	01-00-00
2 It[e]m two feather beds in the hall with its appurtenances, Chaires tables & other goods there standing at	03-00-00
3 It[e]m one feather bed with its appurtenances over the hall with Chairs & tables etc	02-00-00

4	It[e]m Two beds with its appurtenances in the Chamber over the shop with other goods etc	02-10-00
5	It[e]m Brass & pewter in the kitchen with tables and other fine goods & materialls	05-00-00
6	It[e]m In the chamber over the kitchen; cheese Butter & pipes etc.	04-00-00
7	It[em] in the store Roome, Iron, leather and other lumber	13-00-00
8	It[em] in the salt Roome i Tunn of salt	08-00-00
9	It[em] in the milking Roome Pannes & pailes etc.	00-05-00
10	It[em] All manner of shop goods at	45-00-00
11	It[em] In Corne of all sorte etc.	07-00-00
12	It[em] five Cows, 49 sheep & a horse	31-00-00
13	It[em] Hey at	07-00-00
14	It[em] a Chattle Lease at	02-10-00
15	It[em] Money due by Bonds	<u>137-10-00</u>
		268-15-00

appraisors Richard Bates Owen Morgans Edward Morgan Richard Jenkin Sworn by Joan John, alias Miles, relict and administratrix, before Franc. Davies, surrogate, 19th December, 1715.

Administration Bond: Richard John: 19th December, 1715

In the Consistory Court of Llandaff, 19th December, 1715, administration of the goods etc. of Richard John, alias Jones, deceased, was granted to his widow, Joan John, alias Miles, alias Jones. Joan John and John Miles of the parish of Porthkerry, were bound by the Court in the sum of £300 for Joan John to make and exhibit a true inventory of the goods etc. of her late husband at or before the 19th March next, to administer according to law, to give a true account of her administration at or before the 19th December 1716, and to present to the Court any last will and testament of the deceased that might appear. Both John John and John Miles signed the administration bond.

[National Library of Wales Document Reference: LL /1715 /27]

A probate inventory was usually taken soon after the death of a person who usually possessed at least some degree of wealth. The date of Richard John's death is not known, and if, as is possible, he was buried in the parish church of Cowbridge, no record of his burial exists, as the burial registers for the parish date from 1735, the earlier registers not surviving. The valuation or 'appraisal' of an estate – Richard John's 'goods, chattles and creditts' – was made by two or more local peers of the dead person, and for Richard John there were four named appraisers. If the deceased person was a tradesman or a specialist shopkeeper, at least one of the appraisers would belong to the trade or craft of the deceased, as the valuation of specialist goods required a good knowledge of that trade and its products or sale goods. It is likely, therefore, that at least one of Richard John's appraisers was a shopkeeper and grocer. Richard John did not leave a will, and consequently, an administration bond was required to grant his wife the legal power to administer his estate.

Item 1 of the inventory values Richard John's clothes at £1. A valuation for clothes is given in 102 out of the 109 inventories in the book, but in 99 of these documents the only information given is, 'his (or her) wearing apparel,' plus a valuation. Clearly, the listing of actual garments owned is a rare occurance. The three inventories that list clothing are those of John Thomas, Thomas Young and Job Hopwell, all shopkeepers, the first of Laleston, the others of Cardiff, who died in 1710, 1760 and 1856 respectively. Of the seven inventories in which no valuation for clothing is given, four are for persons with estate ranging in value from £729 to £1584, very consisderable sums. In 73 documents clothing is valued at £3 or less. In all but two of the remainder, the value of clothing is between £3+ and £11. John Wollrin, a Cardiff salter with considerable farming interests, owning estate valued at £1117-3-0, had clothing valued at £30 when he died in 1673. Henry Hill, a country gentleman of St. Athan, owned estate valued at £1135 and possessed clothing valued at £50 at his death in 1666.

As one would expect, there is a broad positive link between the value of a person's clothing and how wealthy a person was. However, as in the case of Richard John, it was possible to have considerable wealth – £268-15-00 – and still own clothing valued at £1, a valuation typical of persons with total wealth of less than £20. And Richard John's case is far from unique. John Stidder, a Cowbridge shopkeeper (1737), had clothing valued at £2 and estate of £826-12-4. Katherine Hammond, widow (1720), also of Cowbridge, had estate of £883-17-10½ and clothing of £3. In contrast, there are examples of persons with relatively low total wealth but high value clothing, but these are far less common. Richard Jenkins of Llanishen (1698) had clothing valued at £6, almost 25% of his total wealth, but he was a parson and a 'gentleman.' Only 14 out of 102 persons had clothing worth more than £6. Elizabeth Lambert, a Cardiff shopkeeper (1685), had estate of £50 and clothes of £10. Just three people had clothing of greater value. More detailed information relating to clothing can be studied in the first chart in Appendix 4.

Items 2 to 5 of the inventory list Richard John's household goods. This particular inventory only gives the barest details of household goods, but fortunately, this is not repeated in most other documents. As can be seen, all the named household items in John's inventory are basic necessities, essentials for everyday living, and this is a feature of most other inventories, dominated as they are by details of beds, bedding, tables, chairs, stooles, cupboards, fire-irons, grates, cooking vessels, candlesticks, earthenware, metal and wooden kitchen ware. In some documents, however, it is obvious that items of a quality well above the basic are being described, either because of high-quality material, or of skilled workmanship. In Richard John's inventory, there is reference to 'other fine goods & materials,' but, sadly, no detail. In 45 documents, items which at that period were non-essential, even 'luxury' items, are mentioned. Thirteen people listed silver plate amongst their possessions. In five instances, the plate was valued at between £20 and £30, and in each of these cases, the owners had estate valued at between £883 and £1360. Seven people possessed silver goods; six owned rings or jewels; seven owned clocks, and six watches. Three of the watch owners lived in the mid-nineteenth century, and two of the others were mid-eighteenth century mariners. Musical instruments are listed in four inventories: John Wollrin and Henry Hoare each owned a pair of virginals, a spinet and frame was owned by Robert Priest of Cardiff, mariner, (1742), and a citterne was owned by Thomas Spencer of the parish of Penmark, also a mariner, (1681). Only fifteen people owned books, the bible being named in two inventories. Looking glasses are recorded in fourteen documents, with Morgan Jenkins, a Cardiff chandler (1737), owing four, Robert Priest three, and William Hiley, a Cardiff mercer (1723), two. Three people owned maps, two of these being mariners. Sixteen people possessed pictures or prints, and one owned just a picture frame. Out of the 45 people owning these 'non-essential' items, 18 owned just a single item and 13 owned two items, one of these being Robert Hodds of Llandaff, innkeeper (1687), who owned '3 paper pictures,' and '1 bird cage.' Mary Lewis of Cardiff, shopkeeper (1720), owned a Bible [valued at] 9^d, eight large pictures 8^d, five small pictures 3^d, two books 1/-, a looking glass 2/-, and an hour-glass 3^d. Arthur Yeoman of Cardiff, glover (1719), owned 'one Looking glass . . . one Clocke & Case ffive Small maps Seaven pictures.' As well as the four looking glasses he owned, Morgan Jenkins possessed five pictures 'in the Little Parlour,' eight pictures 'in the best Chamber,' 'a Small quantity of Plate at £2,' and 'a Small parcell of Books at 5/-.' Hopkin Williams of Cardiff, maltster (1735), owned 'a Parcell of old Books at £1-17-0,' 'one Silver Watch at £2-12-6,' and 'one Silver Cup weighing 5 ounces at 5^s an Ounce £1-5-0,' and Robert Priest owned a watch valued at £4, three maps, 'a Parcell of Books' at 10/-, 'a brass Door Knocker' at 6/-, three looking glasses, with one of gilt, 'three Clothes Brushes' at 1/-, 'one plate Warmer' at 2/6, as well as 'a Spinet and Frame at Mr William Richard's [at] £2-2-0.' Robert Priest also possessed furniture made of mahogany, and in total, his household goods were valued at £75-4-7. In comparison with the household goods of John Wollrin, this total was small, Wollrin's possessions being valued at £204-18-0, and listing a range of expensive, hand-worked soft furnishings. However, the most interesting and varied list of 'luxury' household goods is found in the inventory of Jonathan Greenfield of Cardiff, even though the total value of his household goods was only £50-12-0. Greenfield is described as a mariner in the documents, but he held significant posts in customs and excise for the Town of Cardiff between 1689 and 1724, and his estate was valued at £4,525 in 1736, three times larger than the estate of any other person recorded in the book. The following provides a 'taster' of the document's contents: 17 alabaster images, 47 pictures, 'a China Punch Bowle,' 'Six Gold Rings one silver Tankard ten Silver Spoons two Silver plates two silver Salts two Silver Porringers two Silver Cupps one Silver Sugar Dish,' 'Glasses and Wax work on the Mantle Piece,' 'one Weather Glass,' 122 pieces of pewter all initialled, 'three whole peeces of Lace marked K:J: and a remnant of Scollup Lace,' and 'a Glass of fflowers.'

All but three of the inventories in the book list and value household goods, but, in the cases of three innkeepers, it is difficult to separate household goods from similar goods that would have been an essential part of the innkeeper's trade goods. Consequently, a valuation for household goods has been obtained for 103 documents, with the lowest total being seven shillings and the highest £204-18-0. 67 of the 103 documents record household goods valued at less than £20, and of these 26 have household goods valued between 0 & £5, 16 between £5 & £10, 13 between £10 & £15, and 12 between £15 & £20. Between £20 & £40 are 15 people; between £40 & £60 8 persons; between £60 & £100 a further 10 people, and over £100 3 people. As with clothing, the link between greater total wealth and household possessions of greater value is clear, but, once again, it is equally clear that the link was broadly based, ensuring that the value of ones household goods was not an immediate indicator of the value of ones estate, as the following three examples illustrate. First, of the 26 people who owned household goods valued between £0-£5, 9 had total wealth of less than £10, 8 total wealth of between £10 & £20, 5 total wealth between £20 & £40, 2 between £40 & £100, and two, Edward Rees and Thomas Gronow, both farmers who died in 1720, with total estate of £109-1-0 and £182-9-10. Second, Rees and Gronow were 2 of 17 persons with total estate valued between £100 and £200. A valuation for household goods could be made for only 15 of these people, and, in the chart below, each of these valuations has been placed, as appropriate, into one of eight 'value of household goods' groups: '0 - £4+;' '£5 - £9+;' '£10 - £14+;' .... '£50 - £55.'

Value of H'se Goods	0-£4+	£5-£9+	£10-£14+	£15-£19+	£20-£29+	£40-£44+	£45-£49+	£50-£55
Number of Persons	2	1	2	3	2	2	2	1

The spread is remarkable, as is its evenness.

Third, out of the 103 inventories, eleven people possessed household goods valued at between £15 and £20. In this £15-£20 group were (i) Henry Spencer, a Llandaff shoemaker (1643), with estate of £30-7-8, and household goods of £16-14-8 (57% of his total wealth); (ii) Thomas Powell, a Cardiff carpenter (1732), with estate of just £22-9-10, and household goods of £19-17-10 (which included ale valued at £1-15-0), 88% of his total wealth; and (iii) Elias Jones, a Cardiff builder (1854), with estate of £729-19-6, and household goods of £17-19-6, 2½% of his total wealth. To repeat, the value of ones household goods was not an immediate indicator of the value of ones estate. In Appendix 4, the second and third tables provide further detail of the relationship between value of household goods and value of a person's estate.

The individuals with household goods valued at more than £100 were: John Wollrin, already mentioned; Thomas Jones, a Cardiff wholesale hosier (1686) – £120-10-0; and Cradock Nowell, Alderman of Cardiff (1709), with business interests in tanning, malting etc. – £140-10-0. In each of these cases, household goods formed approximately 20% of total wealth, small in comparison with the following three estates: John Hammans, a Cardiff cooper (1684), had estate of £38-12-2, and household goods of £28-6-4, 73% of his total wealth; Anstance Wells of Cardiff, widow (1705), had estate of £49-6-6, and household goods of £32-0-6, 65% of her total wealth; and Arthur Yeomans, a Cardiff glover/shopkeeper (1686), had estate of £91-10-0 and household goods of £61-10-0, 66% of his total wealth.

Item 10 of Richard John's inventory is 'all manner of shop goods.' Items 6 & 7 – 'cheese, Butter & pipes,' 'Iron, leather & lumber' – are, at least in part, shop goods held in store. Item 8 – a ton of salt – is undoubtedly salt for sale. Together, these items give a total value for shop goods of £70 – a very considerable sum – and 24% of John's total wealth. It is also possible that 'other fine goods & materials' relates to stored shop goods. Without the detail of Richard John's stored shop goods, the only record of his shop would be 'all manner of shop goods,' together with their very high valuation of £45. 'All the goods in the shop,' however, is not infrequently the only record of a shop found in inventories. Similarly, inventories of craftsman might only record the number of loomes owned (see John Alexander, Llancarvan, 1633; David William, Llanblethian, 1701), or give a list of the tools in a blacksmith's shop (John Thomas, Cowbridge, 1685; Walter Hart, St. Andrew's, 1696). On the other hand, there are inventories of glovers (Samuel William, 1668, Lodwick Gronow 1671, both of Cowbridge), of a chandler (Morgan Jenkins, Cardiff, 1737), of carpenters (Thomas Smyth 1694, Thomas Powell 1732, Edward Evans 1751, all of Cardiff), and of a tanner (William David, Cowbridge, 1690), that give information on shop goods owned, and all the raw materials of trade that these craftsman possessed. Similarly, there are shop inventories that give a finely detailed list of thirty, fifty, a hundred, even two hundred items of shop goods.

The inventories associated with the hosiery trade that are included in the book record all stages of the network associated with this trade, from cottage production (Ann Howell, Peterston-super-Ely, 1715; Mary Miles, Bonvilston, 1725); to local middleman (Richard John St. George's, 1674); to large scale wholesaler (John Jenkins, Cardiff, 1684; Thomas Jones, Cardiff, 1686); to hosiery shopkeeper (Myles Evans, Cardiff, 1665, Job Hipwell, Cardiff, 1856). Local weavers, too, might well have sold their fabric to Thomas Jones as his inventory states, '5 packs of Stokins fflannens and Inkles valued at £150.' The only document giving actual details of locally woven fabric is the inventory of James Richards, tucker, of Llanblethian (1725).

Inventories of mercers figure prominently amongst the documents of highest quality, with that of John Vallence of Cowbridge, who died in 1750, being unequalled, perhaps. Three of the items for sale in Vallence's shop were: '1095 yards of Stuffs at 10^d per yd;' '945 yards of Fustians & Checks at 12^d per yd;' '770 yards of Chinease Berrin crapes and Plads at 12^d per yd.' The quantity of fabric is staggering, and no shop owner would hold such stock unless it sold well. The Vallence document also contains a lists of debtors, recorded in three shop books, and arranged under four headings – 'debtors name,' 'habitation,' good debts,' 'bad debts.' The 159 names listed give clues to the social class of Vallence's clientele, as well as to the geographical extent of the shop's drawing power, which was considerable. The only other document with a list of debtors of similar size is the inventory of Hopkin Williams, a Cardiff innkeeper (1735), which names 143 people who, presumably, had been allowed credit for drink. These too came from far and wide.

As well as the excellent inventories for mercers, there are documents of similar quality for saddler/shopkeepers (David Griffiths, Colwinston, 1719, Thomas Glascot, Cardiff, 1732, Nathaniel Young, Cowbridge, 1842); for a hardware store owner (John Watkin, Cardiff, 1763); for a glover (Arthur Yeomans, Cardiff, 1719); for village stores (Walter Hart, St. Andrews, 1696, Jane Lewis, Llanbleddian, 1696, Joseph Leckey, Llantwit Major, 1708, John Thomas, Laleston, 1710); for general & provision store owners in towns (Henry Hammonds, 1700, Thomas Edwards, 1704, William Foord, 1717, Mary Lewis, 1720, Florence Brewer, 1740, Thomas Young, 1760, all of Cardiff); and for a Cardiff gardener, William Jones (1763). The range of goods available in these shops was truly amazing. It is doubtful whether any glove shop today would match the variety available in Arthur Yeomans' shop in 1719, and the list of raw materials he possessed is equally remarkable. Also, who would imagine that, in Cardiff, 250 years ago, amongst the produce of William Jones would be 172 'holes' of cucumber, and that cherry, peach and nectarin trees were growing 'in the Fryers garden.' No doubt William Jones sold his produce in local markets, and, perhaps, at Bristol, if the practice of Edward Rees, an Ely farmer, who died in 1720, was continued.

There is also excellent detail in the inventories of innkeepers. Richard Sheeres, an alderman of Cardiff (1662), ran a truly 'five-star' inn. His inventory lists the contents of his wine and beer cellars, valued at £95-10-00 and £6-12-00 respectively, with a single item in the wine cellar valued at £54 – 'Three hogseds of Malligo sacke at £18 p[er] hog.' The inventory also lists the furniture and soft furnishings of six named rooms in his inn, each valued separately, and with a total value of £153-13-06. One room, 'the Angell Chamber,' contained items valued at £31-16-04. A photocopy of a small section of the Richard Sheeres' inventory appears on page 29. The full contents of the wine and ale cellars of Robert Hodds of Llandaff (1687) are also recorded and valued (at £45) in his inventory, as is 'the stock in trade' of three nineteenth century Cardiff 'victuallers,' as they were called, Catherine Powell, John Morgan, and John Nisbett. Amongst Catherine Powell's stock was 10 gallons of rum, 4 gallons of gin, 2 gallons of brandy, 1 gallon of peppermint, 2 gallons of raspberry brandy, 3 gallons of whisky, as well as 5 barrels of beer and 1 gallon of porter. The 'Schedule of Debts' of John Nisbett of Cardiff (1846), show that one of his ale suppliers was based in Bath. By the mid-nineteenth century, distance between production and consumption of ale was often considerable, whereas in previous centuries the networks were local as the inventories of Wenllian James and John Vallence show.

The survival of so many high quality documents might give the impression that shop/trade data is plentiful in probate documents. However, out of approximately 1,000 local inventories that have been studied, only a little over a hundred contain any detail relating to shop goods, or goods available from tradesmen. Consequently, an inventory with only a single relevant detail is a comparative rarity and is valuable. 'All ye goods in ye shop;' 'the shop and all that is in it;' 'ye shop goods;' these are the only fragments of evidence for shops at Bonvilston, Merthyr Dyfan and St. Andrews in 1673, 1708 and 1720. They appear in the inventories of Thomas Mawrice, Margaret Richards, and Thomas Gronow, and their shop goods were valued at £5, £15 and £40 respectively. What the actual contents of these shops were will never be known, but with information from contemporary shop inventories in similar rural locations, it is possible to make a good guess at their likely contents. The inventories for seven village shopkeepers are recorded in the book, and apart from those mentioned above, there are records of shops at St. Athan (1642), St. Andrews/Dinas Powys (1696), Llanblethian (1696), Llantwit Major (1708) and Laleston (1710). Dr. Moelwyn Williams states in Volume IV of the *Glamorgan County History* that 'almost every village in the county had its shop.' It seems likely, however, that documentary evidence for many of these shops has been lost or was never recorded.

One other single detail demands mention. In the inventory of Anstance Wells of Cardiff, widow/maltster? (1705), is the following intriguing entry: 'In ye Inner Shopp In plague Water [valued at] £3.'

Items 9, 11, 12 & 13 of Richard John's inventory relate to his farming stock – 'In Corne of all sorte etc. £7;' 'five cows 49 sheep & a horse £31;' 'Hey at

£7;' 'in the milking Roome pannes & pailes etc. 5/-.' Their total value was £45-05-00, or 15% of Richard John's total wealth. The scale of his farming does not seem large, but the total value is twelfth highest out of the 61 persons in the book whose inventories record at least some interest in livestock or crops. The table below provides an overview of the value of the farming element in the estates of these 61 individuals, with number of individuals in each group recorded beneath:

Value of Farm 'Goods'	£452	£195	£118-£134	£53-£76	£45-£49	£30-£40	£20-£30	£10-£20	0-£10
No. of Persons in Value Group	1	1	3	5	3	6	4	10	28

Seven of the 61 persons – Richard John of St. George's (1674), Robert Bawdrey of 'place Turton,' Cardiff (1705), Edward Rees of Ely (1720), Thomas Gronow of St. Andrew's (1720), Morgan Howell of Whichurch (1722), Edward Wattkins of Llanishen (1729), and, William Lee of Cadoxton (1776), – are described as 'farmer' or 'yeoman' in their probate documents, and the value of the farming element in each person's estate was, £53-7-6; £126-8-0; £69-4-6; £75-19-10; £28-7-6; £45-2-8; and £36-1-0, respectively. In addition to their main employment in farming, each one had a commercial 'side-line.' Richard John (of St. George's) was a middleman in the hosiery trade; Robert Bawdrey linked his barley growing with the large-scale sale of brewing mault; Edward Wattkins was involved in the marketing of coal; Morgan Howell sold lime and carried 'Coals and Stones to the furnace;' William Lee produced and sold cider and cider vinegar; Thomas Gonow, like Richard John (of Cowbridge), owned a shop (with shop goods valued at £40); and Edward Rees was involved in the direct marketing of his peas 'in Bristoll & at home.' The inventory of William Lee is particularly interesting, because, although brewhouses and their equipment are frequently listed amongst possessions in inventories, the only one giving details of actual production is that of William Lee, but it is cider production, not beer. The Morgan Howell inventory also has an extra dimension, hinting as it does at the industrial activity that was taking place in Whitchurch parish in the early eighteenth century along the river Taff.

Just as some farmers diversified, so did individuals in other trades. The salter, John Wollrin, who owned at his death 'fffifty eight tonns of french & Spanish Salt,' and 'two Salt pans & Materialls,' valued in all at £230, 20% of his estate, also owned 600 sheep, 30 oxen, 17 swine, 3 cows, 2 yearlings, 60 stone of wool, and £50 worth of mault. The total value of his farming wealth was £452, almost double the value of his salt trade wealth. Of the four people with farming interests valued at between £118 and £134, only one was named a farmer – Robert Bawdrey. The others were Wenllian James of Llandaff (1685), an innkeeper/maltster; Thomas Jones of Cardiff (1686), a wholesale hosier; and Thomas Spencer of the parish of Penmark (1681), a mariner.

The inventories indicate, too, that the trades of weaving and shoemaking married well with small-scale farming. Rees John Hopkin, a weaver of Llanishen parish (1653), owned 'Two weaves or loomes togeather w[i]th all the instruments and appurtenances thereunto belonging,' valued at £1, but he also owned 6 milch kine, 2 heifers, 2 horse, swine and hay, valued at £16 in total, or 84% of the value of his estate. Two other weavers, Morgan Edmund of Whitchurch (1689), and John Tucker of St. Andrews (1691), possessed farming goods valued at £22-5-00 and £14-8-0 respectively, or 48% and 61% of their total estate. Three shoemakers, Edward Matthew of Cowbridge (1667), William Rees of Pyle & Kenfig (1690), and John Griffiths of St. Andrews (1731), owned farming goods valued at £37-10-00, £4-5-0 and £2-0-0, or 58%, 53% and 47% of the value of their total estate. The farm 'goods' of Morgan Edmund consisted of crops valued at £18-5-0, livestock at £0-10-0, and farm machinery at £3-10-0. In only 8 cases out of 61 was the value of crops greater than that of livestock.

Nineteen shopkeepers had some interest in crops or livestock, but, apart from five, their interests were small scale – a working horse or pigs for fattening. Of the twenty eight persons with livestock or crops valued at less than £10, eleven owned a single, or two horses, and seven owned a pig. The autumn slaughter of animals and the preservation of meat through salting, link well with the huge quantities of salt that John Wollrin and Richard John offered for sale locally in the seventeenth and eighteenth centuries.

Item 14 gives a valuation of £2-10-0 for the unexpired term of a chattel lease held by Richard John. Detail of leases owned is found in sixteen other documents in the book, with Richard John's lease being the least valuable. The other leases were valued at £5, £16, two at £20, £32, £37, £40, £50, £60, £64, £65, £73, £150, £180, four, collectively, at £180, and a further four, collectively, at £280. Six of these leases, and probably seven, were for houses in Cowbridge or Cardiff, the remaining leases being for parcels of land, or for whole farms, which included farm house and outbuildings. Chattel leases were held for a fixed term of years. Other leases were often held for a term of three lives, the lease lapsing on the death of the last-surviving, named person. Leases sometimes record the name of the actual farm being leased, and these, of course, are especially interesting. The £150 lease, listed above. was held by Robert Bawdrey, who died in 1705 with estate valued at £693-09-07½. The lease details are: 'one Lease granted by Sir John Aubrey & others to the said Robert Bawdrey in his life time for three lives one of ye lives bee dead and two are in being in a tenement of Land called place Turton valued to £150-00-00.' Today, of course, 'place Turton' is an area of Canton, Cardiff. A photograph of the farm house, taken at the time of its demolition at the end of the nineteenth century by the Cardiff photographer, William Booth, is in the local studies collection of the Cardiff Central Library. The valuation of £150 on the lease of 'place Turton' was an estimation based on the likely profit to be made from the land during the likely period of possession – the two remaining lives. The single lease for £180 was held in 1700 by Henry Hammonds, a Cardiff shopkeeper, and was for a farm called Pentrebane. Pentrebane farm still stands today on the north western edge of Cardiff, and it gives its name to a neighbouring district of the City. One of the four leases owned by Henry Hill of St. Athan, who died in 1666, was on 'lands in the parish of Colwinston in the County of Glamorgan called Claypit.' The four leases valued at £280 were held by a Cardiff tanner, Cradock Nowell in 1709. Two were for houses in Cardiff; one of which was called 'ye little-Angell;' a third was for 'ye fulling Mill;' and the fourth for 'Cross bychan,' a farmhouse in the Cathays area of Cardiff, again demolished at the end of the nineteenth century. Of the six farmers whose probate documents are included in the book, four held leases, and, presumably, farmed leasehold land. There is no mention of land in the inventories of Richard John (of St.George's) or Edward Wattkins, and therefore, it is likely that they farmed freehold land, which unlike leasehold land, was not valued for probate purposes.

Item 15 gives a value of £132-10-0 for money owed to Richard John by Bond. Often in inventories, the detail of each Bond is described separately, giving the amount owed and the name of the debtor. An example of this practice is found in the inventory of Richard John of St. George's (1674). In total, 61 documents record debts owed to the deceased. In five documents, the deceased is recorded as a debtor. John Nisbett, a Cardiff publican who died in 1846, left debts of £183-16-9, more than twice the value of his assets, and David Griffiths, a pedlar of Colwinston parish (1686), owed £17-0-6 and had assets of £18-3-0. In the inventories, debt owing to the deceased is usually described as being 'by Book;' 'by note;' 'by Bond;' 'by

Mortgage;' or 'by Specialities.' It is also usual for each debt to be described as either 'sperate debt,' meaning 'good' or recoverable debt, or as 'desperate debt,' meaning 'bad' or irrecoverable debt. Debt by note or book were the most readily obtainable types of credit, and were, as the records show, available from shopkeepers or alehouse keepers. Debt by bond, mortgage or specialities were more formal forms of debt, and might well involve the writing of legal documents. The £132-10-00 owed to Richard John by bond was 46% of his estate, and, although no indication is given as to whether it was 'sperate' or 'desperate' debt, it is probable that he had lent wisely, like any other good business man.

Richard John's estate was valued at £286-15-0, and the estates of eight other people fall into a £200-£300 'wealth band.' As all but one of these eight estates was owed money in substantial amounts, the choice of this particular group for close examination in relation to debt is particularly apt. The amounts owed to the eight people were as follows: £56-5-3 & £189-10-0 was owed to two innkeepers/maltsters – Wenllian James (1685) & Robert Hodds (1687) – both of Llandaff; £79-12-7, £15, £95-19-8, and £63-5-4 was owed to four shopkeepers – Walter Hart (1696), Joseph Hoar (1707), James Leckey (1708), and Arthur Yeomans (1719) – of St. Andrews, Cardiff, Llantwit Major and Cardiff, respectively; £229 was owed to a felt-maker – William Lewis of Cardiff (1731); and £92-6-10 to a chandler – Morgan Jenkins of Cardiff (1737). The debts owed to Wenllian James were for barrels of ale, much of which was supplied to other innkeepers, and her inventory just states, 'debts due to the deceased.' The £15 owed to Joseph Hoar was 'book debt,' as was the £95-19-8 owed to James Leckey, but in James Leckey's case, the debt is described as 'both sperate and desperate.' The £229 which William Lewis had lent represented 90% of his total assets, and were due 'By Mortgages bonds and book,' but no indication is given of the extent to which they were recoverable. In the four remaining cases, the amount of good and bad debt was clearly stated. Every penny of the £189-10-0 owing to Robert Hodds was desperate debt, 66% of his total wealth, and a fraction less than half of the £79-12-7 owing to Walter Hart was desperate. £17-17-2 of the debt owing to Arthur Yeomans was irrecoverable, as was £19 owing to Morgan Jenkins. Out of total estate of £2266-11-8 for the 9 persons in the £200-£300 wealth group, £853-10-4 (37%) was debt owing to them. The total trade goods of these people was £650-9-0, and the total of their trade goods plus farming stock was £860-18-0. Debt owing was, therefore, almost exactly equal to their 'trading' assets. In the last table in Appendix 4, the 'debt' data for the £200-£300 'wealth group' is given in tabular form, and is placed alongside that of ten other 'wealth groups' based on estate value.

The evidence of the inventories indicates that whereas as much as a half of the book debt owed to shopkeepers was likely to be desperate, the considerable sums that businessmen loaned by note, bonds, mortgages or specialities were far more secure. John Greenfield had 'Sperate debts by Bonds and Mortgages' totalling £4,124, as well as £83 'By Notes.' Just £205 of the money loaned by him, 4½% of his total loans, was described as 'Desperate Debts.' Robert Priest died with total estate of £610-5-7, sperate debts of £250, book debts of £25, 'ready money' of £50, and desperate debts of just £2. The £800 loaned by William Richard, a Cardiff mercer (1694) whose estate was valued at £1360, was all sperate debt, as was the £300 loaned by his fellow mercer, Lewis Sheares (1687), whose estate was valued at £926-16-9. Clearly, wealthy businessmen were not reckless with their capital.

The main burden of desperate debt fell upon shopkeepers, tradesmen-shopkeepers and innkeepers. Reference has already been made to the superb shop books of John Vallence of Cowbridge, and to the 'book debt' of Hopkin Williams, innkeeper. In addition to Hopkin Williams' book debts of £133-17-05½ from 143 named persons, he was owed £46 by bond from four named people, £100 by mortgage from Mr. Edward Herbert, £29 by note from seven named people, and had desperate debts by note from nine named persons. Hopkin Morgan was owed £328-2-10½, 68% of his total wealth. Such high percentages of money loaned were not uncommon: Ann Howell, Peterston-super-Ely (1715), loaned £9-15-0, 74% of her wealth; William Owen, carpenter, Cardiff (1712) loaned £69-19-0, 75% of his estate; John Alexander, weaver, Llancarvan (1633), loaned £32-10-0, 86% of his wealth; William Lewis, feltmaker/hatter, Cardiff (1731), loaned £229, 91% of his wealth; and John Greenfield of Cardiff (1736), loaned £4,412, or 98.7% of his estate. Rodolph Williams, a Llancarvan tailor who died in 1661, had loaned £56-7-0, 72% of his estate, but his list of debts is especially significant because it gives a clue to his clientelle, and these were not just locals.

The probate inventories of two other persons demand mentioned in relation to debt: the inventory of Jane Lewis, a shopkeeper of Llanblethian (1696), and the inventory of a parson, Richard Jenkins of Llanishen (1698). The names of 63 persons who owed money to Jane Lewis are recorded in her inventory, many owing just pence or a few shillings. This inventory hints, perhaps, at the 'breadline' existence of many people at the period. The inventory of Richard Jenkins records that he was owed £15-5-4, 64% of his estate, and all was deperate debt. Richard Jenkins inventory contrasts sharply with those of many parish priests of past centuries, who were often very wealthy. The make-up of the debt is unknown, but it seems likely that some was for unpaid tythes, as small bequests to the parish priest are frequently recorded in wills, 'in lieu of tythes forgotten.'

The body of evidence from the probate documents shows that debt was a common part of everyday life in past centuries, and that it was not just confined to the poorer members of society.

Richard John's inventory does not record that he possessed any 'ready money,' However, he must have had 'cash in hand' in order to run his grocery business. The Richard John example is, however, fairly typical, as 'ready money' is recorded in only 25 of the documents. Richard Lewis, a pedlar of Llandaff parish, had four shillings and nine pence in cash when he died in 1684, and four Cardiff shopkeepers of the early eighteenth century, Thomas Edward, William Foord, William Hiley and Joseph Hoar, with estates valued at £48-3-6, £25-4-0, £136-9-6 and £298-8-11, possessed cash of £1, 25/-, £2-10-05 and £66 ('in cash, gold and rings') respectively. Henry Hammond and Robert Bawdrey, both already mentioned, had 30 shillings and £4 in cash, and Jonathan Greenfield, with estate of £4,525, had just £3 in 'ready money.' John Thomas, a shopkeeper of Laleston parish, who died in 1710, had £10 cash, but amongst his possessions were, 'fresh goods bought att St. Pauls faire in Bristol & not Sold or disposed of at ye time of ye deced[en]ts death as appear'd by ye Notes of his Sev[er]al Correspond[en]ts att Bristol to ye Sum of £94-01-01.' These goods must have been paid for in cash, as his inventory does not record that he owed money to anyone. Similarly, in the possession of Lewis Sheares, mercer (1687), were 'all ye goods (all listed) that came home this last Bristol faire,' and these were worth £305-07-06, a truly enormous amount of money. He too had no creditors, and his 'ready money' is recorded as £31. John Vallance, with trade goods valued at £860-13-11 in 1750, possessed £188-17-06 in ready money, and John Stidder of Cowbridge, also a mercer (?), had £80-4-6 cash. Cowbridge was, too, the home of Katherine Hammond, the widow of John Hammond, maltster. She possessed £236-7-6 in 'ready Cash' at her death in 1720, and at his death in 1684, John Jenkins, a wholesale hosier, had £120 in ready money, an amount that would have allowed him to trade in the 'two packs and a halfe of Stockins or thereabouts prized and valued at £100' that he owned at his death. The largest amount of ready money recorded in the documents dates to 1856, when John Penfound Harris, a Cardiff blacksmith, had £280-12-6 in 'cash in West of England Bank, Cardiff.' Two other nineteenth testators. Nathaniel Young, a Cowbridge sadler (1842), and Thomas David, an Ely carpenter, who died on the 26th February, 1850, had £250 and £275-4-7 respectively, 'at interest.' The largest percentage of total wealth held in 'ready money' was the £50 held by Wenllian Hedges of Cardiff in 1709, 76% of her estate.

The book includes the inventories of seven mariners. Testimony to the importance of cross-channel trade with Bristol has already been shown from the inventories of Lewis Sheares, mercer, John Thomas, village shopkeeper, and Edward Rees, farmer, and the will of Richard Powell of Cowbridge, a vintner, who died in 1661, not only shows that such a tradesman operated locally, but also establishes the link with Bistol, the wine trade and the wider world, as John Broadway of Bristol, vintner, probably Richard Powell's trading partner, and clearly his trusted friend, is overseer of his will. The names of trading vessels are recorded in the inventories: the Blessing of Aberthaw and the Elizabeth in the inventory of Thomas Spencer; the Speedwell of Cardiff was the barque of John Brewer; the Lyon, the Speedwell and the Two Brothers were owned in share by Richard Davis, with Nicholas Stidman owing a half share in the Speedwell; the Jaine sloop was owned by Robert Priest. Most importantly, the names of many of these vessels appear in the Port Books, a key source of evidence relating to the imports and exports into and from the ports of the Vale and of Cardiff in past centuries. John Wollrin's inventory is an indication of the considerable quantity of salt that was imported from France and Spain in the later seventeenth century, and the inventories of numerous shopkeepers list the spices and exotic substances used in dyeing, tanning, etc. that were commonly available locally, the spices coming mainly from the East Indies, and many of the dyeing products from the Caribbean region. In the inventory of Richard Sheeres, a Cardiff innkeeper who died in 1662, an entry states: 'adventured in goods sent to sea £8.' Richard Sheeres would not have been the only wealthy local person to be similarly involved. Henry Hill, a country gentleman-farmer of St. Athan, was the owner of a trading barque, the Speedwell, which was valued at £100 in his inventory in 1666, and William Morgan, gentleman, of Coed y Gores [Llanedeyrn, Cardiff], and Cradock Nowell of Cardiff, glover (see page 133), were the principal creditors of John Brewer, mariner (see page 196). Cross-channel trade, trade with the Continent, trade with the wider world: all contributed to the variety of products readily available to people in town and village locally. It is this that makes the inclusion of mariners' inventories in the book particularly appropriate. The estates of the seven mariners were valued at: £381-17-0; £161-2-10; £110-15-0; £58; £4,525; £610-5-7; and £170-14-6.

Shops were obviously the main sales outlet for goods, but pedlars had their rounds in country and town, and there were regular markets and fairs. Also, tradesmen sold direct to customers. An invaluable document relating to the day to day workings of economic life, and included as Appendix 2, is the inventory of Jennet John, a widow of Llancarvan (1733). It gives details of the money she owed at her death to labourers, cobbler, taylor, for spinning and weaving, for candles, as well as for rent, rates, constable rate and widow tax. Few documents provide such insight. David Griffiths, a pedlar of Colwinston parish, 1686, owned 'pedlarie ware' valued at £13 as well as two horses, and Richard Lewis of Llandaff, 1684, possessed 'pedlary ware in the shop with a few small vessels of Brandy and aniseed' valued at £5. Richard Lewis had no horse, and presumably, he carried his wares on his rounds, which were, perhaps, mainly 'urban.' His inventory, also, contains the following entry: 'Item in Logges, towards the raysinge of smale Tilts in the faire, and three or fowre planks to the same use pri[sed]: at £0-2-6.' The fair referred to was almost certainly Llandaff fair. Perhaps, Rice Lewis of Llandaff, gentleman (1685), sold some of the fish and birds he caught, shot or trapped in and along the Taff at Llandaff fair, and at other local markets. His inventory is most unusual and hints at hunting and fishing on some scale.

One probate document from outside Cardiff and the Vale has been included as Appendix 1 – the Inventory of James Harries, a mercer, from Usk, Monmouthshire, who died in 1692. The Inventory lists approximately 200 items of woven fabric of great variety, as well as about 100 items of household provision, hardware and chandlery. No inventory of this period from Cardiff and the Vale matches the detail of this inventory, but there is good reason for thinking that it provides an excellent insight into the probable contents of certain shops in Cardiff and Cowbridge at this time. The total value of James Harries' inventory is £446-07-00½, a total made up largely of shop goods and book debts. In 1694, William Richards, a Cardiff mercer, died leaving 'Goods in Shopp & Warehouse' valued at £450-08-00. The James Harries inventory, as well as that of Lewis Sheares, another mercer (1687), are likely to be good clues as to the detail of William Richards' goods. No doubt, too, the small town of Cowbridge had, at this time, a mercer's shop similar to that of James Harries, just as it had in 1750, as the dazzling John Vallence inventory testifies. James Harries's inventory also provides concrete evidence relating to debt recovery, as the following two entries from his inventory indicate: 'Debts Due to ye Deced[en]t James Harries att ye time of his death and received by Mary Harris his relict & executrix Since – £89-15-11;' 'Book Debts Due to ye said Decead[en]t att his Decease still Due & unpayed £100-01-10.'

An attempt has been made to record each document exactly as it was written originally – letter for letter, mark for mark – except, of course, that modern type has been used. You will discover that: (i) the same word might well be spelt in two or three different ways in the space of a few lines of text; (ii) that punctuation was often totally absent; and (iii) that capital letters are used for almost every other word in some documents. It would have been far simpler to use modern spelling and punctuation throughout the work of transcription, but if this had been done, insight into the changing face of written English over the centuries would have been lost, as would a glimpse into some of the problems that are an integral part of transcribing old documents. Levels of appreciation, independent of document content, would have been lost if present custom had been adopted. However, to make the reading of unpunctuated text easier, spaces, not in the original text, have often been included as thought necessary

Roman numerals were in common use in the early and middle seventeenth century, and still appear in late seventeenth century documents. In the inventory of David Lewis, a shopkeeper in St. Athan (1642), Roman numerals record the values of his goods, and in the inventory of Henry Spencer of Llandaff, shoemaker (1643), modern and Roman numerals are found side by side. Roman numerals are still used in the inventories of Arthur Yeomans, 1686, and Thomas Richards, 1699. Of course, the values of goods are not given in pounds and pence as they are today. From the mid-eighteenth century, money values are recorded under the heading £-s-d, and in earlier documents the heading used is li-s-d (as is the case in the Richard John inventory). Both £-s-d and li-s-d stand for pounds, shillings and pence, when there were 12 pence in one shilling, and twenty shillings in one pound.

It was once common to abbreviate words, particularly in the seventeenth century, resulting in a sort of 'shorthand.' The word parish, for example,

Introduction

was usually written 'pish.' In the transcription, 'pish' is recorded as 'p[ar]ish.' Omitted letters are always recorded between square brackets. Other examples of frequently abbreviated words are: w^{ch} – w[hi]ch; w^t – w[ha]t; pfect – p[er]fect; y^d – y[ar]d. The word 'appertenances' appears in numerous documents. It means the things that belong to, or are usually associated with a particular object or place – a bed, or the dairy, for example. As it is a long word containing 'er,' 'en,' and 'an,' letters which were often omitted, the opportunity for abbreviation in many varieties existed, as you will see in the documents.

All probate documents – inventories, wills and administrations bonds – provide a rudimentary clue to literacy, showing as they do whether the signatories to the documents could, or could not, write their own name.

Probate documents giving details of shop or trade goods are not in plentiful supply. Consequently, there is little opportunity to select – those documents to include and those to exclude – and, as a result, the parishes, occupations and time periods covered by the documents merely reflect those that have survived out of approximately 4,000 that have been studied.

Parishes represented: St. Johns & St. Marys, Cardiff (57); Cowbridge (14); Llandaff (6); St. Andrews (Dinas Powys) (6); Llanishen (3); Llanblethian (3); Bonvilston (2); Colwinston (2); Llancarfan (2); Llantwit Major (2); Pile & Kenfig (2); St. Athan (2); Whitchurch (2); Cadoxton (1); Laleston (1); Merthyr Dyfan (1); Penmark (1); Peterston-super-Ely (1); St. George's (1).

Occupations represented: shopkeepers 33 (13 mercers; 2 hosiers; 1 glover; 4 hardware shops; 13 general goods/provisions); pedlars 2; weavers 4; tucker 1; tailor 1; feltmakers 3; hosiers 2; stocking knitters 2; tanners 3; shoemakers 5; saddlers 3; glovers 5; chandler 1; blacksmiths 2; carpenters 5; cooper 1; sawyer 1; ship builder 1; builder 1; innkeepers/brewers/maltsters 10; vintner 1; mariners 7; farmers with commercial interests 8; gardener 1; salters 4; gentlemen with commercial interests 2; parson with a bookbinder's press 1.

Time periods represented: 1633-1699 – 53 records; 1700-1776 – 45 records; 1777-1838 – no records; 1839-1857 – 11 records.

The National Library of Wales Document Reference is included at the end of each transcription. However, some documents are not listed in the current Index, and for these no reference is given.

Arrangements can be made to examine photocopies of the original documents by contacting the publisher.

Lack of space has made it impossible to include the wills that accompany many of the inventories. A computer floppy disc, with all the wills saved as a Word Document, will be available from the publisher at £1.50, post and package free. Obviously, wills usually provide the family background of the deceased, as well as other invaluable detail.

Peter Bowen

Sections of Original Inventories and Wills

Opening section of the Inventory of Richard Sheeres of Cardiff, dated 19th January, 1659.
(By kind permission of the National Library of Wales).

Opening section of the Will of Richard Sheeres of Cardiff, dated 30th December, 1659.
(By kind permission of the National Library of Wales).

Selected sections of the Inventory of Edward Evans of Cardiff, carpenter, dated 12th November, 1751.
(By kind permission of the National Library of Wales).

Opening section of the Will of Edward Evans of Cardiff, carpenter, dated 10th October, 1751.
(By kind permission of the National Library of Wales).

Sections of Original Inventories and Wills

> Inventory of all the Household furniture and
> Stock in trade the property of the late Mr
> Nathaniel Young of the Town of Cowbridge
> in the County of Glamorgan who died on
> the 8 of March 1842 and Appraised on the of
> 12 May following by John Aubrey Auctioneer
>
> Stock in Trade £
> 46 Cart Saddle trees — — — — — — — — 2 14 —
> 2 Cart Saddle trees partly finished — — — " 8 —
> 24 White Hides 12 Saddle trees — — — 10 2 —
> Quantity of Harness Buckles 3 lb of Hemp — — " 12 6

Selected sections of the Inventory of Nathaniel Young of Cowbridge, sadler, dated 12th May, 1842.
(By kind permission of the National Library of Wales).

> This is the last will and Testament of me Nathaniel
> Young of the town of Cowbridge in the county of Gla-
> morgan Sadler made this twenty ninth day of May
> in the year of our Lord one thousand eight hundred
> and thirty eight. I give and devise all those my five
> freehold messuages or dwelling houses with their appur-
> tenances situate in Church Street in the said town of
> Cowbridge, and also my leasehold interest in a certain
> Dwelling house called The Old Workhouse in Church

Opening section of the Will of Nathaniel Young of Cowbridge, sadler, dated 29th May, 1838.
(By kind permission of the National Library of Wales).

The Evidence:
The Inventories of Local Shopkeepers and Tradesmen, 1633-1857

1. Village Shops

A true and p[er]fect Inventorie of all the goods Cattles & Chatells of David Lewis late of St Tathans in the county of glamorgan and dioces of Landaff, deceased, taken, vewed, and appraised the xii[th] daye of Aprill *in the eighteenth year of the reign of our Lord Charles King of England etc. in the year of our lord (in latin)* 1642 by the p[er]sons whose names are subscribed.

Imprimis twoe feather beads w[i]th the clothes thereunto belonging aprised at	ii^{li}	
Item one Table boord and frame and one Cubbard aprised at	[lost]	?
Item Twoe Trunks aprised at	[lost]	?
Item Twoe Coffers or chestes	[lost]	?
It[em] in Brasse and pewter apprised at	i^{li}	
It[em] Tenn peeces of holland & stuff apprised at	xii^{li}	
It[em] some p[ar]cels of ware viz knives, silcke and other such like	i^{li}	
It[em] three peeces of Saye, twoe pieces of fine holland, and other peeces of Stuff & small wares, apprised at	vii^{li}	
Item some p[ar]cells of laund? cambricke Tiffetie and Ribbands at	viii^{li}	
Item in Soape, fruits, and Spices apprised at	iii^{li}	
It[em] his wearing apparrell apprised at	i^{li}	x^s
Sum tot[al]	xxxvii^{li}	[lost]

Apprised the daye above written by us:
John David   Robert Corrick   John Mathew   Cradock: Griffith

[National Library of Wales Document Reference: LL/1642/44]

————————

The Inventory of all ye goods & Cattle of Thomas Mawrice of Bonvilston within the Diocesse of Landaffe Made prised and valued by ye p[er]sons undernamed ye Sixth Day of 8ber A[nno] D[omi]ni 1673.

	li - s - d
Imp[rimi]s we prise his wearing apparell att	01-10-00
It[em] one cow & one old horse att	02-00-00
It[em] three ewes att	00-10-00
It[em] we prise all ye ware in ye shoppe att	05-00-00
It[em] one rike of oates & barly att	02-00-00
It[em] barly in ye barne att	03-00-00
It[em] in ye hall one table & fowr stooles att	00-10-00
It[em] one cupboard one pewter platter two beakers two earthen platters two bottles & three earthen cupps att	00-05-00
It[em] one Settle three Small chaires & one chest att	00-10-00
It[em] one frying pan tongs & Andirons & Spitts att	00-02-06
It[em] one Smoothing iron att	00-00-06
It[em] in ye two upper roomes two feather beds with their appurtenances att	02-10-00
It[em] one livery cupboard 7 peeces of pewter one tanket & three candlestickes	00-10-00
It[em] one trestle two chaires, butter & cheese att	00-17-06
It[em] two iron crockes two cauldrons & two skillet att	00-10-00
It[em] in ye upper house one cauldron one brandiron one chaire & a few old potts & tubbs att	00-06-08
It[em] a small p[ar]cell of wool att	00-05-00
It[em] a brass mortar & pestle	00-03-06
It[em] a small Rick of hey att	01-00-00
It[em] piggs & poultrey att	00-12-00
Sum	22-00-08

Despratt? Depts due to ye Deceadent
on Mrs Eliz: Jones	01-05-00
on Gilian Bowden	02-10-00
on Jenett Griffith al[ia]s W[illia]m	01-10-00

p[ri]sers   Jo:? Thomas   ye M[a]rk of William Phillipp
John Hawkin

[National Library of Wales Document Reference: LL./1673/21]

An Inventory of all & Singular the Goods Cattle & Chattles of Walter Hart of the parish of St. Andrews within the diocesse of Landaffe Blacksmyth deceased Apprized the fifth day of December Anno D[omi]ni 1696 by the p[er]sons und[er]named in manner & forme following.

Imp[rimi]s his wearing apparell apprais[e]d to	02-00-00
Three feather bedds, two bolsters & two pillowes weighing 246^{li} at 5d. p[er] [pound]	06-03-00
Six Ruggs, an old peece of Arras & seven blanketts	03-00-00
A p[ai]re of fine sheets, three p[ai]re of Course sheets & five pillow Cases	03-00-00
one p[ai]re Curtaines, two bedsteeds mattresse & Cords	01-00-00
one Diap[er] table cloth, six Diap[er] Napkins, three Course table Cloths, six Course Napkins & two towells	01-00-00
one Chest, one little Cupboard, one table & frame, 2 Joynt Stooles, ffoure chaires, one bench, one lookeing glass, one window Curtaine & an houre glasse	02-00-00
Sixteene pewter dishes, one pewter Candlestick, two pewter Gunns, two pewter plates, three pewter porring[er]s, one pewter coffin seven pewter spoons weighing 68^{li} at 8d. p[er] [pound]	02-05-04
Three brass panns, three brasse Caldrons & one skellet weighing 89^{li} at p[er] [pound]	04-09-10
Three brasse Crocks, two brasse Candlesticks weighing 57£. at 6d. p[er] [pound]	01-08-06
ffoure milke Cowes, three yearlings and hay	12-00-00
All the Corne w[i]thin doores and without	05-00-00
seven stones of Cheese at 3s. a stone, one stone fine wool & one stone 6^{li} coarse wool the one at 17s. p[er] [stone] and ye other at 7s. p[er] [stone]	02-05-00
one ffirkin of Butter	00-16-00
sixteene sheepe five piggs one horse one mare	08-03-00
In the Kytchin Two Kitchin boords with fframes, one bin, one Cheese wring two chaires a p[ai]re Andirons, a fryeing pann a fender, a Candlestick with several small Lumber stuffe	01-00-00
In the forge An Anvill, a pair of Bellowes, a pick iron a pair of tongues, a Grindstone with all appurtt[enance]s, two Vices, two sledges, three new shovells, two new plough shares with other Implements	05-00-00

In the shopp
A Buffe britches   9 y[ar]ds ¾ of simpl fustian at 1s. p[er yd.] 01-07-09
10 y[ar]ds plaine fustian at 13d. y[ar]d   14 y[ar]ds German
    holl[and] at 15½d.   01-08-11
9 y[ar]ds broad dowlas at 17d. p[er]   6 y[ar]ds ¾ coarse
    dowlas at 1s.1d. p[er]   01-00-00¾
7 y[ar]ds ½ painted linen at 11d. p[er]   2 y[ar]ds painted
    fustian at 1s. p[er]   00-08-10½
7 y[ar]ds ½ painted Callicoe at 2s.   22 y[ar]ds painted
    Strip't tyke at 1s. p[er]   01-17-00
3 y[ar]ds blew chequer at 1s. p[er]   5 y[ar]ds ¾ Stript
    tyke at 1s. p[er]   00-08-09
6 y[ar]ds fine Tyke at 1s.1d. p[er]   18 y[ar]ds Russia
    at 4d. p[er]   00-13-00
3 y[ar]ds ¼ painted callico at 1s. p[er]   42 y[ar]ds browne
    fflaxen at 6d. p[er]   01-04-06
18 y[ar]ds browne fflaxen at 7½d. p[er]   18 y[ar]ds ½
    of ye same   01-02-09¾
9 y[ar]ds ¾ German linen at 10d.p[er]   10 y[ar]ds ¾
    fliwr'd fustian at 1s. p[er]   00-18-10½
2 y[ar]ds ½ browne fflaxen at 7d. p[er]   9 y[ar]ds blew
    German at 8d. p[er]   00-07-05½
30 y[ar]ds Russia at 4d. p[er]   11 y[ar]ds ¼ Ozenbriggs
    at 8d. p[er]   00-17-06
15 y[ar]ds ½ painted ozenbriggs at 7½d. p[er] 6 y[ar]ds ¾
    painted linen at 14d.   00-12-09½
47 y[ar]ds Coll^d Ozenbriggs at 7½d.   2 y[ar]ds painted
    Callicie at 1s. p[er]   01-09-09½
2 y[ar]ds ½ blew painted Cloth at 16d.   11 y[ar]ds ¾
    painted Kentins at 16d.   01-00-11½
24 y[ar]ds blew ozenbriggs at 7d.   18 y[ar]ds Strip't
    Callimancoe at 2s. p[er]   02-10-00
18 y[ar]ds ½ broad stripte at 2s. p[er]   2 y[ar]ds blew
    linen at 7½d. yd   01-18-03
11 y[ar]ds callimancoe at 20d. p[er]   35 y[ar]ds strip't   02-04-07
44 y[ar]ds stipt stuffe at 11d.   13 y[ar]ds ¾ browne
    ozenbriggs at 7d. p[er]   02-16-00
2 y[ar]ds ½ browne ozenbriggs at 7½ p[er] 11 y[ar]ds
    fine searge at 2s. p[er]   01-03-04¾

3 y[ar]ds ½ Course searge at 18d. 13 y[ar]ds ½ Coll^d Searge at 2s. p[er]	01-12-03
18 y[ar]ds Drugget at 1s. p[er] 27 y[ar]ds Sad? Coll^d searge at 2/- [yd]	03-00-00
13 y[ar]ds Drugget at 14d. p[er]	00-15-02
20 y[ar]ds Carzey at 4s. p[er] 28 y[ar]ds Carzey at 3s. p[er]	08-04-00
2 shirts, 9 bodis & six quilted capps	02-03-00
6 y[ar]ds ½ Coll^d fustian at 1s. p[er] with sev[era]l other small ware	01-16-00
10 y[ar]ds sewing silke at 2s. p[er]	01-00-00
Knifes Combes packing? Needles Bees wax & other small ware	03-04-00
8 grose ½ Buttons at 1s 6d [gross] 2 gross of Tipt? buttons at 3s. p[er] [gross]	01-04-09
A Case of Drawers w[i]th small wares	00-10-00
six looking glasses; Cords & Bellices?	01-10-00
4^li white sugar at 8d p[er] [pound] 3^li hopps at 1s. p[er] [li.]	00-05-08
4^li currance at 5d. p[er] 4^li malligoe reasins at 4d. p[er] [li.]	00-03-00
10^li meire sugar at 5d. p[er] [li.] 30^li candles at 11d. p[er] [li.] & nayles	02-10-04
7^li starch at 5d. p[er] [li] 3^li copperas at 4d. & Locks & Keys	00-10-07
two small Casks of Oyle, one Gallen Anniseed water	01-03-04
two Gold Rings 1^li. 5^s. & ½ Guinea 11^s.	01-16-00
in money	02-00-00
in farthings and half pennyes	00-01-10
scales and weights	00-05-00
6 y[ar]ds redd searge at 2s. p[er] 16 yds ¼ druggett at 18d.	01-16-03
27 y[ar]ds Druggett at 15d. p[er] burkram 4d	01-14-01
11 y[ar]ds ¾ Linsey wolsey at 12d. p[er] 3 y[ar]ds ½ redd cottin at 1s. p[er]	00-15-03
9 y[ar]ds ½ blu: Clo:[th] at 5/- p[er] 5 y[ar]ds blu. Clo:[th] at 5s. p[er]	03-12-06
3 y[ar]ds cottin att 6d. p[er] 16 y[ar]ds ½ serge at 2s.4d. p[er]	02-00-00
2 Remn[an]ts Clo:[th] 1s. 20 y[ar]ds Linsey wollsey at 1s. p[er]	01-01-00
7 y[ar]ds bro: Clo:[th] at 5/- p[er] 4 y[ar]ds coarse at 2s. p[er]	02-03-00

16 y[ar]ds carsey at 2s. p[er] 13 y[ar]ds cotton at 1s. p[er]	02-04-00
20 y[ar]ds bro: Clo:[th] 2s. p[er] 11 y[ar]ds ½ Carsey at 3s. p[er]	03-14-06
6 y[ar]ds ½ Cottin at 12d. p[er] 7 y[ar]ds ½ Cottin at 12d. p[er]	00-14-00
6 y[ar]ds Cottin at 12d. p[er]	00-06-00
upon ye shop books of good depts the sum of	40-05-00
of desparete depts on ye books the sum of	<u>39-07-07</u>
The sum totall is	<u>220-01-04 ½</u>

Appraisers names: Francis Richards   John Jones   Thomas Arle
Exhibited at Llandaff, 16th February, 1696/7, by George Tristram, administrator.

Administration Bond: Walter Hart, blacksmith: 16th February, 1696/7
In the Consistory Court of Llandaff, 16th February, 1696/7, administration of the goods etc. of Walter Hart, deceased, was granted to George Tristram alias Thomas, of Michaelston le Pit, yeoman, administrator, with the will annexed, 'to the use and during the minority of William Thomas, the executor named in the will of the deceased.' George Tristram, Philipp White and William Jenkins, both yeomen of the parish of St Andrew, were bound in the sum of £1,000 for George Tristram to make and exhibit a true inventory of the goods etc. of the deceased at or before the 1st April next, to administer to the use of William Thomas, to pay all debts and legacies, and to render a just account of his administration. George Thomas, Phillip White and William Jenkins signed the administration bond.

[National Library of Wales Document Reference: LL/1696/183]

A true & perfect Inventary of all ye goods and personall estate of Jane Lewis late of ye parish of Lanblethian w[i]thin ye Diocesse of Landaffe deceased made prised & valued by ye persons undernamed on ye fourteenth day of July An[n]o d[omi]ni 1696 followeth

	li - s - d
Impri[mi]s her wearing apparell prised att	01-00-00
It[em] 28 yards of strip stuffe at 10^d per yard	01-03-03
It[em] 4 yards of black crape 9 pence per yard at	00-13-00
It[em] 18 yards of white crape 9 pence per yard att	00-13-06
It[em] 10 yards of course canvas 4 pence per yard att	00-03-04
It[em] 4 yards of cheese cloth 3 pence per yard att	00-01-00
It[em] 1 yard of painted calico att	00-00-07

It[em] 11 strawn hatts 8 pence a hatt	00-07-04
It[em] 3 coloured hats ... children att	00-02-06
It[em] 4 coloured hats at	00-12-00
It[em] 5 neck cloaths att	00-02-11
It[em] 4 paire of course bodices att	00-08-00
It[em] 15 pownds of flax att	00-10-00
It[em] 10 pownds of roll tobacco att	00-07-06
It[em] 6 pownds of tobacco cut att	00-04-06
It[em] 2 pownds press tobacco att	00-01-06
It[em] 3 quires of writing paper	00-01-03
It[em] 8 pownds of candles att	00-02-08
It[em] 38 pownds of black soap att	00-06-06
It[em] 80 pownds of browne sugar att	00-18-00
It[em] 4 pownds of currence att	00-01-08
It[em] 1 pownd of wick yarn att	00-00-05
It[em] 2 pounds of brown sugar Candy att	00-01-06
It[em] 1 pound of Jamaica pepper att	00-01-02
It[em] 4 pounds of turmeric att	00-02-00
It[em] 2 pound of beaten ginger att	00-00-04
It[em] a grose of ……. buttons att	00-02-00
It[em] 2 pownds of thread att	00-03-00
It[em] 7 pounds of Alam att	00-01-09
It[em] 12 pounds of coperas att	00-01-00
It[em] incle & bobin att	00-01-00
It[em] 8 gallons of brandy att	01-05-00
It[em] halfe a hundred of treacle att	00-08-00
It[em] a q[uar]ter of a hundred of ……. ……. att	00-02-00
It[em] one gallon of vineger att	00-01-08
It[em] one gallon of Salett oyle att	00-06-00
It[em] three dozens of pipes att	00-01-04
It[em] two tin trinketts att	00-02-00
It[em] 3 ….. of measures for brandy att	00-01-06
Sum	10-07-10

prizers   John Robert   the mark of Lewis Meirick   Da: Rimberick?

Desperat depts due by shop book	li - s - d
Imprimis on Mr Evan Jenkins	00-04-04
It[em] on Mr Morgan Williams	01-02-07
It[em] on howell anstance	00-14-01

It[em] on David Mathew	00-14-11
It[em] on Elinor Thomas	00-00-05
It[em] on Elizabeth Thomas	00-00-06
It[em] on Watkin Thomas	00-08-06
It[em] on Catherin Treharn	00-00-11
It[em] on Thomas Jenkin	00-02-09
It[em] on Joan Thomas	00-00-10
It[em] Catherin Rice	00-02-03
It[em] Morgan Rice	00-00-09
It[em] Eaustance Richard	00-05-06
It[em] on Henry Milward	00-01-00
It[em] on John Griffith	00-03-06
It[em] on Jenkin Thomas	00-03-03
It[em] on Jenkin Rice	00-02-05
It[em] on David Gibbon	00-06-04
It[em] on Tha...... David	00-00-02
It[em] on Thomas Robert	00-00-03
It[em] on Joan Mathew	00-16-03
It[em] on John Trahern	00-01-00
It[em] on Edward David	00-01-11
It[em] on Edward David	00-01-07
It[em] on Rice Nicholl	00-07-00
It[em] on hanna Morgan	00-01-05
It[em] on Thomas Piers?	00-07-05
It[em] on Mary Thomas wid[ow]	00-02-01
It[em] on Blanch Thomas	00-00-01
It[em] on Alice Christopher	00-00-02
It[em] on Jenet Gibbon	00-00-08
It[em] on Thomas Anthony	00-00-06
It[em] on Evan Gibbon	00-02-06
It[em] on Anne Gibbon	00-05-07
It[em] on Wm Lewis	00-02-01
It[em] John Grant?	00-02-05
It[em] on Wm David	00-06-04
It[em] Phelice Bullard	00-07-07
It[em] on Eaustance Richard	00-00-03
It[em] Jane David	00-01-03
It[em] on Margaret David	00-01-03
It[em] on David Rice	00-04-05

It[em] on Lewis …..	00-01-01
It[em] on Thomas David	00-04-08
It[em] Joan Mr Jenkins	01-00-00
It[em] on Elinor Miles Maidservant	00-00-06
It[em] on Evan Watkin	00-06-07
It[em] Edward Lewis	00-08-08
It[em] on Joan Nicholl	00-02-00
It[em] on Cicill Evan	00-01-06
It[em] on Cicill Thomas	00-01-03
It[em] on Anne Nicholl	00-00-03
It[em] on Evan Hugh	00-01-10
It[em] on Elinor Jones	00-01-10
It[em] on Lidia Thomas	00-01-06
It[em] on Evan Morgan	00-02-02
It[em] on Catherin John	00-13-03
It[em] on Mrs Kemeys	00-16-09
It[em] on Mr Jones Rector	00-01-06
It[em] on Richard Bassett	00-03-00
It[em] on Mr Humphrey Mathew	00-04-00
It[em] on Wm Rice	00-00-11
It[em] on Evan Lewelin	00-11-06
Sum	11$^{li.}$ 17$^{s.}$ 9$^{d.}$
Sum tot[al]	22$^{li.}$ 4$^{s.}$ 7$^{d.}$

John Robert   L Ludovici Meirick   Da Rumberick?

Exhibited at Llandaff, 16th July, 1698, by Anna Lewis, mother & administratrix of the deceased.

Administration Bond: Jane Lewis: 16th July, 1698

In the Consistory Court of Llandaff, 16th July, 1698, administration of the goods, chattells and credits of Jane Lewis, deceased, was granted to her mother, Ann Lewis of the parish of Llanblethian. Ann Lewis and Richard Deer of the parish of St. Georges, were bound by the Court in the sum of £100 for Ann Lewis to make and exhibit a true and perfect inventory of the goods etc. of her late daughter at or before the 1st August next, to administer according to law, to give a just account of her administration at or before the 16th July, 1699, and to present to the Court any last will and testament of the deceased that might appear. Ann Lewis recorded her mark on the administration bond: Richard Deer signed the document.

[National Library of Wales Document Reference: LL/1698 /143]

Inventory of Margaret Richard late of Merthyr Dyfan, made by William Howell, Robert Thomas and John Richard on the 9th December 1708.

	li - s - d
her wearing apparrell vallued att	03-00-00
all the pewter and brass in the hall att	01-05-00
one bedstead and one feather bed with all its appurtananccs att	03-00-00
all the rest of the goods in the chamber att	01-00-00
the goods in the hall att	01-10-00
the shop and all that is in it att	15-00-00
two acres of freehold lands valued att £20 Total	24-15-00

[National Library of Wales Document Reference: LL/1708/]

An Inventory of all and Singular ye the goods Ch[att]ells and p[er]sonall estate of James Leckey late of ye p[ar]ish of Lantwit Major in the County of Glamorgan & dioceses of Landaffe dese[ace]d mad[e[valued & apprized by John Deere, Robert Kerr & John Maxwell apprizors the ninth day of June 1708 as foll[ows] vizt

	li - s - d
Impr[ini]s his wearing apparel valued at	01-10-00
It[em] bedding and Lynen at	10-00-00
It[em] Tables Chaires & other household stuff at	03-00-00
It[em] brasse and peauter at	03-00-00
It[em] one old mare at	01-10-00
It[em] two p[iece]s of garlick Holland at	02-16-00
It[em] one p[iece]s of dowlas at	02-00-00
It[em] 46. y[ar]ds of Scotch cloth at 1^s 3^d p[er]	02-17-06
It[em] 21 yds holland at 1^s 8^d p[er]	01-15-00
It[em] 11 yds & … holland at 2^s 6^d	01-08-06
It[em] 33 Ells of holland at 2^s 6^d p[er]	04-02-06
It[em] 7 yds of Holland at	00-10-00
It[em] 20. Ells Narrow Holland at	01-03-04
It[em] 16. Ells & ½ of Narrow holland at	00-16-06
It[em] 3. yds of narrow holland at	00-04-03
It[em] 2 p[iece]s of kentin at	00-17-00
It[em] 16 yds ¾ Camerick at	02-17-06
It[em] 8. yds of diaper at	00-12-00
It[em] 20 yds of Muzlin at	03-10-00

It[em]	19 yds of Stript muslin at	03-16-00
It[em]	13. yds of Indian demity at	01-12-00
It[em]	3 yds of Demity at	00-03-00
It[em]	11 yds of fustian at	00-07-06
It[em]	10 Ells of Silke at	01-12-06
It[em]	10 Ells of Dowlas at	00-15-00
It[em]	12 ells of narrow Dowlas at	00-10-00
It[em]	39. yds of fflaxen at	01-19-00
It[em]	32 yds & ¾ of Calicoe at 2^s p[er]	03-05-06
It[em]	17. yds ½ of Calicoe at 14^d p[er]	01-00-05
It[em]	19. yds of blew at 14^d p[er]	01-02-02
It[em]	14 yds of blew at 7^d p[er]	00-08-02
It[em]	34 yds of checquer linnen at 18^d p[er]	02-11-00
It[em]	8 yds of checquer linnen at 20^d p[er]	00-13-04
It[em]	13 Silke handerchiefes at 21^d p[er]	01-02-09
It[em]	34 ditto at 14^d p[er]	01-19-08
It[em]	11 ditto of Cotten at 9^d p[er]	00-08-03
It[em]	58 yds of checquer linen at 9^d p[er]	02-03-06
It[em]	ten yds of plush at 3^s p[er]	01-10-00
It[em]	8 yds & ¾ of fustian at 12^d p[er]	00-08-06
It[em]	10 yds of minko at 2^s p[er]	01-00-00
It[em]	2 p[iece]s of Single stuffe at	01-14-00
It[em]	50 yds of crape	02-10-00
It[em]	86 yds of Cantilon stuffe at	01-19-05
It[em]	a p[iece]s of Serge at 22^s p[er]	01-02-00
Item	8: yds of Serge at 15^d p[er]	00-10-00
It[em]	for Small remnants	02-00-00
It[em]	for a Small box of lace	06-00-00
It[em]	for Buttons, thread, and small things at	05-00-00
It[em]	for Tobacco	04-00-00
It[em]	for Sugar and Currans	05-00-00
It[em]	for Liquors	01-00-00
It[em]	for hopps	01-00-00
It[em]	for Nayles and other small goods	02-00-00
It[em]	Debts due by note and booke Sperate & desperate	<u>95-19-08</u>
	Total	<u>202-13-07</u>

Exhibited at Llandaff, 1st December, 1708, by Mary Leckey, relict and executrix.

[National Library of Wales Document Reference: LL/1708/157]

A true and perfect Inventory of all & Singular ye Goods, Ch[att]ells & Credits of **John Thomas** late of ye p[ar]ish of Laleston in ye County of Glamorgan and Diocese of Llandaff Shopkeeper dece[ase]d, made valued and appraised ye 30th day of May Anno D[omi]ni 1710 by Robert Thomas Arthur Richard and Richard Leyson Appraisers as follows Viz^t.

£ - s - d

Inp[rimi]s his wearing Apparell consisting of 4 Coats, 4 wastcoats, 3 or 4 pairs of Breeches, ab[ou]t 6 Shirts, 8 Cravatts, 3 or 4 Shams, 8 or 9 paire of Stockins, ab[ou]t 3 paire of Shoes, 3 hatts, a Cap & a hatt-brush valued att	02-00-00
Item one feather Bed w[i]th 3 bolsters and 2 Pillows two Ruggs, 2 paire of blanketts, 3 paire of Sheets, 4 pillow-Cases, a paire of Curtains & Vallians & two bedsteads w[i]th their app[ur]tenances att	02-00-00
Item two dust Beds one Bolster, three Coverlids, 3 paire of blanketts & 2 Matts att	01-00-00
Item 4 old Table Cloths & ab[ou]t a dozen Napkins & Towells	00-05-00
Item two Cup-boards att	00-07-00
Item a Table and five Coffers att	00-15-00
Item 4 rush bottom Chaires att	00-03-00
Item one brass Caldron 6^s & a brass skillett 3^s	00-09-00
Item two brass Crocks att	00-10-00
Item two Iron Crocks, one Iron Caldron two frying Pans & an Iron Skillett att	00-07-00
Item 5 pewter platters, 10 pewter plates, 4 pewter porringers, two small pewter porringers, 18 Spoons, a brass Morter & pestle & 3 brass Candlesticks att	00-15-00
Item one pewter Pint and two halfe-pints w[i]th other smaller pewter measures att	00-01-06
Item 6 paire of brass Scales and weights att	00-12-00
Item one Iron Grate, 4 paire of Tongs, two Slices, 2 paire of Potthooks & hangers & a Toaster att	00-10-00
Item all ye Poultrey consisting of a goose, a gander & ab[ou]t 6 Goslings att	00-01-00
Carry over	09-15-06
Item 19 old dry Casks 3 Trindles 3 pailes one washing Tubb & a dough Tubb att	00-06-00

Item 3 dozen & 9 Trenchers, 6 little wooden Measures, 7 wooden dishes, 2 Ladles, 3 wooden Spoons & 4 three legged Stools att	00-03-00
Item one Cheese vate & its Cover, two bowls, one wooden platter, 2 Standards, one Chopping-board, 2 Spades & a Bitle att	00-01-06
Item a few glass Bottles att	00-01-06
Item all Sort of small Glasses att	00-02-00
Item Tyn Vessells, 2 Truels one smoothing Iron & neaters att	00-02-06
Item 2 wooden Tundishes, 3 old meal-Sives & one old wooden Morter & pestle	00-00-04
Item a little Cupboard by ye fire side att	00-00-06
Item 3 old Mill baggs att	00-00-06
Item 2 Spinning Wheels & Cards, a paire of Gobbards & 2 binches att	00-01-00
Item 5 Mannes or flasks att	00-00-05
Item an Ax & a Bill att	00-00-08
Item two old horses, a Sadle, 2 packsadles, one Pad, two Bridles, a paire of horse-Potts, a paire of hampiers? w[i]th some old Cloaths to cover em & a paire of Poutches	02-00-00

Shop-Goods

Ab[ou]t 46 Yards of Shalloon att 12^d p[er] Yard	02-06-00
Ab[ou]t 17 Yards ½ diamond Shagg att 16^d p[er] y[ar]d	01-03-08
Ab[ou]t 67 Yards of damask Stuffe att 10^d p[er] Yard	02-16-10
Ab[ou]t 78 Yards of worsted Stuffe att 6^d p[er] y[ar]d	01-19-00
Ab[ou]t 54 Yards of Slight worsted Stuffe att 5^d p[er] y[ar]d	01-02-06
Ab[ou]t 59 Yards of black Taramin att 8^d p[er] y[ar]d	01-19-08
163 Yards ⅓ Cantaloon & other Stuffe att 4^d p[er] y[ar]d	02-14-07
10 Yards ½ Linsey blew & green 12^d p[er] y[ar]d	00-10-06
2 Yards ¼ Say att	00-05-06
53 Yards Sarges att 15^d a Yard	03-06-03
7 Yards ⅓ broadCloth att 5^s p[er] y[ar]d	01-18-09
A remnant of druggett ab[ou]t 6 Yards att	00-08-00
7 Yards of frise at 20^d p[er] y[ar]d	00-11-08
60 Yards of broad colour'd Linnen 8^d p[er] y[ar]d	02-00-00
4 Yards blew ditto	<u>00-02-08</u>

carried over	<u>36-01-00</u>
2 Yards ½ colour'd dimity at 10ᵈ p[er] y[ar]d	00-02-01
2 Yards ½ narrow buckram att 6ᵈ p[er] y[ar]d	00-01-03
7 Yards of blew broad Callicoe att 18ᵈ p[er] y[ar]d	00-10-00
3 yards of Plush att 2ˢ 6ᵈ p[er] y[ar]d	00-07-06
163 Yards of Cantaloons att 4ᵈ p[er] y[ar]d	02-14-04
7 Yards ¾ narrow Tick att 10ᵈ p[er] y[ar]d	00-06-05 ½
7 Yards ¾ coarse ditto	00-06-05 ½
9 Yards broader ditto att 12ᵈ p[er] y[ar]d	00-09-00
17 Yards ¼ broad ditto	00-17-03
16 Yards Chequer Linnen att 8ᵈ p[er] y[ar]d	00-10-08
13 Yards ½ Striped Chequer Linnen att 10ᵈ p[er] y[ar]d	00-11-03
9 Yards of white Slisy damnify'd Holland 9ᵈ p[er] y[ar]d	00-06-00
14 Yards ½ fine Cheese-Cloth att 4ᵈ p[er] y[ar]d	00-04-10
13 Yards of Oseenbrig att 7ᵈ p[er] y[ar]d	00-07-07
3 Yards ½ coarse ditto att	00-01-09
3 Yards ¼ garlick holland att 12ᵈ p[er] y[ar]d	00-03-03
5 Yards ½ flaxen Cloth att 8ᵈ p[er] y[ar]d	00-03-08
8 Yards ¾ broad Canvas att 12ᵈ p[er] y[ar]d	00-08-09
one Yard stamp'd Cotten 18ᵈ 2 y[ar]ds fine Cheque 3ˢ	00-04-06
9 colour'd Linen hankerchiefs att 8ᵈ a piece	00-06-00
8 Yards ½ Cloth Sarge att	00-15-07
13 Yards Buckram att 10ᵈ p[er] y[ar]d	00-10-10
10 Yards ¾ blew Harfoard att 6ᵈ p[er] y[ar]d	00-05-04 ½
3 Yards colour'd Crocus	00-01-03
45 Yards Crape att 10ᵈ p[er] Yard	01-17-11
58 Yards ¾ colour'd Harford & remn[an]ts of Osenbrig	01-09-04
Earthen Ware att	00-05-00
12 Pound Rosin	00-03-00
12 Pound Stone pitch 3ˢ ab[ou]t 100ˡⁱ Barrill pitch 15ˢ	00-18-00
Ab[ou]t 10£ redwood 5ˢ & ab[ou]t 6£ Allom 1ˢ	00-06-00
16 Pound of Wick Yarn att	00-06-00
Ab[ou]t 3 gallons af Tarr att	00-04-06
Old Nailes, a few old buckles, two or three Iron Candlesticks, a few knives & Scissers w[i]th other small rusty Iron Ware att	00-05-00
Old decay'd Remn[an]ts of Manchester Goods as Buttons, thred, moehaire, Inckle, Tape etc.	00-10-00
11 ordinary Bodics & Stomachers att	01-10-00

A small quantity of Tallow att	00-08-00
Ab[ou]t 15£ Loggwood 3s & ¼ hundred Copperas 2s 4d	00-05-04
Carry over	55-02-08 ½
Item 4 old haire Baggs att	00-05-00
Item a quantity of old coarse wool worth	00-03-00
Item a few small Remnants of Sowing Silk, a few Shotts, a small quantity of brandy and other distill'd liquors, a small quantity of oyle, and other small and inconsiderable Remnants and Trumperies belonging to ye shop vallued att	00-05-00
Item a small quantity of Indigo and Gauls, Verdigrass & white Copperas, Senna, Salt Peter, a little Madarn & fustick att	00-04-06
Item 5 barrs or Sticks of Wax & ab[ou]t halfe a Bottle of Syrop of Buckthorn att	00-01-06
a few pieces of Plaister w[i]th 2 or 3 pound of white & red Lead	00-01-06
Item a few old Cords and bagg Strings w[i]th a small quantity of hemp & flax att	00-01-00
Item 6 or 7 Books of Silver leaf and two Books of gold leaf att	00-02-00
Item ye Shopboard and shelves att	00-02-00
Item Seaven old Boxes, one Desk, two little Nests of Boxes w[i]th six other Boxes & a Standish in ye Shop att	00-03-06
Item 3 dozen & 4 paire of Cards att	00-03-00
Item a small quantity of Cantharides att	00-00-06
Item a small quantity of Chalke att	00-00-06
Item old Books att	00-02-06
It[em] Booke Debts ye sum of	32-02-11
Item fresh goods bought att St. Pauls faire in Bristoll & not Sold or disposed of at ye time of ye deced[en]ts death as appear'd by ye Notes of his Sev[er]al Correspond[en]ts att Bristoll amounted to ye Sum of	94-01-01
Item in ready money the Sum of	10-00-00
Sum total	193-02-02 ½

Sworn by Elizabeth Thomas, before William Howard, surrogate, 26 September, 1710.

Administration Bond: John Thomas, shopkeeper: 26th September, 1710

In the Consistory Court of Llandaff, 26th September, 1710, administration of the goods etc. of John Thomas, deceased, was granted to his widow,

Elizabeth Thomas. Elizabeth Thomas and Richard Leyson of Laleston, gentleman, were bound by the Court for Elizabeth Thomas to make and exhibit a true inventory of the goods etc. of her late husband at or before the 31st October next, to administer according to law, to render a true account of her administration at or before the 30th September, 1711, and to present to the Court any last will and testament of the deceased that might appear. Both Elizabeth Thomas and Richard Leyson signed the administration bond.

[National Library of Wales Document Reference: LL/1710/54]

2. Pedlars

A true and perfect Inventory of all the goods Cattles and Chattles of Richard Lewis Late of Landaff in the County of Glamorgan and Diocess of Landaff yeoman, made and apprised the 19th day of May 1684

	li - s - d
Imprimis his wearinge apparrell prised at	1 - 0 - 0
Item one feather bedd with Curtaines and Vallianes & other appurten[an]ces thereunto belonging prised att	1 -10- 0
Item one bedsteede, and old feather bedd, and the appurten[an]ces thereunto belonging prised at	1 - 4 - 0
Item in the Chamber sume old Trumpery stuff at	0 - 6 - 0
Item one Cubboord in the Lower roome at	0 - 6 - 8
Item one Chest, two Coffers, two Chaires and an old fowrme prised at	0 -12- 0
Item one old Cradle, and other wooden Trumpery prised at	0 - 6 - 0
Item one glass Cage, with some earthen vessells prised at	0 - 1 - 0
Item in the roome called the shopp one Table & frame, with an old Coffer and 2 boxes	0 -10- 0
Item in Pedlary ware in the shopp with a few small vessells of Brandy and anniseed water prised at	5 - 0 - 0
Item two Iron Crocks, two brass Kettles and one skillett prised at	0 -15- 0
Item two Spitts, 2 payre of Pott hookes, and one paire of old dogges in the Chimney or hearth, and one brandiron prised at	0 - 6 - 0
Item in pewter, six platters, 2 fflagons one Beaker three pewter Candlesticks, two sausers and a pewter	

Porrenge dish, two little pewter noggins, 3 pewter spoones, and a Tinn Tundish prised at	0 -15- 0
Item in Linnen, one payre of dowlas sheetes	0 - 8 - 0
Item a Ragg over the fire whereon a Small p[ar]cell of dryed beefe, and a little bacon towards provision prised at	0 - 2 - 0
Item wheat as it weare in grasse 5 quarters of an Acre at	1 - 0 - 0
Item one quarter of an Acre of beanes prised at	0 -10- 0
Item one Acre and a halfe of Barely prised at	1 - 0 - 0
Item in Logges,? towards the raysinge of smale Tilts in the faire, and three or fowre planks to the same use pri[sed]: at	0 - 2 - 6
Item one Small Pigg prised at	0 - 6 - 8
Sume tot[al]	15 - 1 -10

Prisers William George Morgan Morris Thomas Morgan Thomas Edward

Administration Bond: Richard Lewis: 19th May, 1684

In the Consistory Court at Llandaff, 19th May 1684, administration of the goods etc. of Richard Lewis of the City of Llandaff, deceased, was granted to his widow, Anne Meyrick alias Lewis. Ann Meyrick, William Vucles, gentleman, and Morgan John Morris, victualler, both of the City of Llandaff, were bound by the Court for Anne Meyrick to exhibit a true inventory of the goods etc. of her late husband on or before the 19th of August next, to administer according to law, to render an account of her administration on or before the 19th May, 1685, and to present to the Court any last will and testament of the deceased that might appear. Both Ann Meyrick and Morgan John Morris recorded their mark on the administration bond. William Vuckles signed the bond.

[National Library of Wales Document Reference: LL /1684 /67]

A true and p[er]fect Inventorie of all the goods Cattles Chattles and Creditts of David Griffith of the p[ar]ish of colwinston and dioceses of Landaff deceased the 28th day of June Anno dom[ini] 1686 and prized by the p[er]sons undernamed the first day of July Anno 1686 as followeth

	li - s - d
Imp[rimis] his wearing apparel prized to	00-10-00
Itt[em] two small Cettles and 3 Iron crock prized to	00-06-06
Itt[em] five pewter platters one pewtter bottle three pewter candlesticks one pewter Beggar one pewter tankard six	

pewter disches two pewter saucers two dozen pewter spoones	00-07-06
Itt[em] one tinn tancard one erthen Joog one erthen bowl three erthen platters six glass bottles & one ……. glass & two wooden cupps	00-01-06
Itt[em] 2 horses	03-00-00
Itt[em] two dust bedds two coverleds fower sheets two bedsteads two bowlsters two blancetts	00-06-08
Itt[em] one iron bakeston one Iron crock and hanging one frying pan one bellows one Chaire	00-02-00
Itt[em] three payles one trendle one looking glass two standards.	00-01-06
Itt[em] three binches two billhooks one hatchet two pack sadles two old baggs	00-01-00
Itt[em] one silk seeve one ranger and two seeves one slicking Iron	00-01-00
Itt[em] the pedlarie ware in the hows	13-00-00
Itt[em] debts due to testator	00-05-04
sum total is	18-03-00
debts due upon the testator	17-00-06

Appraisers Thomas Bowen   sign[um] Edward E N [his mark] ……
             sign[um] Tho. T [his mark] Griffith   William Thomas

[National Library of Wales Document Reference: LL/1686/57]

---

3. General/Provisions Stores in Towns

A true & p[er]fect Inventory of all and Singular the goods Cattles and Chattles moveable and unmoveable of Elizabeth Lambert late of Cardiff in the County of Glam[or]gan Spinster deceased made & duely Appraysed by the severall p[er]sons hereafter subscribing their severall names here-unto taken the 4th Day of December *in the first year of the reign of our Lord James the second King of England etc. in the year of our Lord 1685 (in latin)* in manner and forme following vizt/

	li - s - d
Imp[rimi]s the said decead[en]ts wearing apparell appraysed att	10-00-00
It[em] All her shopp goods of all maner of sorte whatsoever except Brandy and Annyseed water appraysed att	30-00-00

It[em]   The before mentioned Brandy and the said Annyseed
   water appraysed att   10-00-00
                                                    tot[al]   50-00-00
Appraysers names   Will Lambart Seniar   William Lambert ....

Administration Bond: Elizabeth Lambert: 11th November, 1685
In the Consistory Court at Llandaff, 11th November, 1685, administration of the goods etc. of Elizabeth Lambert, spinster, deceased, was granted to her sister, Charity Lambert. Charity Lambert, William Lambart, Senior, cordwayner, and William Morgan of Lanederne, gentleman, were bound for Charity Lambert to exhibit a true inventory of the goods etc. of her late sister at or before the 1st January next, to administer according to law, to render a true account of her administration at or before the 11th November, 1686, and to present to the Court any last will and testament that might appear. All three boundens signed the administration bond.

[National Library of Wales Document Reference: LL/1685/33]

A true and p[er]fect Inventory of all the Goods Cattle Chattles p[er]sonall Estate and Credits of Henry Hamonds late of Cardiff in ye County of Glamorgan and in the Diocesse of Landaff dec[eas]ed, appraised by us the p[er]sons subscribing as followeth (vizt) this p[re]sent 17 of March 1700/1

	li - s - d
Imp[rimis] His wearing Apparell	04-00-00
One silver hilted Sword	02-00-00
In the forestreet chamber in the new house one feather Bed Bedsteed and Bolster	02-10-00
Two Pillopers one Rugg one pair of Curtaines & vallians w[i]th its app[ur]ten[a]nces	10-00-00
Six Cane Chairers 4 Rusha Leather Chairers	01-04-00
One Case of drawers Table & Stand	01-00-00
One Lookeing Glasse and 2 Pictures	01-00-00
A pair of Andirons Grate, felder tongs, Slice and window Curtaines	01-00-00
att the head of the staires one large Chest in the little Chamber next to the forestreet chamber	00-10-00
one Bed one Boulster and pillowper	01-10-00
one Pair of Curtaines and Vallians & Bedsteed and Quilt	02-10-00
ffour Chairers and a little Table	00-05-00
in the upper Chamber	

one Bedsteede one Trunk one Powdering Tubb	00-00-00
In the Parlo[ur]	
Two Case of drawers Bedstead & one Bed Bolster & Rug	01-15-00
Six Leather Chairers	00-06-00
one Clock & Case	01-05-00
one Child's Chaire and Glasse Case	00-02-00
one Round Table board	00-05-00
Carpenter Tooles for his owne use	00-02-00
In the Scullery	
one Crock and Board	00-03-00
Two Brasse Scilletts one Kettle & some small things	00-07-00
In the Citching	
Six old Rusha bottome Chaires	00-01-06
One Racke and Small Table	00-05-00
One Warmeing panne Bellacis?, Grate, tongs Slice and Spitts and Andirons & Smoothing irons and ffour Iron Candlesticks	00-16-00
In Earthen ware and tinning things	00-05-00
In Pewter three hundred & three pound w[eigh]t att 6½ld	09-03-06
In Brasse Candlesticks & 2 pair of Brasse Andirons	07-00-00
	49-05-00
In the Royall oake Parlo[ur]	
A Bed Bedsteed Boulster Curtains & Vallians Rug	02-15-00
one Twigg Chaire and Barrs	00-02-00
In a bye Roome	
One fflock Bed and some old Cask	00-05-00
In the Salt Roome	
one Salt panne three butts and its app[ur]ten[a]nces	02-10-00
The bruehouse	
one Mill one small furnase 4 vattes & 2 tubbs	02-14-00
one Cubb and stilling	00-07-00
In Stone Coale	00-12-00
In Mault in one little Chamber by ye Kill 46 Welsh Busshells	11-10-00
One Hair Cloath & three small Shovells and Peacke	00-16-06
In another Chamber an hundred Welsh Bushells of Mault	25-00-00
In Beanes 5 Welsh Bushells	01-05-00
In the Mault house	
Green Mault 20 Welsh bushels	05-00-00
In dry Barley 30 Welsh bushels	03-05-00
one press cubboard	00-02-06

One stilling & two half barrell	00-03-06
Eight old Sacks	00-08-00
Bucket Shout[?] and Rope	00-04-00
Stock in Salt Rock	01-16-00
Salt upon Salt	00-10-00
six boxes of Cutt Tobacco weighing 193 neate	06-08-08
ffive pounds of the best Tobacco	00-06-06
a hundred of Roll Tobacco	03-14-00
one stilling & vinegar Cask	00-02-00
A bagg of hopps	04-11-00
one Mare Saddles Bridle and Hay	06-00-00

In the shopp

In white Salt	02-00-00
five Loafes of Sugar	00-13-04
28 pound of Meavis Sugar at 5^d	00-11-08
Halfe a hundred of brown sugar	00-19-00
Maligo Reysons	00-12-00
a hundred and quarter of Raisons of the same att	01-15-00
Six pound of powder Sugar at 8^d	00-04-00
22^{li} of Currence at 6^d	00-11-00
halfe a hundred of Browne Sugar at 42^d	01-01-00
7^{li} of the blacker pepper & 7 of Jaymaco at 17^d.	00-19-10
Six ounces of Cloves at 8^d	<u>00-04-00</u>
	<u>139-04-02</u>
Two ounzes of Large maze	00-03-00
One pounde of Nutts	00-09-06
a quarter of Synamon	00-02-00
halfe an ounze of Safforne	00-02-00
two pounds of sugar Candye	00-01-08
two pounds of Anniseed	00-01-04
Six pounds of Ginger	00-02-00
3 quarters of an hundred of Allume	00-15-00
28^{li} of Copras	00-02-00
tenne pound of powder att 8^d	00-06-08
one hundred of Shott	00-10-00
a Reame of writing paper	00-10-00
5 Reames of browne paper	00-10-00
7 Lamblack Barrells	00-07-02
6 pound of twine	00-02-06

a doz[en] of Candles	00-04-06
9 pound of Treagle	00-02-03
turnbrick and sannders	00-04-08
7 pound of Rice	00-02-04
2 doz[en] of Cards	00-04-00
3 pound of thread	00-05-00
3 quarter of browne Sugar at 46	01-14-09
Tapes and Inkles	00-10-00
Scales and weights	00-10-00
one large pair of Scales	00-04-00
one pistle and Mortar	00-01-06
one Brasse candlestick	00-01-06
2 pounds of fflicke	00-00-06
a hundred and a halfe of Soape att 30 p[er]	02-05-00
a tubb a peck a quarte and a Stricker	00-02-00
Sheles boxes and counters	01-00-00
4 Grose of Pipes	00-03-04
	151-04-04
Linnen and Woollen	05-00-00
a Lease of p[ar]bitts on a house	30-00-00
in Spearat debts	162-03-06
in desparatt debts	78-02-05
In ready Money	01-10-00
a chattle Lease held from Richard Lewis Esqr called Pentrebane valued in p[ar]bitts twenty nine pound p[er] Ann[um] but Morgaged to Mr Dear for two hundred pound	150-00-00
Item two piggs sold ye tenant for	00-14-03
sum total	578-14-03

Geo: Stephens   Tho Williams   John Archer   Joseph Hoare

Exhibited at Llandaff, 18th March, 1700, by Anne Hammonds, relict and administratrix.

Administration Bond: Henry Hamonds: 18th March, 1700

In the Consistory Court of Llandaff, 18th March, 1700, administration of the goods etc. of Henry Hamonds, deceased, was granted to his widow, Anne Hamonds. Anne Hamonds, Nathaniel Wells, cordwainer, and Christopher Wells, all of the town of Cardiff, were bound in the sum of £800 for Anne

Hamonds to make and exhibit a true inventory of the goods etc. of her late husband at or before the 1st of June next, to administer according to law, to render a true account of her administration at or before the 18th March 1700, and to present to the Court any last will and testament of the deceased that might appear. The administration bond was signed by all three boundens.

[National Library of Wales Document Reference: LL/1700/26]

A true and perfect Inventory of All & Singular the Goods Ch[att]elles Rights and Creditts of Thomas Edwards late of Cardiff in the County of Glamorgan Dec[eas]ed: Made valued & Appraised the Seven and twentyeth day of October An[n]o Domini 1704 by Us the persons Undernamed as followeth vizt.

	li - s - d
Inprimis All his Wearing Apparell valued att	01-00-00
Item fifteen Pewter Platters weighing 50li at 6d. p[er]li valued att	01-05-00
Item four Pewter Candlesticks four Porrengers two old Basons one Salt & one flagon	00-02-06
Item one Brass Warming Pan & three Brass Candlesticks att	00-02-06
Item one Brass Kettle one Bellmettal Skilett & one Iron Pott or Crock att	00-06-00
Item one Brass p[ai]r of Andirons att	00-03-00
Item Ten Earthen Platters or Plates att	00-05-00
Item one Jack & App[urtenance]s one paire of Andirons & one frying Pan att	00-05-00
Item one Cupboard five Chairs & one Chest	00-06-00
Item one feather bed one Bedstead & Clooths	01-05-00
Item Six p[ai]rs of Sheets one Dozen of Napkins and one Table cloeth at	01-00-00
Item one Silver Tankard att	03-00-09
Item two Silver spoones att	00-06-00
Item One old feather Bed one Boulster one Pillow & Curtains att	00-10-00
Item One Cupboard one Chest & four chaires	00-04-00
Item One other feather Bed & bedstead one Boulster & one Coverlid att	00-15-00
Item one Cupboard one Chair one Table One Chest & one Trunk att	00-02-06

Inventories of Village Shopkeepers and Tradesmen: Provision Stores in Town

Item one old Brewing Kettle att	00-10-00
Item One Cask of Sugar weighing 100^{li} at 5^d p[er]^{li} Appraised	02-01-08
Item one other Cask of Brown Sugar weighing 84^{li} pounds at 4^d p[er]^{li} att	01-08-00
Item One Cask of Soap wighing 50^{li} at 3d. p[er]^{li}	00-16-04
Item fifty Pounds of Raisons of the Sun at 5^d p[er]^{li}	01-03-04
Item The Remainder of a Cask of Malaga Raisons & figgs att	00-10-00
Item Twelve Pounds of Logwood att	00-02-00
Item five Rolls of Tobacco weighing 60^{li} at 8^d p[er]^{li}	02-00-00
Item Twelve pounds of Leaf Tobacco	00-08-00
Item All the Rosam Pitch & Coppras	00-04-00
Item four Dozen of Wickyarne at 4^s per doz.	00-16-00
Item All the Thread Laces & Inkle at	00-10-00
Item All the Sainen? Twine	00-01-00
Item The Cutt Tobacco	00-05-00
Item The Hemp & fflax valued at	00-07-00
Item Three Pounds of Black Pepper	00-04-06
Item One Pound of Jamaica pepper at	00-02-02
Item The Pinns at	00-04-00
Item the Ginger Turmrick & Sanders at	00-05-00
Item the Knives Nauls & Nailes att	00-05-00
Item the Paper & Mailing cord	00-05-00
Item The Scales & Weights att	00-10-00
Item All the Earthen Ware in the Shopp at	00-10-00
Item All the Earthen Ware in the Chamber	05-00-00
Item the Earthen Ware in the Shopp over the Way	03-00-00
Item One Blind Mare & colt & one horse	03-00-00
Item The Cropp of One Acre of Hay at	00-10-00
Item One Chattle Lease valued at	06-00-00
Item All the Dec[eas]eds Ready Money	01-10-00
Item Debts due to the said Dec[eas]ed	05-00-00
Sume Total	48-05-06

Appraisers   Nath: Wells   Morg: Rees   Rich Gibbon   John Williams
Exhibited at Llandaff, 23rd November, 1704, by John Williams, gaurdian to Thomas, George and Jennette Rees, minors, executors.
[Deceased described in the Will as a 'Cordiner' – presumably, a cordwainer]

[National Library of Wales Document Reference: LL/ 1704/ 24]

An Inventory of all ye Goods & Ch[att]ells of Wenllian Hedges alias Hodges late of ye Town of Cardiffe in ye County of Glam[or]gan and Diocess of Landaffe widdow dec[ea]s[e]d made vallued and apprayzed by ye p[er]sons undernamed as foll[ows]

	li - s - d
Imp[rimi]s her wearing apparell vallued	01-00-00
Item in ye Kitchen one little round table, four old chairs, three joint stools & four small stools, 2 dressers & shelves & an old hanging Cupboard att	00-12-00
Item one Copper Kettle, one brass pott, one middle Size brass Kettle, a brass pan, three small brass kettles a brass skillett & Chaffing dish, a brass Candlestick a brass spoon & a pestle & mortar att	03-00-00
Item 27 small pewter dishes, 17 pewter plates 5 porringers, 5 peawter flagons, 3 beakers, 7 peawter Candlesticks, 3 spitts 2 pair of tongs, 2 slices, 2 frying pans, a fender, 2 small iron potts & a dog wheel & a p[ai]r of bellows att	02-10-00
Item in ye shop five sacks ready made, 2 halfe pieces of sack cloth, a small p[ar]cell of hemp, ab[ou]t a dozen knotts of bed Cords, a small quantity of butter & severall p[ar]cell of sugar & spice in drawers and paper & severall other small odd things as thred, Juite, shoe points or strings, Chalk, redding twine, 2 p[ai]r of scales, an iron pestle & mortar, ab[ou]t 6 pound of Candy, a small p[ar]cell of wickyarn, 6 small empty Casks, ab[ou]t halfe a Roll of Tobacco & some other small things & lumber att	03-00-00
Item in ye best Chamber one Standing Bedstead one feather bed & bed Cloaths & Curtains, one long table, 5 joynt stools, 8 leather Chairs, an old press Cupboard, an old trunk & a box	03-00-00
Item in ye other Chamber an old bedstead a flock bed & bed Cloaths, a Chest, a small Stool an old chair an old iron grate & andirons	00-18-00
Item in ye Garrett an old bedstead & Cradle att	00-02-06
A p[ar]cell of wood & Coal att	00-05-00
Item 3 pair of sheets, a pair of table Cloaths & a dozen Napkins	00-10-00
Item in ready money ye sum of	<u>50-00-00</u>
Tot[al]	<u>64-17-06</u>

Apraysers   Wm Jenkins   Wm Thomas   John Price

Exhibited at Llandaff, 21st March, 1708/9, by William Hodges alias Hedges, son and executor.

[National Library of Wales Document Reference: LL/1708/45]

A true & perfect Inventory of all & singular the Goods, Chattles & Creditts of Richard John of Cowbridge in the County of Glamorgan & Diocess of Landaffe Grocer Lately dece]ase]d, taken, valued & appraised the 24th day of November An[n]o D[omi]ni 1715 by the persons undernamed appointed appraisors

	li s d
Imp[ri]mis His wearing apparel at	01.0.0
It[e]m two feather beds in the hall with its appurtenances, Chaires tables & other goods there standing at	03.0.0
It[e]m one feather bed with its appurtenances over the hall with Chairs & tables etc	02.0.0
It[e]m Two beds with its appurtenances in the Chamber over the shop with other goods etc	02.10.0
It[e]m Brass & pewter in the kitchen with tables and other fine goods & materialls	05.0.0
It[e]m In the chamber over the kitchen; cheese Butter & pipes etc.	04.0.0
It[em] in the store Roome, Iron, leather and other lumber	13.0.0
It[em] in the salt Roome i Tunn of salt	08.0.0
It[em] in the milking Roome Pannes & pailes etc.	00.5.0
It[em] All manner of shop goods at	45.0.0
It[em] In Corne of all sorte etc.	07.0.0
It[em] five Cows, 49 sheep & a horse	31.0.0
It[em] Hey at	07.0.0
It[em] a Chattle Lease at	02.10.0
It[em] Money due by Bonds	<u>137.10.00</u>
	268.15.00

appraisors Richard Bates Owen Morgans Edward Morgan Richard Jenkin Sworn by Joan John, alias Miles, relict and administratrix, before Franc. Davies, surrogate, 19th December, 1715.

Administration Bond: Richard John: 19th December, 1715

In the Consistory Court of Llandaff, 19th December, 1715, administration of the goods etc. of Richard John, alias Jones, deceased, was granted to his widow, Joan John, alias Miles, alias Jones. Joan John and John Miles of the parish of Porthkerry, were bound by the Court in the sum of £300 for Joan John to make and exhibit a true inventory of the goods etc. of her late husband at or before the 19th March next, to administer according to law, to give a true account of her administration at or before the 19th December 1716, and to present to the Court any last will and testament of the deceased that might appear. Both John John and John Miles signed the administration bond.

[National Library of Wales Document Reference: LL/ 1715/ 27]

An Inventory of the Personalls of William ffoord of Cardiff Cordwiner Dece[ease]d

In the Shop

One Peice of Dowlas measur'd 33 y[ar]ds at 10d p[er] y[ar]d	01-09-06
One other Piece Do. measur'd 27 yds att 6d p[er] yd	00-13-06
One other Piece of Do. measur'd 29yds at 8d p[er] yd	00-19-00
One other Piece of Holland measur'd 25yds at 10d p[er] yd	00-18-08
A remnent of Scotch Cloth	00-01-00
One piece of Garlick Holl[an]d measur'd 3yds & a half at 10d	00-02-11
Two Remn[an]ts of Muslin	00-00-06
Three yards of Coarse fustian	00-01-06
Half a Piece of Scotch Cloth measur'd 16 yds	00-10-08
severall small Rem[nan]ts of Muslin Holl[an]d and Dowlas	00-01-06
Two Coarse Kentin Cravatts	00-01-02
Seven y[ar]ds of Cheese Cloth	00-01-09
Six yds of Do.	00-01-06
ffive yards of Do.	00-01-03
six yards of Canvas at 5d	00-02-06
ffour yards of Do. at 3d	00-01-00
Nine yds of Blue Lawn at 8d	00-06-00
ffour yards of Calicoe at 10d	00-03-04
Sixteen yards of Blue Linen at 6d	00-08-00
Nine yds of Blue Check at 5d	00-03-09
A Remn[an]t of Blue Check	00-00-07
one Peice of Blue Check	00-12-00
Several Small Remn[ants]	00-01-06
One Peice of Cantaloon	00-08-00
One Peice of Stuffe	00-12-00

Six Remn[an]ts of Cantaloons	00-08-00
Thread Laces and Bobin and one piece of Cadis	00-06-00
More Thread and Tape	00-00-08
Spectacles, Cases, primers and Pins	00-01-00
One paper of pins & Buttons	00-02-00
Nine peices Lace	01-00-00
Several Small Remn[an]ts of Lace	00-05-00
Three & Twenty Silk Handkerchiefs	01-03-00
Gartering & Cadis & Inkles	00-04-00
Pinnyis?	00-02-06
A small parcel of Earthen ware	00-03-06
Three Small Caggs of Brandy	00-04-00
Eight Quiers of Writeing paper & ffifteen of Capp paper	00-03-06
In the ffore street Room	
the Deced[ent]s wearing Apparell	00-10-00
Ready Mony	01-05-00
ffive Perwiggs	00-00-06
one dust Bed 2 Bolsters two Blanketts Bedstid and Curtains	00-04-00
Two pair of Canvas sheets one pair of Old Blanketts	00-03-00
One old Case of Drawers Table & Chest	00-05-00
One Bird Cage	00-00-01
One Grate	00-00-08
In the Kitchin	
one ffeather Bed and Bolster one flock Bolster and Rug & a pair of Blanketts and a ffeather Pillow	01-16-00
Ten Old Platters	00-12-00
Tenn Old Pewter Plates	00-02-06
Eight Old Earthen Plates most Broke	00-00-04
Two Old Tables	00-02-00
ffour Old Chairs & a Stoole	00-00-08
One Old Jack & one Old Grate	00-04-00
One Toaster Tongues Slice & Grid Iron	00-01-00
One small Brass Pot one Old Iron Pot one Bell Mettle skillet one sauce pan & a Copper Pott	00-06-00
Leather and a New pair of shoes and vamps	00-03-00
One Looking Glass & ffive Prints Three Brass Candlesticks one Brass Spoon & Skimer and Some old Tin Utensills	00-01-06
In the Cellar	
Half a Hundred of Leafe Tobacco	01-05-00

ffive Rolls of Tobacco	02-00-00
a Small Box of White Sope	00-08-00
In Cutt & Dry Tobacco	00-10-00
Half a Barrel of the Best ale three quarters of Two Peny ale	00-15-00
ffour old Casks	00-06-00
In the Back Room	
one Bed of ffeathers and fflocks Bedstid Two Chairs	
one Table one Cast Iron Grate	00-03-00
In the Brewhouse	
one Old ffurnace One ffloate One Vate Two Half Barrells	
Two Casks & ffour Tubbs	01-10-00
One Pigg	00-02-00
One Bowle & Pans?	00-00-06
One Bucket & Rope	<u>00-01-00</u>
	<u>25-04-00</u>

13th August 1717 Appraized by us Wm Hiley Thomas Reece the mark of Richard Jones

Administration Bond: William ffoord: 13th August, 1717
In the Consistory Court of Llandaff, 13th August, 1717, administration of the goods etc. of William ffoord of the parish of St. John's, Cardiff, deceased, was granted to his widow, Maria ffoord. Maria ffoord and Elias Wrentmore, also of the parish of St. John's, mason, were sworn by the Court in the sum of £50 for Maria ffoord to exhibit a true inventory of the goods etc. of her late husband before the last day of October next, to administer according to law, to render a true account of her administration before the 13th August, 1718, and to present to the Court any last will and testament of the deceased that might appear. Elias Wrentmore signed the administration bond: Maria ffoord recorded her mark.

[National Library of Wales Document Reference: LL/ 1717/ 20]

A true & perfect Inventory of all & Singular ye goods Ch[att]ells, & Credits of Mary Lewis late of ye Towne of Cardiffe, in ye County of Glamorgan, & Diocess of Landaffe, widdow dece[ase]d, made, valued & appraised ye 2nd day of December, in the ye year of our Lord 1720 by John Abiss, & George Evans appraisors, as follows, (vizt.)

	li - s - d
Inp[rimi]s Her wearing apparell valued at	00-10-00
Item book debts ye summ of	03-00-00

Item	Goods in yᵉ parlour, one feather bed at	01-00-00
Item	one folding bedstead at	00-04-00
Item	five small bolsters at	00-10-00
Item	one pair of Curtains at	00-04-00
Item	one rugg at	00-02-00
Item	Two round tables at	00-04-00
Item	Eight large pictures at	00-00-08
Item	five small pictures at	00-00-03
Item	one looking glass at	00-02-00
Item	six small earthen plates at	00-00-06
Item	one brasse Candlestick at	00-00-06
Item	one iron candlestick at	00-00-01
Item	one pair of tongs at	00-00-02
Item	two small fire shovells at	00-00-06
Item	Two Joint stooles at	00-00-06
Item	Eight Chairs at	00-04-00
Item	one hour-glass at	00-00-03
Item	Goods in yᵉ Kitchin, eighteen small pewter platters at	01-07-00
Item	Eleven small pewter plates at	00-04-07
Item	Two pewter Candlesticks at	00-01-00
Item	one tin pudding-pan at	00-00-03
Item	one pewter quart at	00-00-06
Item	two pewter quartans at	00-00-04 ½
Item	one half quartan at	00-00-01 ½
Item	one Dresser at	00-04-00
Item	one rack at	00-01-00
Item	one hen-Coop at	00-01-00
Item	one Dog-wheel at	00-01-06
Item	one Spit at	00-00-06
Item	one pair of Andirons at	00-02-00
Item	one toaster at	00-00-09
Item	one frying-pan at	00-01-00
Item	one pair of tongs at	00-00-06
Item	one smoothing iron at	00-01-00
Item	four small Chairs at	00-01-04
Item	one pair of bellows at	00-00-06
Item	one Small Square table at	00-01-00
Item	Goods in yᵉ back-Kitchin Seven pewter dishes at	00-02-06
Item	Six pewter spoons at	00-00-06

Item	one skillett at	00-02-00
Item	oneSmall iron marmant	00-01-06
Item	one Small brass Candlestick at	00-00-06
Item	one fire-pott at	00-02-06
Item	one boyler at	00-12-00
Item	one small brass brewing vate at	00-01-00
Item	one Tub at	00-00-06
Item	Goods in ye Chamber two small beds	01-10-00
Item	one bolster at	00-02-06
Item	five pillows at	00-02-06
Item	Two ruggs at	00-10-00
Item	one pair of Sheets at	00-03-00
Item	Two pair of old Curtains at	00-02-06
Item	five pair of blanketts at	00-05-00
Item	one Square table at	00-01-00
Item	two other small Square tables at	00-02-00
Item	four Chairs at	00-03-00
Item	Two Joint stools at	00-00-06
Item	Two Chests at	00-05-00
Item	one trunk at	00-01-00
Item	one bible at	00-00-09
Item	two other books at	00-01-00
Item	0ne small Grate at	00-02-00
Item	shop goods, five hundred, one quarter, & thirteen pounds of sugar at	05-03-00
Item	one hundred, one quarter & thirteen pounds of raisons of ye Sun at	01-15-00
Item	One hundred, one quarter, and two & twenty pounds of Soap at	02-00-00
Item	Seale tobacco at	01-02-00
Item	one quarter & 18 pounds of Currants at	00-16-00
Item	Seven pounds of ginger at	00-01-06
Item	two pounds of Sanders at	00-01-00
Item	12 pounds of Starch at	00-03-00
Item	Seven pounds of gunpowder at	00-04-02
Item	two rhemes of pound paper at	00-03-00
Item	a q^r of Cynamen at	00-01-06
Item	a q^r of Cloves at	00-02-04
Item	two ounces of mace at	00-02-00
Item	half a pound of Nutmegs at	00-04-00

Item	Two dozen of green hemp at		00-12-00
Item	A small box of Manchester ware		00-10-00
Item	four pounds of Glue at		00-00-09
Item	28 pounds of stone pitch & rosum at		00-03-00
Item	Tarr at		00-02-00
Item	Marlins at		00-02-06
Item	earthen ware at		01-00-00
Item	a pestle & Mortar at		00-02-00
Item	one pair of Scales & weights at		00-02-06
Item	black pepper & Jamaica pepper at		00-12-00
Item	twenty six pounds of rowl tobacco at		00-12-00
Item	4 pounds of aniseed at		00-01-06
Item	twenty eight pounds of Leaf tobacco		00-14-00
Item	six Lambs at		00-12-00
Item	forty sheep at		06-10-00
		Tot[al]	35-15-10

Exhibited at Llandaff by Elizabeth Lewis, daughter and administratrix, 12th January, 1720.

Administration Bond: Mary Lewis: 12th January, 1720

In the Consistory Court at Llandaff, 12th January, 1720, administration of the goods of Mary Lewis, deceased, was granted to her daughter, Elizabeth Lewis, of the town of Cardiff. Elizabeth Lewis and George Evans of Cardiff, feltmaker, were bound by the Court in the sum of £70 for Elizabeth Lewis to make and exhibit a true inventory of the goods, etc. of her late mother at or before the 12th of July next, to administer according to law, to give a true account of her administration at or before the 12th January, 1721, and to present ot the Court any last will and testament of the deceased that might appear. Both Elizabeth Lewis and George Evans signed the administration bond.

[National Library of Wales Document Reference: LL/1720/41]

A true and perfect Inventory of the Goods and Chattles Rights and Credits of fflorence Brewer late of Cardiff in the County of Glamorgan Widow deceased taken and appraised the Eighth day of August 1740 by us whose Names are hereunto Subscribed as followeth

	li - s - d
Imprimis Her Wearing Apparel at	01-10-00
Item In the Shop	
24li ½ Lump Sugar at 6d	00-12-03

6^{li} ¾ double refine Sugar at 9^d	00-04-09
5^{li} pound Sugar Candy at 8^d	00-08-04
4^{li} ¾ Single refined Sugar at 7^d	00-02-09
7^{li} ½ Course brown Sugar at 3^d	00-01-10
7^{li} more Sugar Candy at 8^d	00-04-08
1^{li} ½ Lump Sugar Candy at 6^d	00-00-09
9^{li} ¼ Powdered Ginger at 3^d	00-02-04
6^{li} ¾ black pepper at 10^d	00-05-05
2^{li} Jamaica pepper at	[blank]
3^{li} Blew at 8^d	00-02-00
2^{li} Blew at 1^s	00-02-00
23^{li} ½ reasons of the Sun at 4^{d}½	00-08-09
22^{li} ½ of Currants at 4^{d}½	00-08-05
1^{li} Sannders	00-00-02
1^{li} ¼ red Lead at 3^d	00-00-04
½^{li} Turmerick at	00-00-06
2 Ounces & ¼ Mace at 1: 6	00-03-04
3 Ounces of Nutmegg at 7^d	00-01-09
3½ Cloves at 7^d	00-02-00
1½ Cinamon at 7^d	00-00-10
1^{li} fflower of Brimstone	00-00-10
¼ of an Ounce Saffron	00-00-06
1^{li} ¾ Starch at 4^d	00-00-07
1^{li} ½ rack Ginger at 4^d	00-00-06
8 ounces AniSeed	00-00-02
2^{li} ½ White Soap at 6^d	00-01-08
6^{li} ½ Roll Tobacco at 7^d	<u>00-06-09</u>
	£5-08-11
4^{li} Black Soap at 4^{d}½	00-01-06
21^{li} Leaf Tobacco at	00-14-00
3^{li} ½ Salt Peter at 10^d	00-02-11
7^{li} ¼ Hemp at 6^d	00-03-07 ½
33^{li} Cut Tobacco at 10^d	01-07-06
a Ream of White Cap Paper at	00-05-00
a Ream of brown Pound Paper	00-01-08
12^{li} ½ Stone Pitch at 1^{d}½	00-01-06 ¾
52^{li} pound Chalk at ¾	00-03-03
6^{li} pound stone BrimStone at 2½	00-01-03
60^{li} pound Stone Reding at ¾	00-03-09

Inventories of Village Shopkeepers and Tradesmen: Provision Stores in Town

a Bushell of red Scouring Sand	00-01-06
2 English Pecks of Calis? Sand	00-00-08
10^{li} ¾ of rotten stone at 4^d	00-03-07
2^{li} brown Sugar at 3^d	00-00-06
135^{li} Whiteing 4^s p[er] Hund[re]d	00-05-00
a Basket and Cover	00-00-07
1^{li} ¾ Sugar at 7^d	00-01-00
2 Doz[e]n & one brown Quarts	00-04-02
4 Doz[e]n & 3 Pints	00-04-03
2 Doz[e]n half Pints	00-02-00
2 Doz[e]n & Seven Yellow Dishes 2 Handles	00-01-11 ½
a piece and a half ffilleting	00-03-00
a piece & ½ Tape	00-01-03
2 pieces Tape	00-01-02
a piece and a half of Tape	00-01-03
2 pieces Tape	00-01-04
1 piece Tape	00-00-05
2 pieces Tape	00-01-08
2 piece Tape	00-00-08
1 pieces Tape	00-00-05
Remnants of Tape	00-00-10
2 pieces Tape	00-01-03
2 piece Tape	00-01-03
1 pieces Tape	00-00-07
1 piece Gartering	00-01-00
3 pieces and ½ Cadiz	00-03-06
a piece of Tape	<u>00-00-07</u>
	10-00-06 ½
A piece of Tape	00-00-06
3 yards Goloom	00-00-03
2 pieces Robin	00-00-07
6 pound of Thread at 1: 8	00-10-00
3 Ounces Thred	00-04-00
½ an ounce Thread	00-00-06
8 Ounces Thread	00-00-09
5 Doz[e]n & 10 thread Laces at 3^{d}½	00-01-09 ½
6 Papers of Pins at 5^d	00-02-06
11 Papers Pins at 3^{d}½	00-03-02 ½
4 Papers Pins at 5^d	00-01-08

¾ of a Rand of Twine   00-00-07
4 Doz[e]n & 4 Knots Twine at   00-02-02
3 Doz[e]n & 9 Knots Twine   00-03-09
9 Doz^n & 6 knots Twine   00-02-05
1 Doz^n & 8 thread Laces   00-00-04
Course Inkle   00-00-04
6 pieces of flat earthen Ware   00-02-02
18 Yellow Cups   00-06-00
28 Yellow Cups   00-01-02
5 Chamber Pots   00-00-06
2 Doz^n & 9 Glasses at 4^s p[er] Doz^n 00-09-06
2 Jars of Oyle   00-10-06
a Bushel of red Scouring Sand   00-01-06
9 pound of Shot   00-01-01
5 hair Brushes   00-02-11
4 hair Brushes   00-01-08
11 p[ai]r ½ glass Decanters at 8^d 00-07-08
17 pound Treacle   00-02-10
fflax   00-00-03
6 Halters   00-01-03
10 Hundred a quarter & 9^d Salt at 7^s 03-12-03
2 Groze & ½ Short Pipes at 10^d 00-02-01
a Groze & a Doz^n long Pipes at 1^{s}4^d 00-01-05
2 Doz^n & ½ Ginger Bread at 1^s 00-02-06
10 Cabbage Nets   00-00-05
Ash Balls   <u>00-10-00</u>
                                                                  18-13-06¼

In the Kitchen
8 p^d of Brass at 6^d 00-04-00
9 Pewter Dishes 23 Pewter Plates & 1 Cullinder wt. 73^{li} at 7^d 02-02-07
3 Iron Candlesticks at 2^d 00-00-06
an Iron Toaster & a stand for a Smoothing Iron   00-01-02
2 Dripping Pans a flower Box & Grater   all Tin   00-01-03
a pair of Andrions   00-02-00
a Kitchen Grate an Ash Grate a paire of Tongs & fire Shovell
    a flesh fork   Grid Iron pot hooks and an old Jack at   00-10-00
Six old Chairs at   00-04-00
An Oval Table a Square Table & an old Coffer at   00-08-00
an old Dresser & 4 earthen fruit Dishes a looking Glass   00-01-00

66

In the best Chamber
one Slope Tester bedstead & furniture and Window Curtains   02-10-00
a Case of Drawers & 2 looking Glasses   01-00-00
a Stove Grate Tongs Shovell poker & fender   00-15-00
10 old Cane Chairs at   00-16-00
In the Room over the Parlour
A Bedstead Curtains and Window Curtains   00-16-00
a Dressing Table & 6 old Chairs   00-10-00
Barrs in the Chimney   00-01-00
In another Chamber
An old Bedstead and other Lumber   00-05-00
Barn & Stable Earthenware   02-00-00
Part of a Barrel of Tar   00-02-00
a ffeather Bed Boulster & 2 pillows belonging to the
best Chamber weighing 122p^d at 6^d 03-01-00
a pair of Sheets and two old Quilts   00-04-00
a ffeather Bed belonging to the other Chamber wt. 75p^d at 4^d 01-05-00
an old Rug   00-01-06
    35-16-06 ¼

In the Brewhouse
A ffurnace and Barrs   01-02-00
1 ffat and two Tubbs   00-05-06
a brass Kettle   00-04-06
a Copper Saucepan   00-01-06
At Leckwith
a Bedstead & Curtains   00-08-00
ffeather Bed & Boulster wt. 70^l at 4^d 01-03-04
An Oval Table & an old Chair   00-04-06
a Corner Cupboard   00-03-00
a pair of Sheets   00-03-00
a Rug and Quilt   00-03-06
a ffrying Pan & Candlestick   00-01-08
a pair of Bellows   00-00-09
an Iron Marmar   00-01-06
2 pewter Plates   00-00-09
2 Pailes   00-01-00
a Cheese fat & butter Plate   00-01-00
A Copper Saucepan   00-01-06
a Silver Cup and Spoon w[eigh]t 13 Ounces at 5^s 4^d 03-09-04

13 Towells at	00-02-00
a pair of Holland Sheets	00-12-00
1 Sheet Holland	00-04-00
a pair of Cotten Sheets	00-04-00
3 Course Sheets	00-03-00
7 Blanketts	00-15-00
1 Quilt	00-12-00
1 ffeather Bolster wt. 15p^d	00-05-00
a pair of Scales and Beam	00-02-00
28p^d of Lead w[eigh]ts at	00-02-04
Two old Cows at	05-00-00
one Dry Cow at	03-00-00
One Heifer two year old	02-10-00
	57-04-02 ¼
Two Heifers one of three and the other of two years old	04-10-00
one yearling Bull at	01-00-00
two Sucking Calves at	00-16-00
1 old Mare at	00-15-00
two small Piggs at	00-13-00
The Hay in the Barn and Rick Yard at	04-04-00
a fat Calf	00-08-00
The Sperate Debts due to the deceased	20-00-00
Desperate Debts due to her	10-00-00
Cupboard Door in the Kitchen	00-03-06
Counter and Shelves in the Shop, Drawer etc.	00-07-06
Chimney Piece in the Parlour	00-05-00
a Rack in the Kitchen	00-01-00
a Horse for drying of Cloaths	00-00-06
3 Doz^n of Quart Bottles	00-03-00
2 Doz^n Pint Bottles	00-00-06
2 Cupboards in the Back Chamber	00-05-00
a Calf at	00-11-01 ½
	102-08-03 ¾

Appraisers   Thomas Seabrook   the mark of Nicholas N [his mark] Jayn
'Exhibited at Cardiffe upon the Twentieth day of October 1740 by Dorothy Brewer the Principal Creditor and Administratrix for a true and perfect Inventory etc.'

Administration Bond: Florence Brewer: 20th October, 1740

In the Consistory Court of Llandaff. 20th October, 1740, administration of the goods, chattles and credits of Florence Brewer, widow, deceased, was granted to Dorothy Brewer, widow of the Town of Cardiff, the principal creditor of the deceased. Dorothy Brewer, John Thomas, Maltster, and Thomas Deer, Perukemaker, both of the Town of Cardiff, were sworn by the Court in the sum of £250 for Dorothy Brewer to make and exhibit a true inventory of the goods etc. of the deceased, to administer according to law, to make a true account of her administration before October 31st, 1741, and to present to the Court any last will and testament of the deceased that might appear. All three boundens signed the administration bond.

[National Library of Wales Document Reference: LL/ 1740/ 25]

An Inventory of all the Goods and Chattels of Mr Thomas Young Now Deceas'd, Apprais'd by Thomas Seabrook and John Jenkin   March the 24th 1760: as followeth

	£ - s - d
Mr Thomas Young's Wearing Apparel Consisting Cloths Shirts, Cravatts, Coats, Wastcoats, Breeches, boots, Shoes, Stockings, Hatts and Wigs etc.	02-10-06
one old Silver Watch, and an old pair of Silver Buckles	01-10-00
In Mr Young's Bed Chamber Two feather beds and bedsteads one feather bed and bolster, weight, 70^{li} att 6^d p[er] pound	01-15-00
one bedstick, Curtains, and all its Appurtenance	01-10-00
another feather bed and bolster 49 pound att 6 per]	01-04-06
one small bedstick without any curtains	00-03-06
5 pair of Ordinary Sheets valu'd to	01-00-00
4 pair of Blankettts	01-00-00
2 old Rugs and one Cover Led	00-18-00
one old Quilt 6^s one small Deal Square Table 2^s in all	00-08-00
one Deal Screntore 1£ 1^s Two Deal Boxes 4^s in all	01-05-00
Six Rush bottom Chairs 9^s one Small Looking Glass 4^s 6^d	00-13-06
In the Next Chamber	
one feather bed 69 pound att 5 the pound	01-08-06
one old bedstick 12^s one small square Table 5^s in all	00-17-00
on Close stool 2^s one old Trunk and one old Deal box 1^s 6^d in all	00-03-06

In the Kitchin

Six Wooden bottom Chairs 6^s one Square Table and a Stand 6^s in all	00-12-00
seven small Iron Candlesticks 1^s 6^d one frying pan and great Iron 2^s	00-03-06
Three Cast Smoothing Irons 9^d Three Small prints 1^s in all	00-01-09
52^{lb} of pewter att 6 p[er] 1£ 6^s Bacon 40^{lb} att 4^d ½ the pound 15^s in all	02-01-00
Half a Dozen knifes and forks 1^s 6^d Two old pails 1^s in all	00-02-06
one old billows 6^d an old Tin Cover 3^d Tin oven 8^d Lanthorn 10^d in all	00-02-03
Tongs, Shovel and pocker 2^s Six old Spoons 6^d 4 old books 2^s	00-04-06

In the Back Room

one old Lave binch and Mr Young's Chest of Carpenters Tools	<u>03-00-00</u>
Please to Turn over Tott[al] sum	<u>22-14-06</u>

In the Shop as followeth

53 Yards of Cheque att 1^s the yard	02-13-00
34 y[ar]ds of Cheque att 7^d comes to 19^s 10^d 26 y^{ds} Rusha Cloth att 5^d comes to 11^s 10^d	01-11-08
38 yards of Irish Cloth att 1^s 3^d the y[ar]d	02-07-06
90 yards of Corce Irish Cloth att 1^s 1^d the y[ar]d	04-17-06
42 yards of Dowlas att 10^d the yard	01-15-00
32 yards of Corce Sheeting att 9^d the y[ar]d	01-04-00
10 yards of Yallow Canvas at 10^d the y[ar]d	00-08-04
17 yards of ordinary Cloth for Wiping the hands att 8^d the y[ar]d	00-11-04
3 yards of Tickin 2^s Eight handkerchiefs 8^s	00-10-00
10 yards of fustian att 8^d p[er] y[ar]d	00-06-08
47 yards of Cheese Cloths att 3^d the y[ar]d	00-11-09
28 yards of Rusha Cloth att 4d. the yard	00-09-04
35 yards of Rowl'd Canvas att 4^d the y[ar]d	00-11-08
40 yards of Crape att 10^d the yard	01-13-04
20 Small handkerchiefs at 6^d Each	00-10-00
26 Ordinary Small Locks att 4^d Each	00-08-08
9 Setts of Tongs Shovels and pockers	18-00-00
31 pound of ordinary Common Thread	01-00-00

12 Hour Glasses 4^s, in a small Neast of Drawers Consisting

Inventories of Village Shopkeepers and Tradesmen: Provision Stores in Town

of flower of Brimstone, Caraway Seeds, Aniseeds, and Salt petre	00-03-00
In a Drawer Some Loose Thread, gartering, and some Tape	00-12-00
In a Drawer A Small parcell of Paddisway and Some Felletting	00-05-00
18 Papers of Horn buttons	00-05-00
In 8 Drawers a Small Quantity of brown Sugar a little rice, blew, starch, and some Lump Sugar	00-05-00
In 4 Papers, Stay Laces to the Amount of	00-08-00
Please to turn over	£47-01-03
36 yards of Corce Crape att 8^d the yard	01-04-00
4^{lb} of Black, and jameco Pepper, att 10^d the pound	00-03-04
3^{lb} of aniseeds att 8d D[itt]o. 6^{lb} of Brimstone att 3^d Do. 5^{lb} of Salt Petre att 10^d	00-07-08
5^{lb} of Worsted att 1^s 12 Quier of Weiteing paper att 6 the Quier	00-11-00
7^{lb} of rond Twine att 9^d four knotts of beggars Tape att 4^d five Saddle girses	00-07-07
100^{lb} of brown sugar att 52^s Twenty eight pounds of Lump Sugar att 8^d	03-05-01
40^{lb} of Tobacco att 13^d Cheese 93^{lb} att 26^s ye Hundred in all comes to	03-04-11
13^{lb} of Sun Raisons at 4^d ½ p[er] Curance 25^{lb} att 4^d ½ p[er]	00-14-03
one Hundred of Spanish White att 3^s	00-03-00
Marling 42^{lb} att 3^d p[er] Tarr in a Cask 7^s 6^d Treacle 2^s 6^d	01-00-06
8^{lb} of gunn powder att 8^d rosome 2^s 6^d Black pitch 2^s 6^d	00-10-04
54^{lb} of Scouring Sand att ½ five pound of rotten stone 5^d	00-02-08
4^{lb} of Hemp att 6^d the pound 4^{lb} and a ½ of Sugar Candy att 6^d ye lb	00-04-03
3^{lb} of Ginger att 8^d p[er] 42 Dozen of Tin plates for Coffins att 6^d	01-03-00
6 Dozen of Tin plate Locks 6s. 9 Dozen Squares and letters 4^s 6^d	00-10-06
9 Cloathes Brushes 3^s Three Dozen of small Scutcheons 2^s 6^d	00-05-06
49 Jack knifes att 3^d Each 19 ordinary knifes without Sheaths at 2^d	00-10-11
62 ordinary pen knifes att 2^d Each 15 common razors att 2^{d}½ Each one Dozen and a ½ of black Common paper Ink horns	00-02-00

11 Black Snuffers att 1^{d}½ one Sugar knife 6^d	00-01-10½
Three Dozen Copasses att 2^d Each	00-06-00
one dozen of Springs for Latches	00-01-00
99 pair of Hinges of Differend sorts att 4^d p[er]	<u>01-13-00</u>
Please to turn over	£64-09-10½
52 Pair of Small box Hinges att 2^d the pair	00-08-08
2 Dozen plates for Carpenter's Planes att 2^s 6^d p[er]	00-05-00
72 pair small Different Sort of Hinges att 4^d p[er]	01-04-00
80 small files att 2^d Each	00-13-04
35 Small flatt Locks att 3^d Each	00-08-09
one Dozen of Hamers att 5^s p[er] Dozen	00-05-00
one Large Lock 2^s 6^d One brass Lock 4^s 6^d	00-07-00
one Dozen of Spring bolts att 4^s p[er] Dozen	00-04-00
8 small Hatchetts 5^s Do. 5 of a Larger Sort 5^s	00-10-00
2 Dozen of Shoemaker's knifes att 3^s the Dozen	00-06-00
17 pound of fire Shovells att 6^d the pound	00-08-06
16 Mouse Traps 1^s 6^d Do. 79 Small brushes att 2^d Each in all	00-14-08
17 Large rubers att 5^d Each 6 Large rubers att 6^d Each	00-10-01
6 Thousand of Six penny Sprigs and Nails att 3^s p[er]	00-18-00
9 Thousand of four Sprigs and Nails att 2^s 3^d p[er] Thousand	01-00-03
11 Thousand of Lath Nails att 10^d p[er] Thousand	00-09-02
12 Thousand of 3 penny Nails att 1^s 6^d p[er] Do.	
28 all hafts att 1^s in all	00-19-00
4 Groce of Wood Screws 6^s Do. 8 Billows att 8^d Each 5^s 4^d	00-11-04
14 brass handles and Scutcheons att 3^d the pair	00-03-06
42 small brass handles and Scutcheons att 3^d the pair	00-07-00
6 pair of brass Hinges att 3^d the pair	00-01-06
6 handles and nine Scutcheons att 1^{d}½ p[er]	00-01-10½
one Dozen of Hinges at 2^d Each 2 dozen of brass buttons 1^s	00-03-00
200 Weight of Nails att 3^d the pound	02-10-00
one garner's Sapade 2^s Three great Irons 2^s Three House Mops	<u>00-05-06</u>
Please to turn over	£78-05-00
Two frying Pans 13 pound att 4^d the pound	00-04-04
80 pounds of Steel att 4^d the pound	01-06-08
65 pounds of Mixt Twine att 9^d the pound	02-08-09
18 Small Tooth Combs	00-04-06
14 Small brass Hinges att 2^d Each	00-02-04
6 pair of brass Hinges at 4^d the pair	00-02-00

6 brass bolts 1^s 6^d nine Screws and Scutcheons 1^s: 4^d	00-02-10
12 Rings for Turn Up? Tables	00-03-00
3 Dozen Scutcheons at 1^s the Dozen	00-03-00
21 Cast Iron potts Weight 220^{lb} att 1^{d}½ p[er] pound	01-07-06
26 Dozen of Eartin Ware att 6^{d}½ p[er] Dozen	00-14-01
6 Tin kettles valued Separately and comes to	00-08-00
3 pudding pots 3^s one strainer 1^s Three Candleboxes 3^s	00-07-00
2 Cheese Tasters 1^s 4^d five Skemers 1^s four fish spoons 1^s	00-03-04
2 large Watter potts 4^s Two Do. 3^s Two Do. 2^s 6^d in all	00-09-06
900 of Hops att £1 3^s 4^d comes to	10-10-00
The Work Shop	
9 Thousand of Laths att 7^s the Thousand	03-03-00
17 Boards of 12 foot Deal at 2^s p[er] Each	01-14-00
10 of 7 foot Deal 10^s one Hundred and a half of raffters 12^s	01-02-00
72 foot of ordinary Walnutt att 1^{d}½ Some Loose Timber £1 10^s	01-19-00
150 of raffter att 8^s the Hundred	00-12-00
Three hundred of Bricks att 3^s the Hundred	00-09-00
66 pan Tyles 2^s 6^d Do. 32 foot of Walnutt Tree att 2^d p[er]	<u>00-07-10</u>
	106-08-08

Witness   Thomas Seabrook   John Jenkins   Appraisers

Administration Bond: Thomas Young: 8th March, 1760

In the Consistory Court of Llandaff, 8th March, 1760, administration of the goods etc. of Thomas Young, deceased, was granted to his widow, Jane Young. Jane Young, Edward Young, shoemaker, and Thomas Seabrook, joiner, both of Cardiff, were sworn by the Court in the sum of £220 for Jane Young to exhibit a true inventory of the goods etc. of her late husband on or before the last day of June next, to administer according to law, to give a just account of her administration on or before the last day of March, 1761, and to present to the Court any last will and testament of the deceased that might appear. All three boundens signed the administration bond.

[National Library of Wales Document Reference: LL./1760/23]

Memorandum made this Twentieth day of August, one thousand eight hundred and fifty one by me Noah Jones of the Town of Cardiff in the County of Glamorgan Appraiser etc. of the Goods & Chattels of John Howells, Grocer deceased, late of Union Street in the Town and County

aforesaid, who died on the third day of August one thousand eight hundred and fifty one a Schedule of which goods is as follows

	£ - s - d
Kitchen	
4 Beech Chairs 8/- 1 rocking chair 1/6	00-09-06
1 Square deal table	00-06-00
1 Deal dresser & Shelves	01-05-00
8 small Pictures & frames	00-03-06
1 lot common ware	00-04-00
1 sett of Tea ware	00-03-06
Tray & Bread Basket	00-02-00
Common fender & fire Irons	00-02-00
Sundry Chimney ornaments	00-02-06
In the Shop 1 Counter	01-00-00
Lot of shelves	00-08-00
2 small scales & weights	00-06-00
Flour Scale & weights	00-04-06
9 Tea Cannisters 13/6 1 Beech chair 2/-	00-15-06
9 lbs [pounds] Tea at 4/- £1-16-0 1 Cwt [hundredweight] Sugar £1-15-0	03-11-00
1 Cwt Soda 5/- ½ Cwt Soap £1-1-0 6lbs Tobacco £1-4-0	02-10-00
9lbs Cocoa 6/- 5 lbs Starch 1/8 2 Reams Paper 10/-	00-17-08
25 lbs Candles 8/4 10 lbs Butter 5/10	00-14-02
first Bedroom Mahogany Pembroke Table	00-16-00
Old Chest Drawers	01-00-00
Stump Bedstead 5/- Feather Bed Bolster & Pillows £3-10-0	03-15-00
1 Blanket 2/- Drugget 1/- 2 Sheets 3/6	00-06-06
2 Dressing Glasses 4/- Tea tray 1/-	00-05-00
on Landing 1 Cradle, mattress & small Blanket	00-04-06
second Bedroom ½ Doz[en] Beech Chairs	00-15-00
1 Tent Bedstead 7/-	00-07-00
Millpuff Bed 8/- Feather Bolster 5/-	00-13-00
Pair Sheets 2/6 Blanket 2/-	00-04-06
Round Deal Table 2/- Painted Washstand 3/-	00-05-00
Sundry Chimney ornaments	00-02-00
3 pair Sheets 6/- 1 Quilt 3/-	<u>00-09-00</u>
	<u>£22-07-04</u>

Noah Rees   Cardiff   August 20th 1851

Administration Bond: John Howells: 20th August, 1851

In the Consistory Court of Llandaff, 20th August, 1851, administration of the goods etc. of John Howells, grocer, who died on the 3rd August, 1851, was granted to his widow, Margaret Howells, of 33, Union Street, Cardiff. Margaret Howells, William John of Tredegar Crescent, Cardiff, grocer, and William Price of Bridge Street, Cardiff, carpenter, were sworn by the Court in the sum of £200 for Margaret Howells to exhibit a true inventory of the goods etc, of her late husband on or before the last day of February next, to administer according to law, to render a true account of her administration on or before the last day of August, 1852, and present to the Court any last will and testament of the deceased that might appear. All three boundens signed the administration bond.

[National Library of Wales Document Reference: LL/ 1851/ 48]

---

4. Hardware Shops/Chandlery/Blacksmiths

The Inventory of the goods & Chattles of Thomas Richards Senior, of the towne of Cowbridge w[i]thin the diocesse of Landaph deceased, made & appraised the first day of May: An[n]o d[omi]ni (1699) by the p[er]sons who have hereunto subscribed their names etc.

	li - s - d
His wearing apparel appraised to xx^s	01-00-00
It[em] one featherbedd & boulster with their app[ur]tenances to	01-00-00
It[em] one dustbedd boulster with the app[ur]tenances and a bedsteed to	00-10-00
It[em] one ….. Table one Cubbord: fower old Red leather chaires one old coffer to	01-00-00
It[em] his Brasse and pewter and 1 p[ai]r Iron Andirons 1 frying pan 1 p[ai]r of Iron tongs, firepan and other small utensils to	01-00-00
It[em] his shop wares being Leather nailes & hemp valued to	10-00-00
It[em] debts due by book to the testator	04-00-00
Sum	18-10-00

Appraisers   John Morris   Lewis Evor   Hen: Richard
            Signum   Morgan   M B [his mark] Bassett

Exhibited at Llandaff, 8th May, 1699, by Joan Richards, daughter and executrix.

[National Library of Wales Document Reference: LL/ 1699/ 35]

A true and perfect Inventory of all Such goods Chattles as were found in the possession of Katherine Bassett of the towne of Cowbridge in the County of Glam[or]gan widow at the time of her decease Made and appraised by the persons under named the first day of October Annoqe D[omi]ni 1707

	li - s - d
Her wearinge Apparell	01-00-00
In the Hall	
1 old feather bed, 2 small bolsters, 1 p[ai]r of sheets 1 rugg & Cov[er]lid, old Curtains & Vallions	01-08-00
1 old bedstead 8^s 1 Cubbord 7^s 1 longe table with 5 joint stooles 8^s	01-03-00
1 Chair & table, 1 Small old oval Table 3^s 6^d 6 old Chairs 5^s 2 old Coffers 3^s	00-11-06
1 Small old Coffer & 1 old trunke 1^s 8^d, 1 Clock 1^{li} 5^s, 1 glass Cage 2^d	01-05-02
1 Small lookinge glass 1^s, 5 Small stooles 1 …. & 2 little benches 1^s 3^d	00-02-03
3 old painted papers 2^d, 1 Bible, 2 Common prayer books & 3 other small books	00-05-02
pewter as weighed 1^{li} 9^s 2^d Cast Brass 1^s 9^d, 2 old Spitts 1^s 3^d old AndIrons 3^s	01-15-02
1 old frying pan 9^d tongs and slice 1^s 6^d, 1 old warminge pan 2^s	00-04-03
2 pott-hooks and Crocks 2^s, 1 Small Skimmer 4^d, 1 flesh fork 3^d, 1 old toster 9^d	00-03-04
1 old Smoothinge Iron & heaters 1^s, 2 old Iron Candlesticks 4^d old tins 1^s	00-02-04
1 old p[ai]r of bellows 6^d in Small Chamberly things besides 1^s	00-01-06
In the Buttry	
in Earthen ware as dishes platters juggs, Muggs and pans	00-04-00
wooden dishes & Trenchers 1^s 6^d pewter as weighed 1^{li} 8^s White brass 1^{li} 3^s 4^d Cast brass 13^s	03-05-10
In the Chamber ov[er] the Shop	
2 feather beds, 1 bolster, 3 pillows, 2 old Ruggs, 4 blanketts, 1 old Curtains & vallions	04-00-00
1 old bedstead, 6 old Chairs, 3 old Coffers and a stoole box?	00-08-00
3 old painted papers & 1 Small bench 6^d Linnen of all Sorts 1^{li} 5^s	01-05-06

In the salt house
Salt ab[ou]t 2 hundred & a halfe 1^li   2 old Spimminge
    wheeles & Cardes 2^s   01-02-00
In the Shop
A parcel of old fustian buttons 5^s hempe 16^s
    Wykyarn 1^s 3^d remnants of inkle 6^d   01-02-09
Thred of all sorts 2^s 6^d, thred laces 6^d, tape 1^s, 5 Ends of
    Cadys 6^d, 5 Ends of fireet ribbon 5^s   00-09-06
Small remnants of old fustian golooms 1^s 6^d, fragments of
    old Sewinge Silks 2^s   00-03-06
Ab[ou]t halfe a hundred of Roll tobacco 1^li 17^s 4^d   remnants
    of all sorts of nails   2^li 5^s   04-02-04
1 winnowinge sheet 5^s, 3 haire Sacks 6^s, 5 Remn[an]ts of
    Col[oure]d Linnen & oxenbrigg 10^s   01-01-00
a Small remnant of Crape & flannen 10^s, 2 broken
    lanthorns 1^s, 3 frying pans 4^s   00-15-00
1 Small bellows 8^d, 2 Small fetter locks 8^d   00-01-04
2 nests of old drawers, broken Casks & boxes, 1 old Coffer
    w[i]th other old lumber not worth the valueinge   00-06-00
2 old p[ai]r of brass Scales and Small weights thereto
    belonginge   00-03-00
In the Cellar
In Backs of Leather and small pieces of Leather   10-10-00
9 hundred & a halfe weight of all Sorts of workinge
    Iron 7^li 12^s, 1 Iron Crock & Marmett 12^s   08-04-00
2 old Anvils & 1 old sledge 5^s , One End of pitch rope 5^s   00-10-00
In the lower house
1 p[ai]r of Scales and weights   00-15-00
in Specialties 118^li 02^s 8^d   in Speratts by booke 4^li &
    desperate 6^li   128-02-08
In Coale and wood for fireinge   00-03-06
                                              Tot[al is   174-16-07

Appraizers   Edward deer   Richard Bates   Jenkin [his mark J S] Savors

The Particulars of the Specialties within menconed
[in the Will] are as foll[ows]   li - s - d
Richard Savors   70-00-00
William Lewelin   15-00-00

William Lewis	10-00-00
John Jenkins	10-00-00
Estance Richards	10-00-00
Morgan Williams	<u>03-02-08</u>
	<u>118-02-08</u>

sig[num] Thomas   T P [his mark] Pierce

Addenda
Item 2 Ch[att]ell Leases att   20-00-00
Sign[um] Thomas   T P [his mark] Pierce
Exhibited at Llandaff, 24th October, 1707, by Thomas Pierce, brother and executor.

[National Library of Wales Document Reference: LL/ 1707/]

An Inventory of all and Singular the Goods, Chattels, and household Stuff of late John Watkin Deceas'd Appraised the 11th Day of March 1763. by William Powel and Thomas Mathews Appraisers

	£ - s - d
In the shop	
3 Dozen of Tin Locks and keys	00-03-00
3 Dozen of Large Do:	00-03-09
½ a Dozen Cherubims & ½ a Dozen Locks Do:	00-01-00
A Parcell of Letters and figures	00-02-00
4 Pair of H.L. Inges	00-02-00
1 Dozen of Spring Bolts	00-03-00
A Parcell of white Bullim	00-01-00
A Parcell of black Do:	00-00-09
A Parcell of large wood Screws	00-01-00
8 Paire of Butt Inges	00-04-00
A Dozen of Small Chisels	00-01-00
Trunknails and Springs	00-01-00
3 Adses 4 Augers 4 Socket Chisels and one Hatchet	00-08-00
3 Reep Hooks	00-02-03
8 Truels	00-04-00
7 Brushes	00-01-09
20 feet of Tin ribbons	00-01-08
6 Pounds of Rozin	00-00-09
6 Mouse Traps	00-00-09
4 Mice Cages	00-01-00

4 Stock locks	00-02-00
16 old Box locks	00-04-00
3 small Parcells of wood Screws	00-04-00
½ a Dozen pair of Coffin handles	00-01-00
A Parcell of Pins	00-01-00
2 Quire of writing Paper	00-01-06
3 pounds of Sparables	00-00-06
11 Padlocks	00-02-09
2 Dozen and 5 Pair of T Inges	00-14-00
3 Bedcords and Ropes	00-03-00
4 Dozen of Sash Sheaves	00-04-00
½ a Dozen of Spit Blocks	00-01-00
Marlin Twine	00-01-00
5 hand Brushes	00-00-10
Spanish brown and whiteing	00-01-06
4^d Sprigs	00-01-00
28 Iron Crocks weight about 2^{lb}	01-00-00
Corks and Chalk	<u>00-00-06</u>
	<u>05-04-09</u>
In the Kitchen	
An old Case of Draws and looking Glass	00-07-06
4 Small Tables	00-06-00
2 Cubboards	00-04-00
2 Chests	00-05-00
7 Pewter Dishes and a Dozen Plates D^o:	00-12-00
2 hand Irons	00-02-00
An Iron Dripping-pan, 7 Old Candlesticks 2 old Spits, an Old Grate & a Toaster	00-05-00
½ a Dozen Old Chairs	00-01-00
an old Vate	00-00-06
In the little Parlor	
A Bed, bedstead, Bolster, Quilt, & Blankett	01-01-00
3 Chairs	00-01-06
A Corner Cubboard	00-01-00
An Oval Table	00-03-00
In the little Room behind the Parlor	
An old Bed and Bedstead	00-15-00
In the best Chamber	
An old Buroe	00-07-06

½ a Dozen cane Chairs	00-03-00
3 Pictures	00-01-00
1 Table	<u>00-01-00</u>
Total	<u>10-01-09</u>

Thomas Mathewes   William powell

Administration Bond: John Watkin: 16th April, 1763

In the Consistory Court of Llandaff, 16th April, 1763, administration of the goods etc. of John Watkin, deceased, was granted to his widow, Ann Watkin. Ann Watkin and James Thomas, Town Carpenter, were sworn in the sum of £100 for Ann Watkin to exhibit a true inventory of the goods etc. of her late husband on or before the last day of July next, to administer according to law, to give a just account of her administration on or before the last day of April, 1764, and to present to the Court any last will and testament of the deceased that might appear. Before Nathaniel Wells, surrogate, Ann Watkin recorded her mark on the administration bond, and James Thomas signed the document.

[National Library of Wales Document Reference: LL/ 1763/ 19]

An Inventary of all and Singular the Goods Cattle Chattles and Creditts of Morgan Jenkins late of the Town of Cardiffe in the County of Glamorgan and Diocess of Landaffe Chandler deceased made, Vallued and appraised the third day of June in the year of our Lord God One thousand Seven hundred thirty and Seven by George Evans and Walter Rosser appraisors as follows, That is to say.

	£ - s - d
First his Wearing Apparel valued at	02-02-00
In the Kitchin Twelve pewter platters three Dozen and a halfe of Pewter Plates at	00-15-00
Allso four pair of Brass Candlesticks and one Pestle and Mortar at	00-05-00
Allso One Brass Pott, two Iron Potts and Six old Wooden Chairs at	00-05-00
Allso three old Tables two old Dressers and two old Cuppboards at	00-02-06
Allso the Fire utensils and one small Looking Glass at	00-07-06
Allso one Dog wheel, two Steel Irons & seven Earthen Plates at	00-02-06

In the Hall Four Tables, five Chairs, one Large Chest with a small quantity of Oates, one small Looking Glass and three old Benches at	00-07-06
In the Outward Roome One large Table One Chest three old Benches at	00-03-00
Allso two old Chairs at	00-00-06
In the Little Parlour One Oval Table Five leather Chairs and five Pictures at	00-02-06
Allso some drinking Vessels and two pair of old window Curtains at	00-01-06
In the Back Chamber One ffeather Bed with the appurtenances at	01-10-00
Allso three Chairs, One Small square Table One Tongs and one Slice at	<u>00-03-00</u>
Carry over	<u>06-07-06</u>
Allso a pair of Window Curtains at	00-00-06
In the best Chamber One Feather Bed with the appurtenances at	02-10-00
Allso two Oval Tables and Nine Chairs at	00-09-00
Allso One Looking Glass and eight Pictures at	00-10-00
Allso One Grate with its appurtenances at	00-05-00
In the little Forestreet Chamber one Oval Table and six old Cane Chairs at	00-07-06
In the Middle Chamber one little Square table and seven Cane Chairs at	00-10-00
Allso two looking Glasses and one Chest of Drawers at	01-00-00
Allso five small Iron Barrs One Tongs amd one Fender at	00-02-00
Allso one Bedstead and Curtains and two window Curtains at	00-10-00
In the 2 South Chambers Four ffeather Beds with their apputenances at	06-00-00
Allso One long Chest two old Chairs and a close stool at	00-05-00
Allso two window curtains at	00-00-06
Allso all the Table Linnen at	01-01-00
In the Cellar two Barrels of Ale at	02-00-00
Allso twelve Dozen of Cyder at	02-00-00
Allso a few Bottles of Ale at	00-10-00
In the Brewing house one Furnace at	02-10-00
Allso all the Brewing vessels at	02-10-00
In the Workbouse four small Iron Furnaces at	01-10-00

Allso	one Brass Kittle and one Brass Pann at	01-10-00
Allso	a quantity of Ashes	02-00-00
Allso	other materials belonging to the Trade at	04-00-00
In the Shop	ffifteen Dozen of Candles or thereabouts at	02-00-00
Allso	about four hundred weight of Soap at	05-00-00
Allso	One old Chest at	00-01-00
Allso	One hundred weight of Wick Yarn at	01-10-00
Allso	three pair of Scales with all the weights at	00-10-00
Allso	one long Table with two small Benches at	00-02-06
Allso	two Black horses at	05-00-00
Allso	three old Mares at	02-10-00
Allso	One three year olf Colt at	01-01-00
Allso	One two year old Colt at	00-15-00
Allso	two yearling Colts at	00-10-00
Allso	a Small quantity of old hay at	02-00-00
Allso	one Lease from Mr William Miles at	10-00-00
Allso	a Small quantity of Plate at	02-00-00
Allso	a Small parcell of Books at	00-05-00
Allso	all the horse furniture at	01-00-00
Allso	all the Lumber at	01-00-00
Allso	ready money in the house the summ of	48-00-00
Allso	due by the Shop Books being Sperate Debts the summ of	73-06-10
Allso	due by the shop Books being Desperate debts the summ of	<u>19-00-00</u>
	Summ Total	<u>216-09-04</u>

Exhibited at the Consistory Court Llandaff, 3rd June 1737, by Mary Jenkins, widow and executrix.

[National Library of Wales Document Reference: LL/1737/35]

A True and perfect Inventory of All the goods of John Thomas of Cowbridge Blacksmith late deceased prized on the fourth day of January in the first yeare of the Reighn of o[ur] Soveraign Lord King James the second of England, Scotland, france etc. Anoqe D[omi]ni 1685 by the persons hereunder named as followeth

                                                                                    li - s - d

Impri[mi]s all his weareing Apparell   00-10-00

itt[em] in the Hall one Cubbard with three small boxes,
one small Chest one little Table with thre turne stools   00-10-00
itt[em] one Table more three Joint stooles two benches,
two old Cofers with Two old Chaires   00-05-00
itt[em] one grate two small Andirons one spit one frying pan
2 Iron candlesticks 2 paire of little pothooks two little racks
two tosters two payre of tonges and two fire shovels   00-06-08
itt[em] Eight small pewter platters, 3 pewter saucers eleven
pewter Spoons, two little Beakers one little Saltseller one
half pint one pewter flagon, one chamber pot one
pewter Tanket   00-04-06
itt[em] one small brass pot two brass Ketls one small brass
pan 3 small brass skillets one brass Candlstick one
small brass basteing spoon with one little Iron dripping pan,
and one little Iron Crock   00-08-00
In a little Roome Joineing to the Hall
Impri[mi]s two feather beds with one bedsteed two blanckets
two feather boulsters One small pillow two Ruggs,
3 pieces of Curtains and one piece of vallion   01-10-00
itt[em] in A Roome overhead the Hall one dust bed
one feather boulster one Rugg one bedstead five blankets
2 douzen of wooden dishes and Trenchers   00-02-06
itt[em] 2 old Chairs one small bench one small old Coffer
one small old box one old Table 4 small standards
one paile one old backstone   00-01-06
In the Shopp   Impri[mi]s one bellows two anvils
two vices two sledges five hammers, two Pareing knifes
3 paire fire tongs six files one Chisle, one ....., two
hundred of Iron with two grinding stones   02-10-00
                              The totall summe is   06-08-02

The Praisers Names
William Bucley   Griffith David   Thomas ....   Christo[pher] William

Extract from the Will of John Thomas, blacksmith, 30th December, 1685

'I give to Katherine my said wife the Anvil, the Tools and all the Iron that is in the shop where I used to work and all my moneys as well what I have lieing within my house as those that are due to me from others'

[National Library of Wales Document Reference: LL/ 1685/ 50]

Inventory of Goods, Chattles & Effects of the late Mr John P Harris [blacksmith] of No. 30 North Church Street, Cardiff   Nov[ember] 13th 1856

Old Sofa 10/- Clock 10/- Drawers 10/-	01-10-00
Old Desk 3/- Table 3/- Glass 2/6 Clock 5/-	00-13-06
2 Trays 1/6 Fender & Fire Irons 1/-	00-02-06
14 Pictures 4/- 5 Chairs 5/- 13 glasses 5/-	00-14-00
6 Cups, Basins, Plates etc. 2/-, Desk 3/-	00-05-00
5 Ornaments 1/- 2 Pieces of Carpet 2/-	00-03-00
7 Chairs 10/6 Fender & Stand 3/-	00-13-06
Kettle, Saucepan & Pan 2/- Table 2/6	00-04-06
Timepiece 14/- 4 Candlesticks 2/-	00-16-00
2 Irons 1/- Kettle & Stand 2/-	00-03-00
4 Trays & 2 Bowls 1/6 Lot of Ware 3/6	00-05-00
2 Chairs 2/6 + Bedstead 4/-	00-06-06
Lot of Files & Shackles 30/- Tent Bedstead 10/-	02-00-00
Bed & Bedding 30/- Stand & Table 7/6	01-17-06
3 Chairs 3/- Box 1/- Bedstead 10/-	00-14-00
Bed 20/- Bed & Bedding 30/- Table	02-12-00
Glass 2/- 1 Chair 1/- Silver Watch 40/-	02-03-00
Lot of Wearing Apparel 30/- 4 Sheets 4/-	01-14-00
3 Bellows 90/- 6 Anvils 110/- 50 Blacks 150/-	17-10-00
4 Vices 30/- 9 Pieces of Chain 90/-	06-00-00
6 Gins 30/- 1 Scales & Weights 30/-	03-00-00
2 Forges 10/- 5 Winches 130/-	07-00-00
5 Small Kedge Anchors	06-10-00
Lot of Bar & Scrap Iron	07-10-00
Lot of Hooks & Thimbles	01-15-00
12 Shackles 7/6 4 Sledges 4/-	00-11-06
2 Hammers 1/6 20 p[ai]r Tongs 7/6	00-09-00
24 Swedges 8/6 1 Set of Stocks and Dies 30/-	01-18-06
Lot of Tools 100/- Lot Sundries 50/-	07-10-00
Lot of Small Coal	00-10-00
Old Timber in Shop	<u>03-10-00</u>
	80-11-00
By Cash in West of England Bank Cardiff	<u>280-12-06</u>
	<u>361-03-06</u>

I Certify the Above to be of the value of Three Hundred & Sixty Pounds & Three Shillings & six Pence   Mark Marks, Auctioneer & Appraiser   9 St Mary Street Cardiff

Administration Bond: John Penfound Harris, blacksmith: 18th November, 1856

In the Consistory Court of Llandaff, 18th November, 1856, administration of the goods, chattels and credits of John Penfound Harris, blacksmith, who died 4th November, 1856, was granted to his widow, Ann Harris, of No. 30, North Church Street, Cardiff. Ann Harris, Harry Penfound, of No. 65, Union Street, Cardiff, smith, and Mark Marks of Cardiff, auctioneer and appraiser, were sworn by the Court in the sum of £900 for Ann Harris to make and exhibit a true inventory of the goods etc. of her late husband on or before the last day of May next, to administer according to law, to make a just account of her administration on or before the last day of November, 1857, and to present to the Court any last will and testament of the deceased that might appear. All three boundens signed the administration bond.

[National Library of Wales Document Reference: LL/ 1856/ 50]

5. Fabric Trades: Weavers/Tucker/Tailor

Diosis Landaffe [Parish of Llancarvan]   An Inventorye of all the goods Chattells utensiles & houshould stuffe of John Alexander weaver Late decessed w[i]thin the said diocis valued & prised the Last day of January 1633 by Jenkin Cradock Geordge Wilkin, …… Smith & Geordge Hullin beinge neere neighbours to the said testator

Imprimis one p[air] of Osett Loomes prised	xx^s
It[e]m vi p[ai]r of Slayes belonginge to the said Lo[o]m[e]s	xv^s
It[e]m other smale implem[en]ts belonginge to the said Lo[o]m[e]s	ii^s
It[e]m his wearinge app[ar]ell prised	xx^s
It[e]m all the reste of his houshould stuffe & implem[en]ts of houshould	xl^s
It[e]m one litell pigge beinge all the movable goods that the said testator had prised	iiii^s vi^d
som totall	v^{li} i^s vi^d

A p[ar]ticuler noate of the deptes owinge To the said testator by Specialties
Inprimis   one bonde upon Wm Alexander penaltie vi^{li} [for the
 payment of] iii^{li} 1st day of the month of May   iii^{li}

It[e]m   one bonde upon Geordge Nicholas penaltie v^{li} [for the payment of] l^s [50s] 23 8ber (October)   l^s

It[e]m   one bonde upon david Gron[ow]? penaltie x^{li} [for the payment of] v^{li} 2nd June   v^{li}

It[e]m   on[e] bonde upon Ann hullin widowe penaltie xx^{li} [for the payment of] x^{li} 1st May   x^{li}

It[e]m   on[e] bonde upon Tho: W^m. penaltie vi^{li} [for the payment of] iii^{li} iii^{li}

It[e]m   on[e] bonde upon Tho: dawkin penaltie v^{li} [for the payment of] l^s l^s

It[e]m   on[e] bonde upon Geordge Nicholas penaltie vi^{li} [for the payment of] iii^{li} 16th 8ber   iii^{li}

It[em]   one bill upon John Evan [for the payment of]   xx^s
It[e]m   one bill upon Geordge hullin [for the payment of]   xx^s
It[e]m   on[e] bill upon W^m deere [for the payment of]   xx^s
It[e]m   lent to Geordge hullin w[i]thout Specialltie   x^s
                      Som[e] totall   xxxii^{li} x^s

[National Library of Wales Reference Number LL/1633/ 10]

****

A true And perfect Inventorie of All the goods implements houshold stuffe Cattell and Chattells of Reece John Hopkin of the parish of Lanishen late deceased   had, taken and prised the Eleventh day of September In the yeare of our Lord 1651

                                                                                      li - s - d

Imprimis   Sixe Milch kine prised everie kowe at one pound thirteene shillings and foure pence Amounting in all to   10 - 0 - 0

Item Two Heifers worth a piece twentie shillings amounting unto   2 - 0 - 0

Item All the Swine And piggs of the said deceadent prised to   1 - 0 - 0

Item One horse of the said decedent prised at   2 - 0 - 0

Item All the Hay of the said Decedent prised at   1 - 0 - 0

Item The Two weaves or loomes togeather w[i]th all the instruments and appurtenances therunto belonging of the said decedent prised at   1 - 0 - 0

Item All the implements And houshold stuffe of the said decedent prised at   2 - 0 - 0

Item The weareing apparell of the said decedent prised at   0 -10- 0
                                            Sum total   19 -10- 0
Prizers   David Lewis   James Edmond   John Rinold

Extract from the Will of Rees John Hopkin, yeoman, 10th July 1651, proved 12th September 1651

'I give and bequeath my brother Rinold John Hopkin my two weaves or loomes w[i]th all implements and instruments belonging therunto or appertenances to the said trade of weaveing lieing and being in the lower house called the weaveing house where I did worke the said trade of weaveing.'

[National Library of Wales Document Reference: LL/ 1651/ 35]

Glamorgan   An Inventory of all the Goods Cattle & p[er]sonall Estate of Morgan Edmond   late of Whitechurch in the said County   made & appraised the Eighth day of July In the yeare of our Lord God 1689 by the persons whose Names are hereunto subscribed as followeth vizt

	li - s - d
Imp[rimis]s the deced[en]ts Wearing Apparell	01-00-00
Item in the Hall one Table Board one Bench one great coffer one wainscote Chair, one Bedsteed on Cuppboard one old Coffer one Table chaire one other wooden chaire, a paire of shelves appraised att	01-10-00
In the two Chambers two old Bedsteeds one longe Coffer two small Boxes	00-10-00
Three dust Bedds one dust Boulster two ffeather Boulsters one pillow seaven Blanketts two Ruggs three Coverletts one Boulster Case & one pillow Case of Dowlas, & one Dowlas sheet	02-10-00
The Cheese in the house	00-05-00
In the lower Inner Roome one old Cuppboard one little Table two old Coffers & two shelves	00-10-00
Item all the deced[en]ts wooden vessells for the dayrie & brewing	00-12-00
Item one old Brasse Pan one small old Brasse Kettle, one Iron Crock one Iron Posnett one Pewter Candlestick, one small Tankerd one Bottle & three Sawcers of Pewter	00-14-00

Item	four Table Napkins & one old Table Cloth	00-02-06
Item	ffive Loomes with their appurtenances	02-00-00
Item	one Iron Tripod	00-02-06
Item	the deced[en]ts corne threshed	02-10-00
Item	the deced[en]ts Implements of husbandry	03-10-00
Item	the deced[en]ts corne in the ground vizt in the lands of John Watkin ffive acres of wheat £6-5-0 ffive acres of Barley £3-15-0 & two acres of oates £1	11-00-00
	More in the lands of Wm. Thomas of Cardiff 1 acre & 3 q[uar]ters of Barley xxv^s one acre & a q[uar]ter of pease xx^s	02-05-00
	More in the lands of Evan Thomas 1 ac[re] & a halfe of oates att	00-15-00
	More the deced[en]ts corne in the lands of Wm Thomas of Eglwysilan three acres & a halfe of oates xxxv^s	01-15-00
Item	the deced[en]ts debts due from Richard David & others	14-00-00
Item	one Sow & his poultry	00-10-00
	Tot[al]	46-01-00

Appraisers Names   Will Lewis   Alexander Lewis   signum Evan Thomas
signum William Harry   William John

[National Library of Wales Document Reference: LL/1689/138]

A True and perfect Inventory of the goods and Chattles of John Tucker of the parish of St Andrews in the County of Glam[or]gan and Diocesse of Landaffe lately deceased, made the 24th day of September in the year of our Lord 1691/2 and prized by us whose names are hereunto subscribed

	li - s - d
Imp[rimis]: his wearing apparrell prized at	00-15-00
itt[em]: in the hall one feather bed and bolster with a coverlid and other appurtenances belonging to it prized at	01-10-00
itt[em]: one table board one presse cubbard one wooden chaire three old offers and 3 old wooden benches prized at	00-15-00
itt[em]: in the chamber over the hall one old bedsted and one trendall prized at	00-03-04
itt[em]: in the shop one weavers loome 3 slaies warpeing bars and a trow at	01-05-00

itt[em]: one little old brasse pan   one old brasse crock
four pewter platters & one brasse mortar prized at   00-15-00

itt[em]: one iron crock   one iron spitt   one brandiron
one hanging hook and one pothook prized at   00-04-00

itt[em]: one tub   four pailes and other vessells belonging
to the dairy prized at   00-10-00

itt[em]: his cheese of all sorts prized at   00-18-00

itt[em]: three cows   three yearlings   three calves and
two pigs prized at   10-00-00

itt[em]: one smal mow of wheat and one reeke of hey
prized at   03-00-00

itt[em]: his share in a mow of pease   00-10-00

It[em]   2 Canvas sheets, 1 old brasse candlestick, a pillow case
halfe a pound of Feathers a poise & a halfe of course
wooll & some old dishes spoones & trumpery   00-06-00

Item   due to ye dec[ease]ed for butter sold ye sum of   01-10-06

Item a debt due to ye dec[eas]ed from Jenkin Thomas 1^li,
from Griffith Jenkin 5^s and from Ann Vaughan 3^s 4^d in all   01-08-04

Sum total   23-10-02

Prizers   Henry David   John Phillip   John Arle   Leomeden Thomas
Sworn by John Tucker, 11th November, 1691.

Administration Bond: John Tucker: 11th November, 1691

In the Consistory Court of Llandaff, 11th November, 1691, administration of the goods etc. of John Tucker, deceased, was granted to his son, John Tucker, weaver. John Tucker, John Arle, carpenter, and John Philip, yeoman, all of the parish of St. Andrews, were sworn by the Court in the sum of £100, for John Tucker to exhibit a true inventory of the goods of his late father before 1th January next, to administer according to law, to make a true account of his administration at or before 11th of August next, and to present to the Court any last will and testement of the deceased that might appear. All three boundens recorded their mark on the administration bond.

[National Library of Wales Document Reference: LL/ 1691/ 109]

A true and perfect Inventory of the Goods and Chattles of David William of the p[ar]ish of Lanblethian in the County of Glamorgan and Diocesse of Landaff   Weaver (late deseased) made and appraised by the Appraisors

who heve hereunto subscribed the fifth day of November Anno dom[ini] (1701)

	li - s - d
his Wearing apparel appraised to	01-10-00
It[em] two feather beds with their app[ur]tenances valued at	03-00-00
It[em] one dust bed with its app[ur]tenanc[e]s vall[ued] at	00-10-00
It[em] his Brasse and pewter and one Iron Crock vall[ued] at	00-15-00
It[em] one table and frame vallued at	00-05-00
It[em] 3 wooden coffers && 3 wood[e]n chairs 1 bible & other small books at	00-10-00
It[em] three wearvers Loomes with their app[ur]tenances vall[ued] at	06-10-00
It[em] one Iron Bakestone a p[ai]r of tongs fire pan 1 Iron Spitt and other small tensills vallued at	00-02-06
Sum	13-02-06

Appraisors the mark of Charles CB Bassett Thomas Tristram the mark of Edmund Thomas

Exhibited at Cowbridge, 14th April, 1702, by Edward David, son and executor.

[National Library of Wales Document Reference: LL/ 1702/54]

An Inventory of all and singular the Goods ch[at]ells & Creditts of James Richards of Lanblethian in ye County of Glamorgan and Diocess of Landaffe Dece[ase]d made vallued & appraiz'd the fifth day of October in ye year of our Lord one Thousand seven hundred and Twenty four by us the Appraisors as follows

	li - s - d
Imp[rimi]s his wearing Apparell vallued att	01-00-00
Item one feather bed and its appurten[an]ces att	03-00-00
Item one Cupboard one Table Two joint stools att	00-18-00
Item seven old chairs one Trunk on Iron Grate	00-05-00
Item four flock beds w[i]th their appurten[an]ces att	03-10-00
Item one hot press one Dresser one Table one Chair one old Cupboard Two pewter platters four pewter plates att	01-02-06
Item one Bakestone one pair of Andirons one spit one frying pan and other Lumbery ware att	00-10-00
Item Two sheares with their appurten[an]ces att	00-10-00
Item Three old Iron Potts	00-05-00

Item one Cow Two Calves on old horse	03-15-00
Item Two small pigs	00-12-00
Item Two small Reeks of hay	02-05-00
Item wool to the value of	00-10-00
Item five yards of cloth at 2^s 6^d p[er] y[a]rd	00-12-06
Item one stone more of wool att	00-05-00
Item Eighteen yards of flanem at 6 p[er] y[a]rd	00-09-00
	19-09-00

Appraisors   William Jenkin   Rees Tuly   Jenkin David
Exhibited at Llandaff, 14th May, 1725, by Ann Richards, relict and administratrix.

Administration Bond: James Richards: 14th May, 1725
In the Consistory Court of Llandaff, 14th May, 1725, administration of the goods etc. of James Richards, deceased, was granted to her widow, Anne Richard. Anne Richard and Thomas Richard of the parish of Llanblethian, tucker, were sworn by the Court in the sum of £40, for Anne Richard to make and exhibit a true inventory of the goods etc. of her late husband at of before the last day of July next, to administer according to law, to make a just account of her administration at or before the 14th May, 1726, and to present to the Court any last will and testament of the deceased that might appear. Anne Richard recorded her mark on the administration bond: Thomas Richard signed the document.

[National Library of Wales Reference Number LL./1725/ 56]

****

A true and p[er]fect Inventory of all the goods, cattles and Chattles of Rodolph Williams of Lancarvan in the Countie of Glam[or]gan taylor deceased taken the eleaventh day of ffebruary 1653 and praysed as followeth,

	li - s - d
Impr[im]is 4 kine	06-00-00
It[em] two bullocks of two yeares old	02-00-00
It[em] three Calves	01-00-00
It[em] one Colt of three years old	01-13-04
It[em] three old feather beds and boulsters	03-00-00
It[em] four pillows	00-04-04
It[em] three Coverletts	01-00-00

It[em] three payre of sheets and 3 payre of blancketts	01-10-00
It[em] two brasse Crocks	00-13-04
It[em] one brasse panne & 2 small kettles	00-15-00
It[em] one French bedstead	00-03-04
It[em] ten pieces of pewter	00-01-00
It[em] a payre of Andiers	00-02-00
It[em] one table 2 Chayres 2 trunckes four Joynt stooles and one Chest	0
It[em] 2 Candlestickes one fryeing pan and one pott hangers	00-03-04
It[em] 2 barrells, 6 milke vessels and one trendle	00-06-08
It[em] his weareing apparel	02-10-00
debts oweinge	
It[em] In the hands of William Roberts of Colwinston	50-00-00
It[em] In the hands of Rice Wilkin of Lancarvan	01-15-00
It[em] John Mathewes of Merthir dovan	01-01-00
It[em] w[i]th Mrs Write?	01-10-00
It[em] Mrs Lewis of Lannissen	00-09-00
It[em] Mr Gabriell Lewis of Lanissen	00-14-00
It[em] Mrs Anne Morgans of St ffagans	00-08-00
It[em] Mr Cutts of Wenvoe	00-10-00
tot[al]	78-19-04

praysers   John Newton   william wilkin   John Thomas
This Inventory was Exhibited upon the xvii[th] day of ffebruary 1653 before Hugh Wood.

[National Library of Wales Reference Number LL/1653/ 21]

****

Mercers

An Invetory of all the Goods and Chattles of Henry Hoare late of the Towne of Cardiff in the Countie of Glamorgan mercer decesed, made and appraised by us the persons subscribing the 26th day of ffebruary In the first yeare of the Reigne of our soveraigne Lord James the 2nd by the Grace of God of England Scotland ffrance and Ireland King defender of the faith etc annoq[ue] d[omi]ni 1684 vizt.

In the Shop	li - s - d
Imprimis In redie money	05-00-00
3 great chests and 3 little chests at	01-00-00

In wollin Cloth as brodcloth carsie & etc	15-00-00
In dowlas Canvas and other linings	15-00-00
In sarge sayes and stuff	06-00-00
In druget and Lyncie	02-10-00
In blew dowlas and dutties	03-00-00
In Teeke and Sackcloth	05-00-00
In fustian and Holland	02-00-00
In Stockins and fflanan	01-00-00
In buttons thred silke ribents & galloom	02-00-00
In bodisis and straw hatts & all small things	06-00-00
2 nests of boxes	00-05-00
Item in the Lower room	
one great press one table boord one settell	01-00-00
one chest and a bedsteed	00-05-00
8 Joint Stooles	00-08-00
In Pewter Bras and Iron things	03-00-00
In earthen vessells	00-03-00
Item in the fore chamber One bedsteed 1 truckle bedsteed	00-06-00
one Cubart, one boxe 3 lether chayers	00-12-00
3 wood chayers 2 long benches	00-05-00
Item in the back chamber 2 bedsteeds 1 truckle bedsteed, 1 chest	00-06-00
one trunke of lining one press 1 table	03-10-00
6 boxes 1 Deske one virginalls	01-10-00
5 feather beds 8 fether boulsters 6 pillows	15-00-00
In curtains vallants & carpets	01-10-00
4 ruges 4 pare of blankets	<u>02-00-00</u>
[total of the above]	93-10-00
In plate and all other things	12-00-00
In aparrell	05-00-00
In Bookes	<u>02-00-00</u>
	19-00-00
	93-10-00
In shop debts	<u>10-00-00</u>
Total	<u>122-10-00</u>

The praysers names   Cradock Wells sawyer Jonathan Jones
Wm Huntly   Thomas Phillips
Exhibited by Joseph Hoare, son, 26th February, 1684.

Administration Bond: Henry Hoare: 26th February, 1684

In the Consistory Court at Llandaff, 26th February 1684, administration of the goods etc. of Henry Hoare, widower, mercer, deceased, was granted to his son, Joseph Hoare, also a mercer of the town of Cardiff. Joseph Hoare and Craddock Wells of Cardiff were bound by the Court for Joseph Hoare to exhibit a true inventory of the goods etc. of his late father, at or before the 26th of May next, to administer according to law, to render an account of his administration before the 26th February, 1685, and to present to the Court any last will and testament of the deceased that might appear. Both boundens signed the administration bond.

[National Library of Wales Document Reference: LL/ 1684/ 30]

A True and perfect Inventory Indented of all ye goodes Chattells Cattles Credits & p[er]sonall Estate of Lewis Sheares late of ye Towne of Cardiffe in ye County of Glamorgan mercer decessed taken & appraysed ye 16th day of february Anno Domini 1687 by us William Richards, George Williams Gabriell Lewis, Thomas Jenkins & Emanuell Miles

	li - s - d
Imp[rimis] It[em] In ye back chamber in Broadcloth	050-00-00
It[em] in searge there	018-13-04
It[em] in stuffes & Silk Ware	005-02-09
It[em] in fustians callicoes colld linins & hollands	010-02-06
It[em] in dowles kentines launds & other linins	015-03-02
It[em] An old bedsteed feather bed and app[ur]ten[an]ces with the Rug blanketts & sheets two old cupboards, one old chest, one old Trunk, 3 old Chaires, 1 old Table a little Stoole 3 old boxes & 4 Joinct stooles	004-00-00
In the forestreett Chamber In Sarges broadcloths hollands dowles Silk ware Crapes Stuffe thrids laces fringes ribonds Stockins hatts hatbands, buttons kerzeys thrid Silk and other mercery, drapery, haberdashery Saltery manchester and other wares being all ye goods that came home this last Bristoll faire	305-07-06

It[em] One standing bedsteed & 1 settle bedsteed, one feather bed, with ye Ruggs Blanketts Sheets & two Suites of Curtains & Vallions with app[ur]ten[an]ces 7 Chaires, 4 Joinct stooles, 1 smale lookeing glasse 1 p[ai]r of Brasse Andirions, 1 p[ai]r of Tongs a fire shovell 2 table boards

Inventories of Village Shopkeepers and Tradesmen: Fabric Trades – Mercers

a Chest a stand, & two paire of store? blanketts & 2 old Arras coverlitts	006-05-08
In ye little forestreet Chamber Over ye little Shoppe 1 standing bedsteed 1 truckle bedsteed, 2 old fether beds with ye Rugs blanketts coverlitts 1 Suite of Curtains vallyons and app[ur]ten[an]ces, 4 old chaires, 1 little side cupboard, 2 p[ai]^r of Andirons & two close stooles	003-10-00
In ye little cogloft 1 old bedsteed & feather bed, with ye Rug Blanketts & app[ur]ten[an]ces	001-05-00
In ye wooll loft a feather bed truckle bedsteed with ye Rug and appurten[an]ces & other lumber	001-02-03
It[em] The wooll there	005-03-05
In ye parlour 1 old bedsteed 1 settle bedsteed, 2 feather beds with ye Rugs Blanketts Curtaines and app[ur]ten[an]ces, 1 old Cupboard 1 old table 1 old chaire & two Cofers	020-10-00
In the ye Shop in all Sortes of goodes there	100-00-00
The linin & napery belonging to ye house	002-00-00
It[em] 10 dozen of hatts of their owne makeing	006-10-00
It[em] Casters and other hatts	003-09-06
It[em] hatband Trimmings and Straw hatts	001-05-00
In ye kitchen his Silver plate, vizt 2 Tankards 4 boules a Candle cup, a Salt Seller, 2 porrengers 1 little dish 17 Spoones & a little dram Cupp	021-00-00
It[em] 2 little tables 2 old chaires 1 p[ai]^r of Andirons & dogs 2 p[ai]^r of Tongs, ye Spitts & other Iron ware & ye pewter Brass, Brass Crocks & earthenware & glasses there	003-04-03
In ye worke house two furnaces 3 basons and some blocks	000-05-00
In ye stable two mares	003-00-00
It[em] Two old saddles & a small p[ar]cell of Hay	000-12-05
Item his wearing apparell and Rings	005-00-00
Item in Ready money	015-00-00
Item in ye cowloft chamber over ye Entry and in ye Entry & backside 1 old bed & bedsteed with app[ur]ten[an]ces one old Cofer & other Lumber	000-15-00
Item debts due to ye Testator	300-00-00
Item desperate debts	<u>000-00-00</u>
	888-19-09

Item In Leases	020-00-00
Item in Ready money	<u>016-00-00</u>
	924-16-09
Item seaven other Rings	<u>002-00-00</u>
	<u>926-16-09</u>

Gabriell Lewis   Tho.Jenkins   Will Richard   Geo. Williams
Exhibited at Llandaff by Elizabeth Shere, widow, 8th March, 1687.

[National Library of Wales Document Reference: Ll/ 1687/18]

A true & p[er]fect Inventory of all and Singular the Goods Chattles rights and Creditts of William Richards late of the Towne of Cardiff in the County of Glamorgan Mercer deceased made taken and appraized by us the persons whose names are herunto Subscribed the Twelvth day of June In the Sixth yeare of the Reigne of our Soveraigne Lord and Lady King William and Queene Mary of England etc. Annoq[ue] D[omi]ni 1694 as followeth viz.

	li - s - d
Imp[rimi]s the decead[en]ts wearing Apparell appraized att	05-00-00
Item the Goods furniture and household Stuff in his house	
In the Severall Roomes or places hereafter mentioned	
viz In the Parlor	06-05-00
Item In the Chamber over the Parlour	07-14-00
Item In the dineing Roome	10-05-00
Item In the Chamber over the dineing Roome	03-05-00
Item In the next Chamber to that	03-05-00
Item In the Garrett	01-10-00
Item In the Chamber over the Kitchin	04-06-00
Item In the Kitchin	08-00-00
Item In the Brewhouse	02-00-00
Item In the Cellar	01-19-00
Item the decead[en]ts Linnen appraized at	10-00-00
Item the decead[en]ts Plate appraized at	20-00-00
Item the decead[en]ts Gold and Silver	20-00-00
Item the decead[en]ts two horses and Sadles appraized at	05-00-00
item the decead[en]ts Goates appraized at	00-10-00
Item the decead[en]ts Bookes appraised at	01-00-00
Item the decead[en]ts Goods in the Shopp and Warehouse appraized at	450-08-06

Item the decead[en]ts Sperate debts appraized at 800-00-00
1360-00-00

John Archer   John Bonner   Samuel Hodges
Exhibited at Llandaff, 15th November, 1694, by Cecill Richards, relict and executrix.

[National Library of Wales Document Reference: LL/ 1694/ 26]

A true Inventory of ye goods and Chattles of Joseph Hoar late of Cardiffe and Diocess of Landaffe deceased made the 18th day of December 1707 by us the persons subscribeing

	li - s - d
Imp[rimi]s his wearing Apparrell	02-00-00
In ye Hall one feather Bed Bolster & appurten[anc]es	01-10-00
in pewter Brass & Iron ware	02-10-00
3 Birding Guns 15^s old Books 5^s	01-00-00
in tin and earthen ware	00-10-00
in paper prints & a looking glass	00-02-00
Tables stooles chaires & an old coffer	00-16-00
in Silver Plate	16-00-00
In ye Inner Room within ye Hall	
1 feather Bed Boulster and appurten[anc]es	00-15-00
one settle small table old chaires empty bottles & other Lumbry stuff	00-07-00
In ye Brewhouse one small furnace vate & coolers	01-10-00
one old cubbord table & other Lumbry	00-02-06
In ye chamber over ye Kitchin a small parcell of wheat & mault	00-10-00
In ye forestreet Chamber	
one feather Bed, curtains vallions Bedstead & apurtenances	03-10-00
12 chaires 2 ovall tables & 1 looking Glass	01-15-00
1 Case of Drawers & 2 trunks	01-00-00
1 fire Grate hand Irons tongs & slice	00-08-00
In ye Back Chamber 1 feather Bed Bolster Curtains Vallions Bedstead & appurtenances	01-00-00
1 side Cubbord 4 old chaires 1 small fire grate & looking glass	00-08-00
In ye further Room above staires mault, wool, truckle Bedstead & other Lumber	01-00-00

a Harpiker	00-02-06
in Linnens of all Sorts	<u>03-00-00</u>
tot[al]	<u>39-16-00</u>

Shop goods in ye shop

in rem[nan]ts about 20 y[ar]ds of Broad cloth	05-00-00
160 yds of serge	14-00-00
30 yds of Kersy	02-10-00
50 yds of shellone	03-00-00
60 yds of Canteloons	01-05-00
108 yds of Dammask	05-08-00
80 yds of Stuffe	02-10-00
60 yds of Sayes	06-00-00
20 yds of linse woolse	01-01-08
40 yds of frize?	03-00-00
180 yds of Bayes	05-05-00
7 vigo? printed coats?	01-15-00
7 yds of Plush	01-02-03
3 Briches 12^s 30 yds p^t calico	03-02-00
3 doz: of wosted stockins	04-10-00
15 yds of cotton chequered	01-10-00
36 yds of Blew chequered	02-14-00
20 yds of Broad Blews	01-00-00
40 yds of narrow Blews	01-01-08
15 yds of Col^d holland	00-12-06
120 yds of Col^d linnens	02-15-00
48 yds of fustian	02-00-00
30 yds of Bookram	01-02-06
120 yds of Broad ticking	06-05-00
50 yds of narrow ticking	02-01-00
80 yds of Broad canvas	<u>04-00-00</u>
	<u>84-18-07</u>
240 yds of course canvas	07-00-00
40 yds of Broad dowlas	02-03-04
70 yds of narrow Dowlas	02-18-04
80 yds of Hagabays	03-06-00
40 yds of check linnen	01-16-08
140 yds of white Irish linnen	05-16-08
30 yds of Hamburgh Holland	01-05-00
15 yds of Isingham Holland	01-02-06

Inventories of Village Shopkeepers and Tradesmen: Fabric Trades – Mercers

40 yds of stayned linnen	01-06-08
20 yds of Printed canvas	00-10-00
12 yds of crape	00-09-00
8 lickings for Dust Beds	02-00-00
50 yds of Russia linnen	00-12-06
140 yds of Innerlings	01-15-00
4 doz[en]: of Sacks	05-08-00
140 yds of sacking	05-05-00
20 yds of course mushings	02-00-00
mornary Bodices	02-00-00
30 women Bodices	10-10-00
12 childrens Bodices	01-10-00
worsted yarn 6^s 8^d	00-06-08
sweet powder Balls & balls for wigs	00-10-00
severall remnants of Ribbands	02-10-00
5 gross of Gallones	07-00-00
2 rem[nan]ts of Kenting	00-08-00
silk laces 5^s cadis 6^s Brays 10^s	01-01-00
Bobins & tapes	00-18-00
1 gross & halfe of laces	00-12-00
in holland & cornation inkles	00-03-00
in mohair 21^s mettle Button etc 6^s	01-07-00
threed silks 42^s in garlring stuff twine marling etc.	02-18-00
a parcell of napkins	00-04-00
3 doz: of threeds	02-14-00
8 gross of coat Buttons	02-00-00
more in Buttons	03-00-00
Straw hatts	02-08-00
Shop Book Debt	15-00-00
in cash rings and other valuable gold & silver things	<u>66-00-00</u>
	167-14-04
on ye other side is	<u>124-14-07</u>
tot[al]	<u>292-08-11</u>

Tho Williams   Richard Gibbon   Richard Bates

Administration Bond: Joseph Hoar: 19th December, 1707
In the Consistory Court at Llandaff, 19th December, 1707, administration of the goods etc. of Joseph Hoare, deceased, was granted to his widow, Elizabeth Hoare. Elizabeth Hoare, Richard Bates of Cowbridge, gentleman,

and Henry Meredith of Cardiff, were bound for Elizabeth Hoare to make and exhibit a true inventory of the goods etc. of her late husband at or before the last day of March next, to administer according to law, to render a just account of her administration at or before the 19th December, 1708, and to present to the Court any last will and testament of the deceased that might appear. All three boundens signed the administration bond.

[National Library of Wales Document Reference: LL/ 1707/ 26]

A True and perfect Inventory of all & Singular the goods and Ch[att]eles Rights and Creditts of William Hiley late of the Towne of Cardiffe in the County of Glamorgan Alderman dece[ase]d Appraised the fourteenth day of ffebruary Anno D[omi]ni 1723 by us whose names are hereunto subscribed

	li - s - d
Inp[rimi]s His Wearing Apparrell att	04-00-00
Item One Bedd & Bolster weighing one Hundred and eighteen pounds another Bedd & Bolster weighing a Hundred & three p[oun]ds another Bedd & Bolster weighing one Hundred and seven pounds and three Bolsters weighing a quarter of a Hundred and eighteen pounds att 6d p[er] p[oun]d	09-07-00
Item One other Bedd weighing halfe a Hundred & seven p[oun]ds & anoth[er] Bedd weighing halfe a Hund[red] & twenty six pounds at 4d p[er] p[oun]d	02-08-04
Item ffive Pillows weighing 14li att 8d	00-09-04
Item his Pewter weighing three quarter of a Hundred & Six pound att 6d p[er] p[oun]d	02-05-00
Item His Brass weighing a quarter of a Hundred & twenty pounds at 9d p[er] p[oun]d	01-16-00
Item His Iron weighing three q[uar]ters of a Hund[red] & 13 pound at 2d p[er]	00-16-02
Item One Warmeing Pann & Coffee Pott att	00-06-00
Item One Close Stool Pann 10d	00-00-10
Item Old Iron weighing 14li att ½ p[er]	00-00-07
Item Two Box Irons a Bell mettall Skillett & a Tea Kettle	00-06-06
Item Two Brass Potts & a Spoon W[eight]: 20li att 9d p[er]	00-15-00
Item Two Christening Mantles & 7 Hol[lan]d Sheets att	02-08-00
Item One Damask Table Cloath & 8 Napkins att	00-11-06

Item	Three Towells 9 Pillow cases & 2 Table Cloaths	00-10-06
Item	Six p[ai]r of Coarse sheets 3 Quilts ffour Ruggs & 4 p[ai]r blanketts	04-00-00
Item	one old Counterpan 2 Suits Curtains & Vall[ians] & 1 Suite India Vall[ians] att	01-02-06
Item	Odd Lineings Books & odd things att	01-02-00
Item	one Gun att	00-08-00
Item	In the Kitchin one Grate & Back Pott Hangings Slice earthen plates & platters, Pictures one Corner Cupboard one Smale hanging Cupboard two oval tables and ffive chairs att	02-11-06
Item	The Window Curtains & Rodd for yᵉ Parlour att	00-01-06
Item	Old Lumber in yᵉ Little room over yᵉ Celler att	00-02-06
Item	ffour Silver Spoons att	00-12-06
Item	two Gold Rings	01-06-00
Item	In the Great Chamber 11 Cane Chairs 6 Black Chairs one Trunk one old Chest 1 Table 1 Case of Drawers & one looking Glass Bedstead Curtains & valliance Window Curtains & Rodds & a grate att	06-15-06
Item	In the Rubb'd Chamber one Bedstead Curtains & vall[iance] one old Bedstead Six Chairs and a Case of Drawers 1 Table Window Curtains & Rodds one frame of a looking Glass & stone Base for a grate att	04-02-00
Item	In the fforestreet Chamber a Case of Draw[er]s Stands and table one large Looking Glass one grate ffive Pictures Window Curtains Vallians & Rodd att	03-03-00
Item	In the little fforestreet Room one Bedstead Hedpiece & tester old Cord & Mattriss? one Dogg Wheel and Chain one Truckle Bedstead four Dozen Bottles ffurnace & Barrs and one Side Table	01-02-00
Item	In the back Chamber old Chairs two old Tables an old Dresser Iron Barrs a Horse for Dryeing of Cloaks the School Benches one Desk two Grates & one Cask att	01-18-04
Item	In Mr Stibles's room one Grate one Head piece & tester old Lumber & two Beere Casks att	00-08-00
Item	one Parcell of small Wares as p[er] Note	13-09-00
Item	One parcell of Dowlas & Hollands att	11-00-00
Item	one parcell of Sugars & pap[er] att	02-10-00

Item	Seven grosse & ½ of Pipes	00-07-06
Item	Two pieces fferretting	00-10-00
Item	halfe a piece narrow Do. att	00-02-00
Item	2 p^s & ½ Silk quality Binding	00-12-06
Item	1 parcell Ribbands	02-10-00
Item	1 parcell Galloons att	00-12-00
Item	10 Girdles att	00-06-00
Item	2 doz[en] Silk Laces & black Cording	00-08-06
Item	½ a p^c narrow Coarse Wigg Ribbones att	00-02-00
Item	1 parcell of Cadis gart[er]ing & binding att	00-10-00
Item	1 doz[en] fferitt Laces & a paire of Garters att	00-01-06
Item	a parcell of ffanns att	00-07-00
Item	10 Trimmers att	00-01-06
Item	Coarse Thread	00-03-00
Item	Coll[oured]? & twist Threads att	00-09-00
Item	Holland Tapes and Dieper att	00-04-00
Item	Bobbins att	00-01-06
Item	Tapes & ffilletting att	00-05-06
Item	Ivory Horne & Box Combs att	00-06-00
Item	1 Doz[en] Scissors	00-01-00
Item	½ doz[en] Haswifes? att	00-01-06
Item	Silke Purses & a p[ai]r of Black Silke Gloves	00-06-00
Item	White Sasnett & Black Silke att	01-04-00
Item	1 Mask & Cypres Hood att	00-03-00
Item	Pin cushions & Patches att	00-01-00
Item	1 parcell Necklaces att	00-12-00
Item	4 ounces Silk at	00-04-00
Item	Linnen Hanckerchiefes att	00-13-00
Item	Silke ditto att	03-15-06
Item	13 Musling Cravatts att	00-13-00
Item	a Kenting Cravatt & 4 twine ……. att	00-06-00
Item	6 y[ar]ds Musling att	00-15-00
Item	13 y[ar]ds Do. att	01-12-00
Item	Remnants att	00-05-00
Item	2 Kenting Cravatts and a work'd ……..	00-04-06
Item	1 y[ar]d Cambrick	00-05-00
Item	7 y[ar]ds stripe & plain Kenting	00-08-00
Item	1 p^s Colloured Check att	01-00-00
Item	1 p^s Do.	01-06-00

Inventories of Village Shopkeepers and Tradesmen: Fabric Trades – Mercers

Item	8 y[ar]ds Linnen Check att	00-07-00
Item	2 Remnants Check	00-04-00
Item	40 y[ar]ds Stripe Holl[and]	02-00-00
Item	13 y[ar]ds Printed Linnen att	01-05-00
Item	10 y[ar]ds Do.	00-15-00
Item	4 y[ar]ds Yellow Cloath for hoop Pettycoates	00-04-00
Item	2 y[ar]ds Canvas & 3 y[ar]ds White Jean att	00-04-00
Item	4 y[ar]ds strip^d Camlett att	00-03-04
Item	6 y[ar]ds blew Dutty	00-10-00
Item	24 y[ar]ds W^t Crepe	00-15-00
Item	8 y[ar]ds Dowlas	00-07-00
Item	2 Remnants Holl[and]	00-02-00
Item	16 Capps	00-08-00
Item	1 Black Velvett Capp att	00-04-06
Item	1 parcell Pinns	00-04-03
Item	1 parcell thread Laces	00-00-06
Item	1 parcell Remnants of Wires	00-03-00
Item	Powder & Bottles of Oyle att	00-08-00
Item	8 Stocks of Cards?	00-05-04
Item	1 parcell of stockins	01-19-00
Item	6 Capps	00-05-00
Item	two Worsted Swathes?	00-04-02
Item	5 p^d ½ Worsted at	00-15-02
Item	Cords Packthread & Brushes	00-16-00
Item	a parcell of Cutt tobacco	00-09-00
Item	½ p^s Leathered Cane	00-01-06
Item	Powd[e]r & Shott	00-06-00
Item	1 Ream & 4 quires Writeing Pap[er]	00-12-00
Item	one Glass of Powatum & the Glass	00-01-04
Item	7 Looking Glasses	00-08-00
Item	Boxes & Babbys?	00-10-00
Item	Snuffe Boxes & Inkbornes	01-10-00
Item	Knifes & fforks Small ….. & Spices att	02-12-06
Item	¼ Blew Pepper & Ginger	00-02-06
Item	4^{li} stone & powe[er]d Blew	00-02-06
Item	21^{li} fflint Glass	00-10-06
Item	18 ordinary Glasses	00-04-06
Item	Earthen ware	01-10-00
Item	3^{li} ½ Bees wax	00-02-04

Item Salt	00-02-00
Item 3 Grosse of pipes	00-02-00
Item a Coffee Mill	00-03-00
Item Shelves Counters & Boxes	01-10-00
Item 1 p^r Pumps	00-00-04
Item for Curtaine Rodds	00-00-09
Item a parcell of Lace	08-06-00
Item His ready money	02-10-05
	136-09-06

Appraizors   Jno Abbis   John Oakey   John Morgan

Exhibited at Llandaff, 17th April, 1724, by Florence Hiley, widow and administratrix.

Administration Bond: William Hiley: 19th April, 1724

In the Consistory Court of Llandaff, 19th April, 1724, administration of the goods etc. of William Hiley of the Towne of Cardiff, deceased, was granted to his widow, Florence Hiley. Florence Hiley, Thomas Glascott of Cardiff, sadler, and Thomas Seabrook of Cardiff, joyner, were bound by the Court in the sum of £300 for Florence Hiley to make and exhibit a true inventory of the goods etc. of her late husband at or before the last day of October next, to administer according to law, to give a true account of her administration at or before the last day of April, 1725, and to present to the Court any last will and testament of the deceased that might appear. Florence Hiley, Thomas Glascott and Thomas Seabrook signed the administration bond.

[National Library of Wales Document Reference: LL/ 1724/ 27]

An Inventory of all & Singular the Goods, Ch[att]ells & Credits of fflorence Hiley late of ye Towne of Cardiff in ye County of Glamorgan & Diocess of Landaffe widow dece[ase]d made, vallued & appraised ye 30th day of September Anno D[omi]ni 1724 by John Willson John Abbis & Humphrey Jones Appraisors

	£ - s - d
Inp[rimi]s her Wearing Apparell Vallued att	02-00-00
It[em] in ye Kitchin 48 £ Brass att	02-08-00
It[em] 1 brass pott & 1 Kettle weighing 16^{li} att 9^d p[er] £ 1 warmeing pann 4s 22 £ weight of pewter 11s	01-07-00
It[em] 73 £ old Iron att	00-07-06¾

It[em]   2 oval Tables, 1 Grate & 1 back, 1 paire of pott
   hangings, Earthen plates, Platters Pictures, 2 Cupboards,
   a dog wheel & Chain   02-10-00
It[em]   one old Gunn att   00-08-00
It[em]   in ye Brewhouse   1 furnace, 1 old table & one
   pail att   01-01-00
It[em]   in ye back Kitchin   1 old Grate & Dresser Shelves &
   one old table att   00-05-00
It[em]   in ye School Roome   1 old Side Saddle & Lumber att 00-10-00
It[em]   in ye Great Chamber   1 bedstead Curtains &
   Vallians, one Chest of Drawers, 2 tables   2 stands,
   11 Cane Chaires, 1 great looking Glass, on old Chest,
   1 old Trunk   1 grate & 2 paire of window Curtains
   & Rods att   07-03-00
It[em]   in ye Rubbed Chamber   one Bedstead, Curtains &
   Vallians, 1 old Chest of Drawers, 6 old Chaires, 1 table,
   window Curtains & Rodds & one old Grate att   01-10-00
It[em]   in ye great forestreet Chamber   one bedstead
   one Chest of Drawers, 1 great Looking Glass, 4 Pictures,
   1 Grate & Curtain Rods & 1 bedstead in ye little
   forestreet Chamber   02-09-00
It[em]   4 feather Beds, 5 Bolsters & 4 Pillows weighing in
   all 446£ at 6^d p[er] £   11-03-00
It[em]   Six paire of Sheets att   02-10-00
It[em]   1 Suit Bed wrought Curtains & Lineings 1 Suit
   window Curtains & Vallians & 8 paire of Pillow Cases
   vallued att   04-08-00
It[em]   4 Table Cloths 14 table napkins & a p[ar]cell of
   broken Towells att   01-00-00
It[em]   4 Ruggs, 2 Quilts & 6 Blanketts att   03-04-00
It[em]   1 Grate in Mrs Stibbs's Chamber att   00-02-00
It[em]   1 Iron Smoothing box, 1 tea kettle & 1 bellmettle
   skillett att   00-06-00
It[em]   Goods in the Shop 1 piece dowlace 32^s 1 piece
   ditto 27^s & 3 Remn[na]ts ditto 9^s 03-08-00
It[em]   19 Yards garlick holland 13^s 2^d 7 Yards ¾
   ditto 10^s 1^{d}½   7 yards ditto 8^s 2^d 01-12-03¾
It[em]   2 yards Irish Cloth 2^s 6^d 6 yards bagg-holland att
   3^s 6^d p[er] yd   1 Remnant ditto 18^d 01-05-00

It[em] 13 Muslin Cravatts att	01-08-02
It[em] nine Yards fine Russia 3ˢ 4ᵈ½ 7 Yards Musling att 4ˢ 4 Yards ditto att 2ˢ 2ᵈ	02-00-00
It[em] 3 yards damaged Str. Musling 6ˢ 8 yds str. Kenting att 11ˢ 4ᵈ 1 yard Cambrick 6ˢ 6ᵈ	01-03-10
It[em] 1 piece white plain fustian 14ˢ 1 piece stripe ditto 15ˢ & 2 Remnants 2ˢ 3ᵈ	01-11-03
It[em] 70 Yards ½ Cotton Check att	04-03-09
It[em] 5 Yards Linnen, 3 Barbers Aprons & 2 Yards yellow Canvas att	00-09-06
It[em] 8 Yards ½ yellow Irish Cloth att 16ᵈ p[er] y[ar]d	00-11-04
It[em] 50 Yards ½ Striped holland att	03-09-09
It[em] 1 Yard ½ Striped Ticking att	00-02-06
It[em] 23 yards printed Linnen at 2ˢ 6ᵈ p[er] y[ar]d 10 yards ditto att 16ᵈ p[er] yard	03-10-10
It[em] 6 Yards ½ blew Dutty 14ˢ 1ᵈ blew Linnen & Bulter 2ˢ 5ᵈ¼	00-16-06¼
It[em] in Silk, Muslin & Susee handkerchiefs	05-01-11
It[em] 1 black Silk bagg 18ᵈ 2 turn over Cravatts 4ˢ	00-05-06
It[em] 10 Girdles, 11 ffans, & some Remn[an]ts of damaged Gause att	00-14-06
It[em] 2 doz[en] ½ thimbles 16 horn Combs & 14 white Combs att	00-16-06
It[em] five box Combs att	00-03-09
It[em] 4 y[ar]ds white Sarsenet 8ˢ 1 Tabby Stomacher 4ˢ 8 Stocks of Cards 4ˢ 8ᵈ 9 primers 3 pin-Cushons & 18 papers of pins 14ˢ 7ᵈ½	01-11-03½
It[em] 8 paire of Children's hose 4ˢ 3 paire woemens & 3 paire Youths ditto & 2 Swaths 9ˢ 6ᵈ Sealing Wax 6ᵈ	00-14-00
It[em] 16 powder boxes, 3 Childrens cotton Waistcoats 13 washballs & 11£ ½ haire powder	00-09-06
It[em] 1£ Nuns thred, 24 twists ditto 2£ bleached & 2£ course ditto	01-00-08
It[em] 7 dozen Silk laces & 3 dozen thred ditto	00-16-10½
It[em] 10 paire wells mettle Shoe buckles & 10 powderpuffs	00-01-11
It[em] Sewing Silk 7ˢ 4£ worsted 8ˢ 2£ Rice 4ᵈ	00-15-04
It[em] 15 dozen Shirt buttons 15ᵈ Nuttmeggs Mace Cloves & Cinnamen 2ˢ 2£ Stone blew 18ᵈ	00-04-09
It[em] 1 doz[en] Inkhorns & 8 pieces quality binding & Gartering att	01-17-00

It[em]   10 pieces holland Inkle   4 pieces of bobin
& 8 pieces coloured tapes att   00-18-02
It[em]   4 dozen ½ Cane hooping,   2 boxes & Needles   00-05-4½
It[em]   12 Vellom pockett books   21 Snuff boxes & 4 Civet
boxes att   01-07-02
It[em]   Necklaces 6ˢ   ½ doz. Silk lauls 12ᵈ   Silk Garters
& Leaders 3ˢ   00-10-00
It[em]   damaged buckles & buttons 10ˢ 10 paire scissors 12ᵈ 00-11-00
It[em]   5 pieces galloon att 4ˢ p[er] piece & 3 pieces
Narrowest Ribbon 4ˢ   01-04-00
It[em]   4 pieces ferrett & Silk binding att 4ˢ p[er] piece   01-00-00
It[em]   7 pieces of fashion Ribbon att 6ᵈ per piece &
1 paire of Silk Gloves 3ˢ   02-05-00
It[em]   2 black Masks 12ᵈ   2 Mens black Velvet Caps &
3 Sattin ditto 12ˢ   Men & childrens Quilt & striped
Silk Caps 8ˢ   Abergavenny Inkle 18ᵈ   01-07-06
It[em]   1 Rheam writeing pap[er] 12ˢ   pepper & ginger 3ˢ   00-15-00
It[em]   damaged Snuff 12ᵈ   2 £ Salt peter 2ˢ   00-03-00
It[em]   9£ ½ Starch & powder blew 7ˢ 11ᵈ   12£ tobacco 10ˢ
18£ Shott 18ᵈ   brushes & whisks 12ˢ   7 paire pattens
att 8ᵈ p[er] p[ai]r   twine 3ˢ   01-19-01
It[em]   25 hemp Collars & 8 Collars ditto att 2ᵈ each   00-05-06
It[em]   26£ loaf Sugar att 12ᵈ   5£ gun powder att 10ᵈ
Corks? & ordinary pin cushions 6ᵈ   bees wax &
powatum 2ˢ   01-12-08
It[em]   2 Groes ½ ordinary Tobacco pipes att   00-01-03
It[em]   in Glasses, Earthen Ware & Hopps att   02-04-00
It[em]   5 C? Weight of Salt att   01-10-00
It[em]   a parcell of Lace   05-13-07¾
It[em]   1 Coffee Mill 3ˢ   9£ Tobacco 6ˢ   00-09-00
It[em]   Counters, Shelves & Boxes   01-10-00
It[em]   Debts due on yᵉ Shop booke yᵉ Sum of   <u>22-00-00</u>
                                                Sum total   <u>133-14-05</u>

Administration Bond: Florence Hiley: 1ˢᵗ October, 1724

In the Consistory Court at Llandaff, 1ˢᵗ October, 1724, administration of the goods of ffloerence Hiley, deceased, was grated to her daughter, Elizabeth Hiley. Elizabeth Hiley, Thomas Seabrook, joyner, and Frances French, were bound by the Court for Elizabeth Hiley to make and exhibit a true inventory of the goods etc. of her late mother at or before the last day of February next, to administer according to law, to render a true account of her administration at or before the 1st October, 1725, and to present to the Court any last will and testament of the deceased that might appear. Elizabeth Hiley, Thomas Seabrook and Frances French signed the administration bond.

[National Library of Wales Document Reference: LL/ 1724/ 26]

An Inventory of all and Singular the Goods Cattle Chattles and Creditts of John Stidder late of the Town of Cowbridge in the County of Glamorgan and Diocess of Landaffe Alderman deceased made, valued and appraised by Watkin Watkins, John Valence, John Jones and John Richards appraisors as follows that is to say

	£ - s - d
First his wearing Apparel valued at	002-00-00
Allso household Goods at	031-07-04
Allso one Horse at	003-10-00
Allso Shop Goods as appears by the amount of particulars	425-17-06
Allso Cash in the house the amount of	080-04-06
Allso one Lease in the parish of Lantrissant from Edmund Says Gent[leman] whereinIs the life of Richard Bates only in being at	060-00-00
Allso one Lease of a house in Cowbridge from Charles Edwin? Esquire wherein is One life in being at	013-00-00
Lastley Book debts sperate and Despearate £238 whereof there is desperate the sum of £115	238-13-00
Summ Total	856-12-04

Exhibited at Llandaff, 13th September, 1737, by Richard Bates, one of the Testamentary Guardians and administrators for a true and perfect inventory.

Administration Bond: John Stidder: 13th September, 1737

In the Consistory Court of Llandaff, 13th September, 1737, administration of the goods etc. of John Styder, deceased, was granted to Richard Bates (with the will annexed) 'to the use and during the minority of Elizabeth Styder, John Styder and Richard Styder, the lawful children of the deceased. Richard Bates, alderman, and Thomas Bates, both of the Town of Cowbridge, were sworn by the Court in the sum of £1,000 for Richard Bates to make and exhibit a true inventory of the goods etc. of the deceased at or before 13th December next, to administer by paying the debts and legacies of the deceased, and to render a just account of his administration when lawfully required. Both Richard and Thomas Bates signed the administration bond.

[National Library of Wales Document Reference: LL/ 1737/47]

A True and perfect Inventory of all the goods Chattles and Credits of John Vallance late of the Town of Cowbridge in the County of Glamorgan Mercer, who died Intestate the Seventh day of June 1750, Exhibited by Jane Vallance his wido[w] and Administratrix and taken and appraised the 9th day of July following by Robert Nelson

	li - s - d
24 yards of Broadshaggs at 2s/6d p[er] yard	03-00-00
44 yards of Broad Napp at 5s p[er] yard	11-00-00
119 yards of Bays at 10d p[er] yard	05-02-06
75 yards of Linceye? at 1s p[er] yard	03-15-00
26 yards of Blanketting at 2s p[er] yard	02-12-00
112 yards of Flannel at 10d p[er] yard	04-16-08
308 yards of BroadCloth at 6s p[er] yard	92-08-00
112 yards of German Serge and Narrow Cloth at 2s p[er] yard	11-04-00
76 yards of worsted and hair Shaggs at 2s/6d p[er] yard	09-10-00
13 Pieces of Duroyes at 10s p[er] Piece	06-10-00
619 yards of shallooms at 12d p[er] yard	30-19-00
679 yards of Camletts and worsted Damaskes at 1s 6d p[er] yard	50-18-06
6 worsted Breeches at 6s p[er] pair	01-16-00
825 yards of Stuffs at 10d p[er] yard	35-16-08
1095 yards of Stuffs at 6d. p[er] yard	27-07-06
945 yards of Fustians & Checks at 12d p[er] yard	47-05-00
7 cotten Gown at 6s p[er] Gown	02-02-00
770 yards of Chinease Berrin crapes and Plads at 12d p[er] yard	38-10-00
170 yards of Printed cottens & Linnen at 2s p[er] yard	18-00-00
Quilts Ruggs Petticoats and Hoops at	11-00-06
7 Pieces and a half of Dowlas at 25s p[er] Piece	09-07-06
2 Horses 2 Mares and 2 Colts at	25-00-00
21 sheep at	05-05-00

5 Cows and two Calves at	16-00-00
A Silver watch and Silver Buckles	03-00-00
To Cash found in the House	<u>188-17-06</u>
	<u>661-03-04</u>
5 Table Clothes at 6^s each one …… Diaper 10^s & 14 yards of Broad Diaper at 2^s/6^d	03-10-00
204 yards of Broad Diaper at 9d. p[er] yard	07-13-00
17 yards Broad Diaper at 19^d	01-06-11
93 yards of Broomsgrove Flaxen at 18d. p[er] yard	06-19-06
27 yards of Holland Ell wide at 2^s p[ar] yard	02-14-00
43 Ells of Holland at 3^s/6^d p[er] Ell	07-10-06
3 pieces of holland 24 yards each at 3^s/2^d p[er] yard	11-02-00
one piece of holland 21 yards at 3^s/2^d p[er] yard	03-06-06
95 yards of Irish holland at 3^s/6^d p[er] yard	16-12-06
145 yards of Irish holland at 2^s p[er] yard	14-10-00
80 yards of Irish holland at 22^d p[er] yard	07-06-08
5 pieces of Irish holland 113 yards at 14^d p[er] yard	06-11-10
23 yards of Irish holland at 10^d p[er] yard	00-19-02
27 yards of Irish holland at 9^d p[er] yard	01-00-03
29 yards of Irish holland at 14^d p[er] yard	01-13-10
55 yards of Irish holland at 2^s p[er] yard	05-10-00
218 yards of Irish sheeting at 10^d p[er] yard	09-01-08
51 Cravatts at 1^s each	02-11-00
3½ yards of Mushing at 15^d p[er] yard	02-12-06
91 yards of Mushing at 3^s p[er] yard	13-13-00
18 white Bordered Handkerchiefs at 2^s	01-16-00
21 Silk Handkerchiefs at 3^s each	03-03-00
22 Silk and Cotton Handkerchiefs at 14^d each	01-05-08
208 Scotch Printed Handkerchiefs at 12^d each	10-08-00
151 Pair of Stockings at	14-02-08
cotton and worsted capps and Gloves	03-08-04
203 yards of Canvas at 6^d p[er] yard	05-01-06
8¾ ^{lb} Silk and Ball Twist at	08-00-00
6^{lb} of twist at 7^s p[er] lb	02-02-00
175^{lb} of snuff at 12^d p[er] lb	08-15-00
29^{lb} of Tobacco Roll at 6^d p[er] lb	00-14-06
34 yards of Wadding at 3^d p[er] yard	00-08-06
110^{lb} of Wick Yarn at 6d. p[er] lb	02-15-00
3 Dozen of hair Cloths	<u>00-12-00</u>
	<u>850-00-04</u>

30^{lb} of Cotton woll at 1ˢ 6ᵈ p[er] lb	02-05-00
33^{lb} of worsted at 20ᵈ p[er] lb	02-15-00
3^{lb} of Hemp	00-02-00
24 shammey skins at 10ᵈ p[er] skin	01-02-00
One piece of Nankeen at	00-05-00
56^{lb} of Rope at 3ᵈ p[er] lb	00-14-00
8^{lb} of Walc Bonc at 4ˢ p[er] lb	01-12-00
91 yards of Yellow Canvas Brown holland and Rusha Drabb at 14ᵈ p[er] yard	05-06-02
55 yards of Ticken at 16ᵈ p[er] yard	03-13-04
18 yards of Coarse Ticken at 8ᵈ p[er] yard	00-12-00
One Bed and Boulster of Flanders Ticken	00-18-00
18 Ells of Russha Cloth at 6ᵈ p[er] ell	00-09-00
20 yards of Buckram and Glazed Linnen at 9ᵈ p[er] yard	00-15-00
58 pieces of Printed Linnen at 2ˢ 6ᵈ p[er] piece	07-05-00
47 yards of Russha Henipton? at 2½ᵈ p[er] yard	00-09-09½
Hatts	02-14-06
61 yards and a half of Loone	15-15-00
7 Loon Handkerchiefs	02-02-00
2 Black Velvett hoods at 10ˢ each	01-00-00
2 Pair of Mens Silk Stockings at 9ˢ p[er] pair	00-18-00
5 pair of Womens Silk Stockings at 6ˢ p[er] pair	01-10-00
2 pair of Gloves at	00-06-00
16 yards of white and Black Tabby at 3ˢ 6ᵈ p[er] yard	02-16-00
151 yards of Pershians of all sorts at 12ᵈ p[er] yard	07-11-00
44 yards of stripe and Plain Silk at 18ᵈ p[er] yard	03-06-00
14 yards of Greys Aramenseens at 2ˢ 6ᵈ p[er] yard	01-15-00
73 yards of Shaggareens at 2ˢ p[er] yard	07-06-00
21 yards of Damasks at 2ˢ p[er] yard	02-02-00
56 yards of Clowded Burdett at 15ᵈ p[er] yard	03-10-00
28 yards of Bengall at 1ˢ 6ᵈ p[er] yard	<u>02-02-00</u>
	<u>932-17-01</u>½
40 yards of Brolia at 2ˢ p[er] yard	04-00-00
44 yards of Irish Stuffs at 10ᵈ p[er] yard	03-13-04
16 yards of 2^{ble} Alapeene at 3ˢ p[er] yard	02-08-00
24 yards of Single Alapeene at 16ᵈ p[er] yard	01-12-00
10 yards of Grey Silk at 2ˢ p[er] yard	01-00-00
25 yards of Velvett at 10ˢ p[er] yard	12-10-00
56 Ells of Black Silk at 5ˢ 6ᵈ p[er] ell	15-08-00

55 Ells of Narrow Silk at 4^s p[er] ell	11-00-00
25 Alamode Silk at 2^s 6^d p[er] ell	03-02-06
3 yards of gold Lace at 14^s p[er] yard	02-02-00
4 yards and a half of gold Lace at 6^s p[er] yard	01-07-00
6 yards and a half of Gold Edging at 3^s p[er] yard	00-19-06
6 yards of Scallop Edging at 2^s p[er] yard	00-12-00
18 yards of Silver Edging at 5^s 6^d p[er] yard	04-19-00
3 yards of Silver Edging at 4^s 6^d p[er] yard	00-13-06
6 pair of Silver Jacks at 2^s p[er] pair	00-12-00
2 Ounces of Gold Cord at 6^s p[er] ounce	00-12-00
3 Ounces of silver Lace	00-07-06
2 Ounces of Gold Thread at 4^s 6^d	00-09-00
24 Dozen of gold and silver Buttons at 2^s p[er] Dozen	02-08-00
Stays and Bodys Stomachingers	11-00-06
159 yards of Rusha at 4^d yard	02-16-00
Sadlery goods	07-02-06
Sadle and Bed Lace	02-00-00
Ribbands Gartering Ferrett Laces Tapes Inkles	07-00-00
Fine and Coarse Thread	07-08-00
Brushes Patterns Gimletts and other small things	01-00-00
Buttons Mettle & Mohair	10-00-00
Cutt Tobacco Powder & Shott	03-12-00
Books	05-00-00
Remnants, Blue Salt Petre hardware & Sciths	03-16-00
Plate at 5^s p[er] Ounce	<u>26-05-00</u>
	<u>1089-12-05 ½</u>
Grey hair and Combings	01-01-00
The Velvett Pall	<u>03-03-00</u>
	<u>1093-16-05 ½</u>
Household goods and Furniture	
In the little Parlour	
5 old chaires 2 little Tables one old Couch old corren Cubboad and a Glass	02-00-00
In the Hall	
3 Tables 6 Chaires one Clock	03-00-00
In the Kitchen one Jack 4 old chaires old Dresser a pair of Bellows, andold Lumber at	02-00-00
105^{lb} of Brass at 10^d p[er] lb	04-07-06
34^{lb} of Bell Mettle at 6^d p[er] lb	00-17-00

112

Inventories of Village Shopkeepers and Tradesmen: Fabric Trades – Mercers

100^{lb} weight of Pewter at 7^d p[er] lb	02-18-04
24^{lb} of Old Iron at 2^d p[er] lb	00-04-00
In the Brewhouse	
Brewing vessells	02-00-00
In the Stable	
2 cheese Presses one Malt Mill sadles and Bridles	02-00-00
In the Room over the Stable	
one Bed and Bedstead with its appurt[enance]s	01-00-00
one Iron Boiler	00-10-00
2 Baggs of Hops	07-00-00
24 Bushells of Malt at 5^s p[er] Bushell	06-00-00
12 Baggs	00-12-00
In the best Chamber	
6 chaires one Dressing Table 2 Glasses old Desk and chest and Drawers 2 Beds Bedsteads bed cloath and old china	10-00-00
5 chaires 2 Chests 3 Beds Bedsteads and Bedcloaths	05-00-00
2 Tables	00-10-00
In the Garretts	
3 Feather Beds and old Lumber	13-00-00
Gloves (omitted in the shop goods)	05-00-00
Table linnen and sheets	<u>05-00-00</u>
	72-18-10

An Account of Debts good and bad due from the persons Under Named to Mr John Vallance late of Cowbridge at the time of his Decease and taken from Lib. D.

Debtors Name	Habitation	Good Debts	Bad Debts
		li - s - d	li - s - d
Mary Jellicott	Cowbridge	00-11-07	
Richard Harrys wid[ow]	St Hillary		01-01-06
Jenkin Thomas	Ty yn y Wern by Neath		00-10-06
Margarett Jenkin	Pendoylan		00-07-11
Llewelni Robert	Pendoylan Tayler		00-17-08
Mrs Deaks	Funmon		00-06-04
Richard Morris	Landough		00-11-06
Robert Thomas	late of Cottrel		01-02-10
Evan Llewis	Cowbridge		01-01-00
Edwd Jenkins	Lysworney		01-10-11

113

Llewellni Evan	Funmon		00-10-08
Wm Roberts	Deceased		00-14-00
Margarett Penry	Roose		00-14-08
Thomas Morris	Landough		02-03-04
Mr Harding	Bristol		00-08-09
Robert Tanner	late Cowbridge		02-03-11
James Morgan Harper	Lantrisent		00-07-05
David Sherry	Colwinston		00-08-05
Richard Saul	Lanillid		00-18-01
Nicholas Evan	Lanblethian		01-06-08
Mrs Lawrence	Neath		09-07-10
		00-11-07	26-13-11

An Account of good and bad Debts Due from the p[er]sons Under Named to M^s Vallance at the time of his Decease taken from Lib. C.

Debtors Names	Habitation	Good Debts	Bad Debts
		li - s - d	li - s - d
Z. Jones	Cowbridge	01-01-11	
Mr James Jones	Boviarton	02-06-00	
David Robert	Lanblethian		01-18-00
David Lewis	Lanblethian	01-14-00	
Mrs Catlem?	late Cowbridge		02-12-07
Lewis Williams	Lansannor	01-03-04	
Thomas Evan	Lanblethian		04-06-05
Thomas Jenkins	late Ogmore		01-06-05
Peggy Leyson	Wick		01-10-00
Mary Pierion	Cowbridge		01-12-11
Edward Nicholl	Siginston		00-16-07
William Llewelin	Cowbridge		03-06-05
Francis Lewis Esq.	Landsoy Monmouthshire		04-11-00
Wm. Lewis S	Saint Mary Hill	01-02-11	
Thomas Wathen	Lantwitt	00-12-11	
Robert Alexander	Penmark	00-14-08	
Wm Hopkin	Lanblethian		03-11-06
David Howell			00-14-08
Charles Lewis	Cowbridge		01-00-00
Mr Phill Jones	Bristol		02-04-08
William Lawson	Lantwitt		00-16-05
Jacob Thomas Junr	Cowbridge	01-16-00	

Sampson Sweeting	late Ewenny		01-02-08
Howell Hopkin	Bonvilston		00-18-00
Mrs Cath Thomas	Cowbridge	00-13-03	
John Evan	Lanblethian	01-02-04	
Mr Perkins	St Nill		01-08-10
Mr George Lewis	late Llanilloyd		18-04-06
M^r Wm. Thomas	Duffrin ffrowd	02-00-08	
Thomas Christopher	Penllyne		02-02-11
Thomas Mathews Esq.	Landaffe	02-13-06	
John Richards	Cottrel	00-19-00	
The Revd Mr John Thomas	Slade	02-08-05	
The Revd Mr John Thomas	Lanblethian	04-13-06	
Cann Wilkins Esq.		17-13-05	
Evan John	Pendoylan	00-13-03	
Mr James Thomas	Lantrissent	05-00-09	
Henry Thomas	Penllyne	01-00-03	
Thomas Lewis Esq.	Lanishen	09-07-06	
Mrs Cecil Williams	Cowbridge	00-19-10	
Mrs Cecil Powell	Landow	06-12-11	
The Rev^d M^r Wm. Harris	Landaffe	06-14-09	
		73-04-04	54-04-06

Good and bad debts from Lib. C continued

Mrs Cath Thomas	Lanvithin		01-08-01
Lewis Thomas	late Bonvilston		02-03-06
Mrs Cath Jenkins	Ogmore		01-01-00
Mr Thomas Hancorne Surgeon		02-07-06	
John Llewellin	Cowbridge	03-16-00	
Edward Jones	Cowbridge		13-05-11
David Jenkin	St Mary Church	01-04-00	
Eliz. Lewis	Lanblethian	02-13-00	
James David	Penllyne	01-05-01	
Mathew	Cowbridge	01-07-02	
Thomas Richard	Cowbridge		01-00-00
Edward Davies	Cowbridge		01-12-06
Joan Lewis	Landough	00-14-03	
Lewis Jenkin	St Donnatts	01-06-08	
William Williams	Landough	02-16-08	
		91-04-07	74-15-09

An Account of good and bad Debts Due from the p[er]sons Under Named to Mr John Vallance at the time of his Decease for Malt Sold & Delivered

		Good Debts	Bad Debts
George John		00-16-00	
Lewis Morgan	Cowbridge		01-12-08
Thos. Bryan	Cowbridge	00-04-00	
Thomas Robert	Ystradowen		02-17-02
John Jukes	Lanblethian	02-02-07	
Llewelin Vawr	Lantwitt		02-05-06
Thomas Tanner	Cowbridge		02-06-06
Wenllian Thomas	Wick		02-07-04
Sciadmore Morgan	Cowbridge		02-02-00
Thomas Richard	Cowbridge		07-13-00
Robert Franklin	Cowbridge	03-12-00	
Thomas Robert	Cowbridge	01-08-00	
		08-02-07	21-04-02

An Account of good and bad Debts Due from the persons Under Named to Mr John Vallance at the time of his Decease and taken from Lib. F

		Good Debts	Bad Debts
John Nuobigging	Cowbridge		07-09-03
Mr Edwd Savours	M. Mawr	04-13-07	
Miss Gregory	Cowbridge	08-18-07	
The Revd Mr Lewis Lewis	Lanillid	00-16-00	
The Revd Mr Carne	St Athan	02-03-06	
Margarett Coffyn	Lanblethian	00-09-00	
Robert Lougher	Cowbridge	01-01-00	
Mr Edwd. Morgan	(School boy)	10-11-07	
Revd Mr James Morgan	Landough	02-16-11	
Mr Edwd Carne	Nash	04-18-06	
Mr Edwd Thomas	Malster	00-07-04	
Madam Morgan	Lanrumney	11-01-00	
Mrs Mathews	Lanrumney	06-05-05	
Edwd Gibbon	Lanblethian	01-06-00	
R. Rurberville Esquire		14-15-00	
Thos. Jones Dr Carnes apprentice		07-03-09	
John Williams (late Mr Durell's servant)			01-16-04
John Carne Esquire	Nash	05-11-00	
Christopher Askins	Aberthaw	00-16-02	

Francis Gwyn Esquire		01-01-00	
Mr Hugh Bowens	Eglwysbrewis	02-12-11	
The Revd Mr Durel		07-10-08	
John Williams	Pendoylan	03-17-10	
William Thomas	Pendoylan	01-00-11	
Isaac Redwood Hatter		01-09-00	
Thomas Mathews	Lantwitt Major	03-08-11	
John Thomas	Cowbridge	06-13-00	
Mr. Edwd. Thomas	Lansannor	09-02-00	
Mr. John Thomas	Penllyne	01-11-06	
Mrs Collins wid[ow]		04-11-09	
Mrs Mary Powell	Wenvoe	01-13-09	
Mrs Jennett Morgan	Ewenny	03-08-00	
Richard John	St Mary Church	04-00-08	
Mr. Taynton		00-03-02	
Thomas David Glazier		01-07-03	
Mr Thos Williams	N. Nottage	02-06-08	
Mr Richard Carne		01-11-09	
Thomas Trueman		00-04-09	
Madam Kemeys		01-02-00	
Stephen Hardwick	Boviarton	<u>00-15-09</u>	
		142-18-07	<u>09-05-07</u>
Good and bad Debts from Lib. F continued			
Mrs Phillipa Jones		01-14-00	
Joan Rees wid[ow]	Cowbridge	01-02-00	
Francis Gamage Sailor	Cowbridge		04-17-06
Pierce Cornish Esqr	Cowbridge	04-02-00	
Mr Edwd Mathew	Abramman?	03-19-04	
Richd Jones	Hensol	00-17-07	
Mr. Edwards ye Officer	Landaffe	03-00-00	
Revd Mr David Pruddio	Colwinston	27-02-08	
Mr Edmunds	Cowbridge	01-17-11	
Mr Thomas Lewis	Cowbridge	06-10-00	
Revd Mr John Nicholl	Lantwitt	01-18-09	
Mary Harry	Cowbridge	01-02-08	
Henry Williams	Marcross	00-07-09	
Mrs Martha Savours		01-11-06	
Miles Thomas	Colwinston	02-03-00	
Joan Mousser		02-15-08	
Miss Turberville		02-05-07	

Mr David Sweeting	Aburthin	02-15-07	
Christopher Wilkins		00-13-00	
Mr Russell	Siginston	03-10-05	
Mrs Savours	Lantrythid	09-13-04	
Capt. Edmond Holland		15-11-07	
Reybold Deere Esqr		05-01-06	
		242-14-05	14-03-01

Good and bad Debts Due by Bonds and promisory Notes to the said John Vallance Deceased at the time of his Death from the persons Under Named Vizt

	Good Debts	Bad Debts
Bond from Mr. John Morgan for		21-06-05
Note from David David for		01-08-11
Note from Thomas James		00-06-02
Conditional Note from Edwd Gwyn		05-06-05
Note from James Todd for		01-01-00
Note from Mr John Tudor Clerk		01-09-10
Note from Mr Robert Atkins of Bristol for	07-07-00	
	07-07-00	30-18-09

Jane Vallance Party Exhibitant

Exhibited at Landaff on the Twenty first day of July in the year of our Lord One Thousand Seven hundred and ffifty by Jane Vallance widow the Relict and administratrix for a true and perfect Inventory etc. but under protestation of adding etc. if any more of the assetts of the deceased shall hereafter come to her hands or possession   Tho: Davies N.P. Dep^ty Register

Administration Bond: John Vallence: 21st July, 1750

In the Consistory Court of Llandaff, 21st July, 1750, administration of the goods etc. of John Vallence, mercer, was granted to his widow, Jane Vallence. Jane Vallence, Pierce Cornish, Esquire, and John Thomas, gentleman, both of the Town of Cowbridge, were sworn by the Court in the sum of £2,000 for Jane Vallence to exhibit a true inventory of the goods etc. of her late husband at or before the last day of October next, to administer according to law, to give a true account of her administration at or before the last day of July 1751, and to present to the Court any last will and testament of the deceased that might appear. All three boundens signed the administration bond, before Thomas Charles, surrogate.

[National Library of Wales Document Reference: LL/1750/42]

Feltmakers/Hatters

A true and perfect Inventory of all the goods and Chattles of George Evans of Cardiffe in the County of Glamorgan ffeltmaker late deceased As they were prized the fift day of June in the year of our Lord one Thousand Six hundred eighty & three by the persons whose names are hereunto Annexed & Sunscribed as ffolloweth   li - s - d

Impr[imis] his wearing Apparrell & money in pockett	01-00-00
Itt[em] in the forestreet Chamber one standing bedstead two feather beds on Table two Chests one Cupboard & two Chaires valued att	02-00-00
Itt[em] In the middle Chamber one bed and bedstead & an old Cupboard att	00-10-00
Itt[em] in the back Chamber one bed & bedstead and Tableboard valued att	00-15-00
Itt[em] In the little buttery one bed and bedstead valued att	00-10-00
Itt[em] In the parlour to Cupboards two Tables Six chairs Six joynt stooles and to benches valued att	01-00-00
Itt[em] one Small brass pott one Small kettle two Ironpotts & twelve peices of pewter one pair of Andirons one pair of tongs & fire Slice and three Spits at	01-00-00
Itt[em] In wooll	01-00-00
Itt[em] 4 dosen of Hatts valued att	02-00-00
Itt[em] His working tooles in the work house valued att	01-00-00
Itt[em] a little hay in ye stable	00-05-00
In all	11-00-00

The prizers names   Tho: Jones   Edward David   James ffoord

[National Library of Wales Document Reference: LL/ 1683/ 16]

A true and perfect Inventory of the Goods and Chattles of Edward Sweete the younger late of Cardiff in the County of Glamorgan ffeltmaker lately deceased made and appraised by the persons whose names are herunto subscribed the seaven and twentieth day of Aprill *in the second year of the reign of our Lord James the second King of England etc. in the year of our Lord [in latin]* 1686 vizt

Imp[rimi]s his wearing apparell appraised att	07-00-00
In the kitchin	
In ready Money	14-00-00

two ffowling pieces appraised att	01-00-00
the pewter and Bras appraised att	08-00-00
One Table Board and fframe ffour joynt stoles three chaires and other small utensills	01-00-00
three Broaches one paire of tongs one slice and other fire utensills appraised att	00-10-00
One silver tanquett eight silver spoones two Dram Dishes & one silver Bowle att	08-00-00

Chamber over y[e] Kitchin

one ffeather Bed with the appertenances appraised	02-10-00
In Earthen Ware in the house appraised att	10-00-00

Parlor

One ffeather Bed with it app[ur]ten[a]nces appraised att	03-00-00
one Round table, six leatherin Chaires two Wooden Chaires, one pres Cubbord, one Chest, one Iron Grate one paire of andirons appraised att	02-00-00

fforestreete Chamber

one Bedsteed one ffeather Bed with its app[ur]ten[a]nces appraised att	03-00-00
one Table Boord & fframe three Chaires, one Chest, one small Cubbord, and one Drawers appraised att	02-00-00

little fforestreete Chamber

one Bedsteed & ffeather Bed with its appurten[a]nces att	02-00-00
In Linnen appraised	02-10-00
one salt pan & y[e] appurten[a]nces appraised at	02-10-00
Hatts and Trimings appraised att	12-00-00
Seaven hundred Winchester Bushells of Salt appraised att	32-18-04
One Horse appraised att	04-00-00
	117-18-04
three Sheepe and a lamb appraised to	00-10-00
Glas Bottles and Glasses appraised to	03-00-00
	121-08-04

Appraisers names	Henrie Sheere	Will Richard	Jonathan Greenfield
	Gabriel Lewis	Thomas James	John Jenkins

Administration Bond: Edward Sweete, feltmaker: 30th April, 1686

In the Consistory Court of Llandaff, 30th April, 1686, administration of the goods etc. of Edward Sweete, feltmaker, deceased, was granted to his widow, Mary Sweete. Mary Sweete, Jonathan Greenfield, and Henrie Murton, salter, all of the town of Cardiff, were sworn by the Court in the sum of £200, for Mary Sweete to make and exhibit an inventory of her late husband's goods etc. at or before the 24th June next, to administer according to law, to give a just account of her administration at or before the 30th April, 1687, and to present to the Court any last will and testament of the deceased that might appear. Mary Sweet and Jonathan Greenfield signed the administration bond: Henry Murton recorded his mark.

[National Library of Wales Document Reference: LL/ 1686/ 42]

An Inventory of all and Singular the Goods, and Ch[att]ells of William Lewis late of the Town of Cardiffe in the County of Glamorgan and Diocess of Landaffe Feltmaker dece[ase]d made valued and Appraised the 28th day of May 1731 by George Evans and Evan Deer Appraisors as follows vizt

	£ - s - d
Inpr[imi]s his waring Apparell valued at	02-10-00
In the Kitchin	
Item Nine pewter dishes att	00-13-00
Item three doz[en] and nine Small pewter plates att	00-10-00
Item two paires of Small Handirons att	00-04-00
Item halfe a Doz[en] of brass Candlesticks one Snuffers three Iron Candlesticks & four old Chairs	00-04-09
Item one pewter tankard four pewter dishes at	00-01-03
Item one brass Spoon att	00-00-02
Item two Tongs two Slices two Spits one toaster one Grate & one Crane att	00-14-00
In the Parlour	
Item one oval table and a Chest att	00-08-00
Item ten Chairs att	00-03-04
Item one Doz[en] of pictures att	00-00-09
Item one small Looking Glass att	00-01-06
In the Chamber	
Item one bed and furniture att	02-10-00
Item one Case of Drawers and two Chests att	00-10-00
Item one Doz[e]n of old Chairs att	00-01-03
Item three old Trunks att	00-02-00
Item one small Glass att	00-02-00
Item three small bars att	00-01-00

Stock in Wool
Item   Stock of wooll valued att   01-03-04
Item   on old founder'd Mare att   01-05-00
In the Buttry
Item   one brass Crock   three small Kettles att   00-11-00
Item   one Skillet att   00-01-00
In the Work house
Item   the tools and things belonging to the Workhouse att   01-00-00
Item   one Small furnace att   00-12-00
Item   the Stock in the Shop   In hats and Hatbands att   10-07-03½
The Plate
Item   one small Silver tankard att   02-03-09
Item   one small Silver Spoon att   00-01-07
Item   in Lumber about the house att   00-07-03
                                              sum total   26-09-02½
By Mortages bonds and book debts ye sume of   229-00-00
                                                               255-09-02½

Exhibited at Llandaff, 31st May, 1731, by Mary Lewis, relict and administrator.

Administration Bond: William Lewis, hatmaker: 31st May, 1731

In the Consistory Court at Llandaff, 31st May, 1731, administration of the goods etc. of William Lewis, hatmaker, deceased, was granted 'with the will annexed,' to his widow, Mary Lewis, 'to ye use and dureing ye minority of Jane Lewis a Miner ye natural & lawful daughter & residuary Legatee named in the last will & testament of the deceased.' Mary Lewis, Marie James, and Morgan William of Radir, yeoman, were sworn by the Court in the sum of £500 for Mary Lewis to make and exhibit a true inventory of the goods and credits of her late husband on or before the last day of August next, to administer to the use and benefit of Jane Lewis, and to give a just account of her administration when required. All three boundens recorded their mark on the administration bond.

[National Library of Wales Document Reference: LL/ 1731/ 34]

Hosiery Trade: Stocking Knitters/Shopkeepers/Wholesalers

A true and perfect Inventory of all & Singular ye goods, Ch[at]ells & Credits of Ann Howell late of ye p[ar]ish of Peterston Sup Eley in ye County of Glamorgan & Diocess of Landaffe dece[ase]d made valued & appraised ye 20th day of June Anno D[omi]ni 1715 by Richard John, Thomas Mathew and Morgan William Appraisors as follows (vizt)

	ll - s - d
Imp[rimi]s Her wearing cloase valued to	1 - 0 - 0
Item one feather bed & all his wearing cloase valued to	1 -10 - 0
Item fifteen paire of Stockings at	0 - 2 - 0
Item Brass, iron & pewter at	0 - 5 - 0
Item All ye rest of her wooden stuffe at	0 -10 - 0
Item Debts due to ye s[ai]d deceased ye Sum of	9 -15 - 0
	Tot[al] 13 - 2 - 6

Exhibited at Llandaff, 29th June, 1715, by Charles Edwards, executor.

Extract from Will of Ann Howell

'I have in the hands of Edward Thomas the Sume of four pounds wich I leave to Charles Edwards   also in the hands of Morgan William two pounds   also in the hands of Will[ia]m John fifteen shillings   Also in the hands of Thomas Morgan one pound   also in the hands of Elizabeth William one pound'

[National Library of Wales Reference Number LL/1715/ 109]

****

A True and perfect Inventory of all & singular the goods Ch[at]ells & Credits of Mary Miles late of the p[ar]ish of Bonvilston in the County of Glamorgan & Diocess of Landaffe Dece[ase]d Made valued & appraised the eight & Twentieth Day of Aprill Anno D[omi]ni 1725 by John Hickes & Thomas Phillip appraisers as foll[ows] (vizt)

	li - s - d
Inpri[mi]s Her wearing apparel valued at	00-07-00
Item Two Coffers att	00-05-00
Item One bed & bedstead att	00-17-06
Item Two Iron Potts att	00-05-00
Item Two Tables att	00-05-00
Item one Coffer att	00-06-00

Item One Trunk att	00-01-00
Item fifteen paire of stockins att	00-06-00
Item One Chaire att	<u>00-00-06</u>
Sum Tot[al]	<u>02-13-00</u>

Administration Bond: Mary Miles: 24th May, 1725

In the Consistory Court of Llandaff, 24th May, 1725, administration of the goods etc. of Mary Miles, deceased, was granted to her niece, Mary David of the parish of Bonvilston. Mary David and William Miles, yeoman, were sworn by the Court in the sum of £10, for Mary David to make and exhibit a true inventory of the goods etc. of her late aunt at of before the last day of August next, to administer according to law, to make a just account of her administration at or before the 24th May, 1726, and to present to the Court any last will and testament of the deceased that might appear. Both Mary David and William Miles recorded their mark on the administration bond.

[National Library of Wales Reference Number LL/1725/ 18]

****

Cardiff   An Inventory of the Goods and Chatles of Myles Evans Late deceased: Appraised the two and Twentith day of January 1665

	li - s - d
Imp[rimi]s his wearing Apparrell valued at	02-00-00
Itt[em] one old feather bed one pare of Canvas Sheets one Red Rugge one fether pillow one standing bedsteed with two old Curtains and valians valued at	02-00-00
Itt[em] more one old feather bed two pare of Canvas sheets one pare of blanketts and one pillow valued at	01-00-00
Itt[em] more Eighteen peeces of pewter small and Graet at	00-18-00
Itt[em] more three litle brass Skilletts and one litle brass Candlestick valued at	00-03-00
Itt[em] more two small Iron Crocks and one litle brass Spoone valued at	00-03-00
Itt[em] more two old Cubbarts valued at	00-05-00
Itt[em] more two Chests & one old box valued at	00-13-00
Itt[em] more three old Chaires three Joynt stooles five Low stooles and one small ironscotte beench valued at	00-05-00

Itt[em] more five porridge dishes fifteene trenchers one old earthen platter with an old baskett valued at 00-01-00

Itt[em] more one frying pan one small Iron grate one small broach 1 small slice one tonges with one iron Marma? one brass Chaffara dish and Eight other small peeces of Iron and one screw candlestick being valued at 00-05-00

Itt[em] one litle Lookeing Glass one old paile one old standerd valued at 00-00-06

Itt[em] one old bible one old Testament valued 00-01-06

Itt[em] Twenty dozen Childrens stockins being valued at 02-00-00

Itt[em] one and Twenty dozen of Midling stockins being at 05-00-00

Itt[em] five pare of Cotton Stockins and one and twenty pare of Cotton Gloves and Tenn pair of yarne stockins being valued at 01-00-00

Itt[em] Eleven dozen of Cabedge Netts and two dozen of wooden buskes being valued at 00-04-00

Itt[em] more one old pack sadle one old Chest one old box and two old baggs being valued at 00-01-06

Ittem] one dozen of strawing hatts valued at 00-02-06

Itt[em] more Twenty Seven Gross of Course Inckle & two & twenty dozen of Small Tobaccoe boxes valued at 01-10-00

The totall sume is 17-13-00

The praisers Names the marke of Thomas Jenkin Tomas Spencer Rich Price Exhibited at Llandaff, 26th January, 1666, by Joan Evans, relict and executrix.

[National Library of Wales Document Reference LL/ 1666/ 15]

May 16th, 1856 Valuation of Household Furniture and Effects, The Property of the late Mr Job Hipwell Taken for the purpose of administration Valued by Mr Abbott, Auctioneer, High St., Cardiff.

Boys and Girles stockings	03-10-00
Mens stockings	04-00-00
Womens stockings	01-16-00
Womens cotton stockings	02-00-00
Mens stockings	05-00-00
Mens stockings	02-00-00
Women's stockings	01-00-00
Boys and Girles stockings	01-10-00
Men's cotton drawers	01-00-00

Men's woollen scarfs	02-00-00
Men's drawers	00-18-00
Morina drawers and shirts	00-12-00
Children's socks	03-00-00
Handkerchiefs	01-00-00
Fancy Goods	00-10-00
Shoes and Braces	01-00-00
Flannells and Checks	01-00-00
Worsted and Yarn	06-00-00
5 Boy's Knitts	00-02-06
4 Pairs Knitts	00-01-00
3 cotton Hose	00-02-06
7 p[ai]r cotton Hose	00-02-06
1 p[ai]r of Girles black cotton	00-02-06
5 p[ai]r of Girles cotton hose Hose	00-00-06
7 p[ai]r Girles cotton hose	00-03-06
6 p[ai]r Girles cotton Hose	00-02-00
3 p[air] Girles cotton Hose	00-01-06
8 p[ai]r Hose	00-04-00
9 pair of hose	00-02-00
3 p[ai]r Hose	00-01-06
6 p[ai]r Hose	<u>00-03-06</u>
carried forward	£39-05-00
12 pair of cotton hose	00-06-00
12 pair of cotton hose	00-04-00
12 pair of cotton hose	00-04-06
6 pair of cotton hose	00-02-00
Straw bonnets and hats	03-00-00
Odd knitting cotton and needles	00-10-00
Odd stockings and sundries	02-00-00
Handkerchiefs and socks	01-10-00
1 desk	00-03-00
Gas fittings	01-10-00
2 small counters	01-05-00
Shelves	00-08-00
p[ai]r of small scales and weights	00-06-00
Sofa	01-16-00
1 round deal Table	00-02-00
1 deal Square table	00-05-00

6 polished Chairs	00-12-00
Odd Books	00-06-00
3 Trays	00-02-00
1 small swing Glass	00-01-00
1 square Glass	05-00-00
2 Pictures	00-02-06
1 arm chair	00-03-00
1 broken arm chair	00-01-00
Deal chest of drawers	00-15-00
4 brass candlesticks	00-04-00
set of fire irons	00-04-06
sundry ware	00-06-00
2 metal teapots and 1 coffee pot	00-04-00
Fender	00-02-06
Drugit	00-04-00
1 Tea Caddy	00-02-00
3 iron saucepans	00-03-00
Bellows, candle box, sundry tins	00-03-00
Iron pot and teakettle	00-02-06
1 X table	00-02-00
Brown Ware	00-02-00
3 broken chairs	00-01-00
steps and cupboard	00-08-00
carried forward	£57-06-06
Sundries	00-03-00
Clothes horse and small cask	00-03-00
Sign board	00-04-00
2 Windsor chairs	00-02-06
1 tent bedstead	00-07-00
Mill-puff matress	00-04-00
8 cotton sheets	00-09-06
3 blankets	00-10-00
1 Quilt	00-01-00
small feather bed	01-05-00
Wash stand and ware	00-04-00
Dressing table	00-02-06
1 swing Glass	00-03-00
2 Boxes	00-03-06
Cap basket and Box	00-01-06

3 pieces of carpet	00-02-06
Roller & Blinds & two curtains	00-01-06
1 old Carpet Bag	00-01-00
1 Umbrella	00-03-06
1 small Bedstead	00-03-00
1 small Mill-puff bed	00-06-00
1 old chair	00-01-00
1 night commode	00-04-00
1 small p[ai]r of steelyards	00-02-00
6 pillow cases	[not valued]
2 Watches	03-00-00
3 p[ai]r of boots	00-06-00
2 pairs of stockings	00-02-00
4 p[ai]r of trousers	00-12-00
4 Waistcoats	00-10-00
6 Calico shirts	00-09-00
2 flannel shirts	00-03-00
3 hats	00-08-06
4 coats	01-10-00
6 handkerchiefs	00-06-00
2 p[ai]r of gloves	00-01-06
1 silver Guard	00-05-00
Men's, women's and children's stockings	03-15-00
20 dozen worsted & cotton socks	03-05-00
Cotton hose	04-00-00
Shirts etc	06-10-00
12 p[ai]r of slippers	00-06-00
	88-05-00

Administration Bond: Job Hipwell, hosier: 16th May, 1856

In the Consistory Court of Llandaff, 16th May, 1856, administration of the goods of Job Hipwell, hosier, who died on the 9th May, 1856 was granted to his widow, Ann Hipwell, of 7, Trinity Street, Cardiff. Ann Hipwell, Samuel Abbott of High Street, Cardiff, auctioneer, and Robert Taverner of Plucca Lane, Cardiff, provision dealer, were sworn by the Court in the sum of £200 for Ann Hipwell to exhibit a true inventory of the goods etc. of her late husband on or before the last day of November next, to administer according to law, to give a just account of her administration on or before the last day of May next, and to present to the Court any last will and testament of the deceased that might appear. Ann Hipwell recorded her mark on the administration bond: Samuel Abbott and Robert Taverner signed the bond.

[National Library of Wales Document Reference: LL/1856/52]

A True and perfect Inventory of all the goods Cattle and Chattles of John Jenkins of Blackffryars in the p[ar]ish of St Maries w[i]thin the Towne of Cardiffe and County of Glamorgan late deaceased; Taken and apprized by us the p[er]sons under named the second day of February in the Thirty fift yeare of the Raigne of our Soveraigne Lord Charles the second Anno D[omi]ni 1683

	li - s - d
Imp[rimi]s his Wearing apparrell prized to	007-00-00
Itt[em] In the Chamber over the Parlour One ffeather Bed and Bedsteed w[i]th Curtaines and Vallians w[i]th its one Bedsteed and dust Bed w[i]th its appurten[a]nces, one ffeather Bowlster	006-00-00
Itt[em] More in the sayd Chamber one great Chest, one Round Table boord, one Trunke, one desk, Two small boxes ffower Chayers, one Cage Glasse	002-00-00
Itt[em] In the Back Chamber One ffeather Bed and pillow Two small Cofers and other small Trumpery vallued to	001-14-00
Itt[em] In the Parlour One standing Bedsteed, one ffeather Bed & Bolster Curtaines and Vallians w[i]th its appurtenances vallued to	004-00-00
Itt[em] More in the sayd Roome one Cupboord, one Table and fframe with three Joynt stooles, ffower Chayers one Chest one Cofer, one payre of Andiarns prized to	002-00-00
Itt[em] In the Kitchin One Table Boord and fframe, one Iron Grate, Two Iron ffire shovells, Two payre of tongs, one ffrying pan, Two Brandierns, Three small Brasse Kettles, Three Iron Crocks, one little Brasse skillett, with severall other small implements of houshould stuffe valued to	002-00-00
Itt[em] All his pewter prized and valued to	003-00-00
Itt[em] In the Slope house of Wood and severall Wooden Trumpery valued to	001-00-00
Itt[em] Two Horses one Mare Two pack saddles and theyr materialls	008-00-00

Itt[em] One Reek of Hay prized to	003-00-00
Itt[em] provision of the House valued to	001-00-00
Itt[em] Two packs and a halfe of Stockins or therabouts prized and valued to	100-00-00
Itt[em] desperate debts due to the deceadent	010-00-00
Itt[em] debts due by Bills and Bonds to the sayd deceadent	207-00-00
Itt[em] In Ready money at his decease	120-00-00
Sum is	<u>478-04-00</u>

Prizers names: Edward E [his mark] Deackon   Row: [his mark] Price
                 Thomas Jones   Robert Bawdrey   Will: Deare

[National Library of Wales Document Reference: LL/ 1683/ 21]

A true and perfect Inventory of Leases, Goodes, Chattles moveables and [un]moveables of Thomas Jones [hosier] of Cardiffe Deceased made the 14th day of may 1686

	li - s - d
Imp[rimi]s 30 weathers vallued at	15-00-00
48 twelve month old sheep vallued at 6^{li} a score	14-08-00
25 yews and Lambs vallued at 8^{li} a score	10-00-00
2 yoake of oxen vallued at	18-00-00
2 cows 1 heyfer and a Calfe vallued at	09-00-00
10 three yeare ould Cattle vallued at	20-00-00
7 Smale Cattle vallued at	06-00-00
4 horsis 1 mare and 3 Coults vallued at	22-00-00
2 Sows vallued at	02-10-00
30 Bushells of wheat vallued at	09-00-00
7 Bushells of Beanes vallued at	01-15-00
13 Accers of wheat in the Ground vallued at 3^{li} p[er] Accer	39-00-00
4 Accers of Barely in the Ground vallued at 40^s per Accer	08-00-00
4 Accers of Pease in the Ground at 20^s vallued p[er]	04-00-00
The moyety of 5 Accers of wheat sowed upon halfe	07-10-00
The moyety of 8 Accers of oates sowed upon halfe	04-00-00
His wearing Apparell vallued at	10-00-00
In the fore Street Chamber 1 Bed and Bedsteed and other furniture vallued at	14-00-00
In the Second Chamber 1 Bed and Bedsteed and other furniture vallued at	10-00-00

In the Third Chamber 1 Bed and bedsteed and other furniture vallued at	08-00-00
In the Garrett 5 packs of Stokins fflannens and Inkles vallued at	150-00-00
In the Garrett and Gallery 1 Bed Steed 1 Close stoole and 1 Chest vallued at	01-00-00
In the Great Parlour 1 Standing bedsteed and 1 Bed 1 press Bed and 2 Beds and other furniture vallued at	20-00-00
In the Little Parlour 1 Bed and Bedsteed and other furniture vallued at	05-00-00
In the Little Chamber 1 Bed and Bedsteed and other furniture vallued at	03-00-00
In the Brew house 1 Brasse ffurnesse and Brewing Vessels vallued at	05-00-00
In the Kitching 2 Dressers 1 Cubb 1 table Board and other furniture vallued at	03-00-00
The plate vallued at	10-00-00
The Brasse Pewter and Iron goodes vallued at	20-00-00
The Linnen vallued at	20-00-00
The two Chattle Leasis vallued at	50-00-00
The Bookes vallued at	01-10-00
The plow harnesse horse harnesse Dung Cart Sadles Bridles and other appurtenances vallued at	05-00-00
Tottall Summe	526-03-00

Praysers names
Cradock Nowell   Will Richard   Will Myles   Edward Dearen

[National Library of Wales Document Reference: LL/ 1686/ 37]

---

6. Leather Trades

Tanners

Glamorgan   A True and perfect Inventory of all the goods and Chatles of William David of the Town of Cowbridge in the County of Glamorgan Tanner late deceased had made and Appraised on the third day of January (in the second yeare of the Reign of our Soveraign Lord & Lady William and Mary by the grace of God of England Scotland etc. King and Queen etc. and in the yeare of our Lord God one thousand Six hundred and Ninetie) by the Appraisers herunto subscribed as followeth (vizt)

	li - s - d
Imprimis his weareing Apparell	02-00-00
In the Chamber over the Entring one feather bed bolster pillows blankets & sheets	01-10-00
two brass pots 2 brass Caldrons & one brass skillet	01-00-00
5 pewter platters one gun and other small pewter things	00-05-00
one Chafing dish one frying pan and dripping pan, one tin Cofin one spit pothoocks Andirons and smoothing Iron	00-03-00
four Chaires	00-01-06
In the inner Chamber 2 feather beds 2 bolsters with Ruggs blankets and bedsteads	01-10-00
In his Tannpitt seaven dickers of leather being seaventy att four pound p[e]r stone	14-00-00
In his lime pits four dickers of skins being forty hides att 20^s p[e]r dicker	04-00-00
the Mill & stone where the bark is ground one horse, hay and one pigg	01-00-00
one fatt & cooler above ground with eight Calve skins	00-07-08
The beame and paring knifes belonging thereto	00-03-00
In bark	01-00-00
in money due out to the said William david late deceased	01-00-00
	28-00-02

Appraisers
the mark of Thomas TP Phillips   Roger RC Clement ffrances G Gybbon   Thomas Morgan   the mark of ffrances R Rees   Christopher William

Administration Bond: William David, tanner: 27th May, 1691

In the Consistory Court of Llandaff, 27th May, 1691, administration of the goods etc. of William David, tanner, deceased, was granted to his widow, Mary David. Mary David and Thomas Morgan, also of the Town of Cowbridge, were sworn in the sum of £100 for Mary David to make and exhibit an inventory of the goods etc. of her late husband at or before 29th June next, to administer according to law, to render a just account of her administration at or before 27th January next, and to present to the Court any last will and testament of the deceased that might appear. Mary David and Thomas Morgan recorded their mark on the administration bond.

[National Library of Wales Document Reference: LL/1691/26]

An Inventory of all & Singular ye Goods Ch[at]ells & Creditts of Cradock Nowell late of ye Towne of Cardiffe in ye County of Glamorgan Alderman dec[eas]ed made, vallued & appraised ye ninth day of March Anno D[omi]ni 1708/9 by William Jones Emanuel Miles, John Sweet & Sherra Sweet Appraisors

	£ - s - d
Inp[rimi]s in ye great forestreet Chamber, a Bed & its Furniture vallued att	15-00-00
Item in ye Wainscott Chamber a Bed & its furniture att	10-00-00
Item in ye hanged Chamber two Beds & their furniture att	25-00-00
Item Linnen att	20-00-00
Item Plate att	30-00-00
Item ye Bed & furniture of a little Roome att	02-10-00
Item ye furniture of ye Hall att	10-00-00
Item ye furniture of ye little Parlour att	03-00-00
Item ye app[ur]tenances of ye Kitchin as Pewter Brass etc. att	20-00-00
Item Malt & Barley att	120-00-00
Item Stock in ye Tann Yard att	200-00-00
Item 3 horses & a Colt att	15-00-00
Item ye Wooll & Sheep att	05-00-00
Item ye Lease of ye dwelling house att	100-00-00
Item ye Lease of ye fulling Mill att	100-00-00
Item ye Lease of Cross bychan att	50-00-00
Item ye Lease of ye house called ye little-Angell att	30-00-00
Item ye Bed & furniture in ye Sev[an]ts Room valued att	03-00-00
Item ye Bed & furniture in ye Chamber over y Kitchin att	02-00-00
Item debts due to ye deced[en]t ye Sum of	150-00-00
Sum total of this Inventory	910-10-00

Exhibited at Llandaff, 12th April, 1709, by Ann Nowell, relict and executrix.

[National Library of Wales Reference Number LL/1709/ 39]

****

A true & perfect Inventory of the Goods Ch[att]ells & Creditts of Thomas Holiday late of Cardiff in the County of Glamorgan Tanner dece[ase]d Appraised by us whose names are hereunto subscribed the fourth day of ffebruary Anno D[omi]ni 1729 (vizt)

	£ - s - d
Impr[im]is His wearing Apparrel	01-05-00

In the best Chamber One Old Ovall table two old black fflagg Chairs one Old Chest One old Bedstead One old feather bed Boulster two small Pillows One Green Rugg one pair of Blanketts & one pair of Curtains & Vallians	02-00-00
In the next Chamber one Dust bed one fflock boulster One old Bedstead & other old Lumber	00-02-06
In the fore Room below stairs two old Square tables one old Cubboard and old Earthen Ware	00-02-06
two old small Brass Kettles	00-06-00
A Small parcell of old Pewter & one old brass Candlestick	00-05-00
In the shop one old Coffer one shop drawer four pounds of Prunes two pound of Gingerbread & seven pounds of Treacle	00-02-00
In the back Room & Coalhouse old Lumber and bottles	00-01-00
one old Little horse	00-15-00
one Broken Winded horse	01-00-00
Sperate debts	
due from Joseph ffarmers widdow	01-00-00
John Price bookbinder	00-05-00
	07-05-00

Appraisers   George Lewis   James Thomas

Administration Bond: Thomas Holiday, tanner: 6th February, 1729

In the Consistory Court at Llandaff, 6th February, 1729, administration of the goods of Thomas Holiday, tanner, deceased, was grated to his widow, Margarett Holyday. Margarett Holyday, William Williams of Cardiff, gardener, and John Williams of Cardiff, labourer, were bound by the Court in the sum of £20 for Margaret Holyday to make and exhibit a true inventory of the goods etc. of her late husband at or before the last day of July next, to administer according to law, to render a true account of her administration at or before the last day of February, 1730, and to present to the Court any last will and testament of the deceased that might appear. John Williams signed the administration bond: both Margarett Holyday and William Williams recorded their mark on the document.

[National Library of Wales Document Reference: LL/ 1729/ 58]

Cordwainers [Boot and Shoe Makers]

A true and p[er]fect Inventorie of all the goodes Cattells amd Chattells moveable and unmoveable of Henry Spencer of landaffe late deceased made and prised the first day of december Anno d[omi]ni 1641./by Morgan Rimbron of fairewater and Thomas William of landaffe

Implements of household stuffe in the Hall

Imprimis one table boord and sixe Joynt stooles prised all		xii^s
It[em] two Cubbords and one great Chest		xxx^s
It[em] one deske and three chaires		viii^s
It[em] two litle round table boords and one binche		iiii^s
It[em] sixe stooles one litle Joynt stoole, one stoolechaire, and one box		iiii^s
It[em] one Carpett and tenn Cushions		x^s
It[em] one pewter basen and ewer, nine great pewter platters, and one pewter flagon		xx^s
It[em] sixe pewter dishes, two pewter Candlesticks, two brasse candlesticks, one pewter saltseller, one quart two tunnes, seaven fruite dishes, two saucers, one pinte, and one tanckett, all of pewter, one brasse mortar and one brasse spoone		xiii^s
It[em] two blacke Andiers, and one fire iron		iii^s
Sum:	v^{li}	iiii^s

In the buttrie

Imprimis two brasse Crocks, and three brasse skilletts		xx^s
It[em] seaven pewter platters, foure pewter fruite dishes one pewter candlestick, and one pewter chamber pott		x^s
It[em] one litle boord, trenchers and other wooden or treen vessells there		2^s
Sum:	i^{li}	xii^s

In the best Chamber

Imprimis one feather bedd, two feather bowlsters three feather pillowes, one dust bedd, two Rugges, with their Appurtenances etc		iiii^{li}
It[em] one standinge bedd and one ffrench bedd		xv^s
It[em] one table boord and frame, seaven Joynt stooles and two binches		x^s
It[em] three Chaires and five litle Joynt stooles		viii^s
It[em] three Coffers, one boxe, one livery Cubbord and Cushion Thereupon	vi^s	viii^d

It[em]   one pair of Andiers, one tonges and a slice   iiii^s
                                            Sum: v^{li} viii^s iiii^d

In the white chamber
Imprimis   one standinge bedd, one table boord, one
   binch, and two coffers   xv^s
It[em]   one dust bedd, one Rugge, with the Appurtenances etc   x^s
                                            Sum: i^{li} v^s

In a litle Chamber
Imprimis   one bedd, one Coverlett with other bedd
   clothers, one tableboord, and one coffer   x^s
In another Chamber
Imprimis   one bedd, a Coverlett with other bedd clothers
   two table boords and one binch   x^s
In another litle roome
Imprimis   one boord and other wodden or treene vessells there   v^s
In the kitchin
Imprimis   one tableboord, one bedd, a Coverlett with other bedd
   clothers and other Implements of small value there   x^s
It[em]   three Iron Crocks   xv^s
                                            Sum: i^{li} v^s

It[em]   one sowe and one pigge   viii^s
It[em]   his the deceadents weareinge Apparell   2^{li}
It[em]   all his leather in the house and Implements or
   tooles belonginge to a shooemaker and to his shoppe   xii^{li}
                                            Sum: xxx^{li} vii^s viii^d

Praisers
Morgan Rimbron   sign[um] Thomas + [his mark] William   Jenkin Richard

[National Library of Wales Document Reference: LL/ 1643/ 27]

A true and perfect Inventory of all the Goods Cattles and Chattles of Edward Mathew of Cowbridg [cordwainer] within the Dioceasse of Landafe deasessed the 2º day of July in the yeare one thousand Six hundred Sixty and seven prized the 4th day of July afores[ai]d by the persons under named as followeth

	li - s - d
Impr[imi]s His Wearing Apparell	05-00-00

Item in the Hall one standing bed w[i]th Curtings & one
   featherbed one boulstar & one pillow w[i]th other

appurten[a]nc[e]s prized to	03-00-00
Item in the said Hall one boord & fframe w[i]th 6 Joint stooles one bench, & one Cupboord one p[air] Iron Andirons	01-00-00
Item in the kitching: one boord & frame w[i]th 2 Coffers one Chaire and other kitching utensils pr[ize]d to	01-00-00
Item in the parlor one standing bed, one feather bed w[i]th its appurten[a]nc[e]s & one pres cupboard, 2 trunckes one Round table 3 Coffers priz[ed] to	02-10-00
Item in the Chamber over ye parlor: 2 ffrench beds one feather bed one dust bed w[i]th its appurten[a]nc[e]s	00-13-04
Item in ye s[ai]d chamber in butter & cheese 20^s In wool 40^s	03-00-00
Item in his shop all his Lasts & seales? w[i]th other Implem[en]ts priz[e]d to	00-10-00
It[em] in the same all his shooes bootes & Leather priz[ed] to	06-00-00
It[em] in Bras and pewter	03-00-00
It[em] 2	01-00-00
	26-03-04
It[em] 3 horses prized to	06-00-00
It[em] 5 Cowes and 2 steeres Six young Cattle 2 caulf?	15-00-00
Item 46 sheepe and 17^{en} lambs	07-10-00
Item Corne in the Ground 2 acres 3qtr of wheate one acre of barly 3 acres of pease and barly prized	08-00-00
	36-10-00
	26-03-04
Sum	62-13-04

Prizers Thomas Richard Geo. Kemyes Lewis Evor Morgan Basett
Exhibited at Llandaff, 6th July, 1667, by Gwenllian Mathew, executrix.

[National Library of Wales Document Reference: LL/1667/30]

The true and p[er]fect Inventory of all the goods of Richard Thomas, Coardwiner, of the towne and Burrough of Kenffigg, the four and twentieth day of x^{ber}, and within the diocese of Llandaff prized by the p[er]sons undernamed the nine and twentieth day of the afores[ai]d Month in the six and thirteeith yeare of our sovereign Lord king Charles the Second of *England, Scotland, ffrance and Ireland, (in latin)* **Annoque domini 1684**//

	o£-os-od
Inp[rimi]s his wearing apparell p[ri]zed to	00-18-08
It[em] stock of leather to	05-13-04
It[em] his Implements for y[e] trade to	00-02-06
It[em] one Coverleat and two sheets to	00-13-04
It[em] six paire of ready shoes to	00-08-08
It[em] his steele heampe? to	00-05-04
It[em] his stock of pitch to	00-02-08
It[em] due to him by his Booke	02-10-00
It[em] in ready money	00-14-09
Tot[al]	10-19-03

Debts

Inp[rimi]s funeral expences	02-00-00
It[em] due to Evan Thomas	00-12-00
It[em] for his service duringe his sickness	00-10-00
It[em] to Katherin Thomas	01-05-00
It[em] to David Thomas	01-01-02
It[em] to Katherin Jenkin	00-05-00
It[em] to Christopher Thomas	00-02-06
It[em] for making y[e] inventory	00-01-00
	05-16-08

p[ri]sors   John Flen   Henry Lydon   John Jenkin
Sworn before David Price, surrogate, by Evan Thomas, 1st January, 1684/5.

Administration Bond: Richard Thomas, cordwainer: 1st January, 1684/5

In the Consistory Court of Llandaff, 1st January, 1684/5, administration of the goods etc. of Richard Thomas, cordwainer, bachelor, deceased, was granted to his brother, Evan Thomas, also a cordwainer of Kenfig parish. Evan Thomas and William Vuckles of Llandaff, alehousekeeper, were sworn in the sum of £100 for Evan Thomas to make and exhibit a true inventory of the goods etc. of his late brother at or before the 1st April next, to administer according to law, to make a true account of his administration at or before the 1st January, 1685, and to present to the Court any last will and testement of the deceased that might appear. Both boundens signed the administration bond.

[National Library of Wales Document Reference: LL/ 1684/ 147]

August the 30th 1690   A true and perfect Inventory of all the goods Catles and Chatles of William Rees of the parish of pile and Kenffigge Cordwiner deceased, made prised & valued by the persons undernamed as followeth;

	li - s - d
Imp[rimi]s one Cow prised at	01-00-00
It[em] one horse prised at	00-10-00
It[em] the yeows and lambes prised at	00-15-00
It[em] all graine of Corn prised at	02-00-00
It[em] small peeces of leather prised at	01-00-00
It[em] Imp[le]m[en]ts belonging to his trade prised at	00-04-00
It[em] the household stuff prised at	01-10-00
It[em] his wearing apparell prised at	00-10-00
It[em] 7 paire of shooes prised at	<u>00-14-00</u>
tot[al]	<u>08-03-06</u>

Prisers   Rich: Lougher   Lewis Aylward   Richard Water
Sworn before William Bean by Margarett Mathew, relict, 2nd September, 1690.

Administration Bond: William Rees: 2nd September, 1690
In the Consistory Court of Llandaff, 2nd September, 1690, administration of the goods etc. of William Rees, deceased, was granted to his widow, Margarett Mathew. Margarett Mathew and Richard Water, yeoman of the parish of Pile and Kenfigg, were sworn by the Court for Margarett Mathew to make and exhibit a true inventory of the goods etc. of her late husband at or before the last day of November next, to administer according to law, to give a just account of her administration at or before the sixth day of August next, and to present ot the Court any last will and testament of the deceased that might appear. Richard Water signed the administration bond: Margarett Mathew recorded her mark.

[National Library of Wales Document Reference: LL/ 1690/ 126]

A true and perfect Inventory of all the goods cattell and chattells of John Griffith of the p[ar]ish of St andrews in the County of Glamorgan and Diocess of Landaff Deceased vallued and apraised By two responsible persons whose names are hereunto subscribed as followeth

	£ - s - d
Impri[mi]s we value and appraise his wearing apparell	00-15-00
Itt[em] we praise his working toules to	00-02-00

Itt[em] an old cupboard	00-02-00
Itt[em] a table board	00-03-00
Itt[em] three old coffers & an old trunk	00-02-06
Itt[em] one Dust bed with ye apurtenances	00-05-00
Itt[em] an old chest	00-02-00
Itt[em] an iron crock	00-03-00
Itt[em] a Little brass Scillet	00-00-06
Itt[em] a little brass kittle	00-00-06
Itt[em] a Little brass porenger	00-01-06
Itt[em] all irons belonging to the fire	00-01-00
Itt[em] for a billhook and a hatchet	00-00-06
Itt[em] a binch	00-00-06
Itt[em] a few old books	00-01-00
Itt[em] an old pick an old rake & an old spade	00-00-06
Itt[em] for a Little old horse	01-00-00
Itt[em] for halfe an acre of wheat grass	01-00-00
Itt[em] we alow towards some things that cannot be found	00-02-00
Tott[al] is	04-02-06

Deductions towards the rent and other Debts

Impri[mi]s house rent	00-10-06
Itt[em] for Land	00-10-00
Tott[al] of Deductions	01-00-06

Apraisors   Edward Edw[ar]ds   James Edmond

Exhibited at Llandaff, 23rd June, 1731, by Thomas Morse, executor.

[National Library of Wales Document Reference: LL/ 1731/ 174]

Sadlers

A True and Perfect Inventorye of all the Goods Cattle and Chattles of David Griffiths of the p[ar]ish of Colwinstone in the County of Glamorgan Sadler w[i]thin the Diocese of Llandaffe lately dece[ase]d, Taken valued & appraized this Twelfth day of october one Thousand Seven hundred and Nineteen by us the Appraizors hereunto subscribeing as followeth.

	li - s - d
Imp[ri]mis The deceased's Weareing Apparrell valued att	01-00-00
Item Household Goods valued att	01-00-00
Item Two Cowes & Three Heyfers valued att	05-10-00
Item Two Horses valued att	01-00-00

Inventories of Village Shopkeepers and Tradesmen: Leather Trades – Sadlers

Item fourteen Sheepe & Twelve Lambs valued att	02-12-00
Item Hay valued att	02-00-00
Item one Pigg valued att	00-01-06
In the Shop	
Item Twelve saddles valued att	02-08-00
Item fourteen Whipps valued att	00-07-06
Item Two Leather Halters valued att	00-01-00
Item Twenty Two Bridles valued att	01-00-00
Item fifteen Crowpers valued att	00-05-00
Item Tenn Gurdles valued att	00-03-04
Item Eight Gurfes valued att	00-03-04
Item four Gurfes valued att	00-00-08
Item Eight Thongs valued att	00-01-04
Item five paire of Stirrup Leathers valued att	00-02-01
Item Leather valued att	00-04-00
Item one Pillion Cloath valued att	00-02-00
Item Webb valued att	00-03-00
Item Three Padds valued att	00-09-00
Item Twenty Two paire of Iron Stirropps valued att	00-09-02
Item Twenty Eight Saddle Trees valued att	00-09-04
Item Sadlers Tooles & other Lumbery old ware in the shopp valued att	00-06-00
Tott[al]	18-17-03

Appraizors   David John   Sign[um] Evan William   John Thomas   Sign[um] David John   Griffith David

Exhibited at Llandaff 20th October, 1719, by Thomas Griffith, joint executor.

[National Library of Wales Document Reference: LL/ 1719/ 37]

A true and perfect Inventory of All and Singular the Goods Chattells Rights Creditts and personall Estate of Thomas Glascot late of Cardiffe in the County of Glamorgan and Diocesse of Landaffe Sadler dece[ase]d made Valued and Appraised by us Whose Names are Subscribed the Seventh day of November in the year of our Lord One thousand Seven hundred and Thirty two.

In the Kitchen	£ - s - d
Eighty pounds weight of Pewter at five pence per pound	01-13-04
Forty Pounds weight of Brass at Seven pence per pound	01-03-04

141

Twenty & Six pounds of Bell-Mettle at four pence per pound	00-08-00
One hundred & Eight pounds weight of Iron at five farthings per pound	00-11-03
One Warming-pan and Copper Pott	00-01-06
One Dog-wheel & Chain, one pair of Bellows & a Chopping-knife	00-03-00
In Tin-ware	00-00-06
In the fore-street Chamber one feather Bed & two Bolsters being fifty Pounds weight at 4 pence p[er] pound	00-16-08
one Bed-stead & Curtains	00-10-00
Two p[ai]r of old sheets & two p[ai]r of Blanketts with six Napkins	00-16-00
Six old Chairs & two old Tables	00-10-00
An old Chest	00-02-00
four fire-Barrs	00-01-00
An old Cupboard	00-01-00
In the Back Chamber one feather-Bed of fifty pounds weight at four pence per pound	00-16-08
one Bed-stead & Curtains	00-10-00
An old broken Table	00-01-00
Three fire-Barrs	00-01-00
A Chest of Drawers & looking-Glass	00-08-00
five Chairs very old	00-01-00
six prints	00-00-06
In the Garrett An old feather Bed and Bolster fifty pounds weight at four pence per p[oun]d	00-16-08
In the Cellar	
One old Barrell & three small Casks and an old Stilling	00-12-00
Sperate Debts in Dec[eas]ed's Book	02-10-00
The deceased's Wearing Apparell	<u>00-10-00</u>
	<u>13-05-01</u>

The Goods in the Shop

Four Sadles with Flaps & without Pannells	01-12-06
Two Sadles without Flaps	00-10-00
Two Bridles with Snaffles	00-03-06
Two Bridles without Snaffles	00-02-06
five p[ai]r of Stirrup-Leathers	00-03-04
One Collar	00-01-00
four double Girts	00-02-06

four Girdles	00-02-00
Sixteen Curry-Combs	00-10-06
Twenty Brushes	00-11-08
three p[ai]r of stirrup-Irons y[e] French Make	00-03-00
Two p[ai]r of Bull-hide stirrup-Leathers	00-01-04
one p[ai]r of ordinary stirrup-Leathers	00-00-04
three Double-Chain Bitts	00-03-00
two Woman's Bitts	00-01-06
two Morocco Bitts	00-01-02
two hollow French Bitts	00-01-00
four Women's Stirrups	00-02-00
five Snaffles	00-01-06
a piece of Streyning-Webb	00-02-00
three Quarters of a piece of ordinary Webb	00-01-06
Two yards of double Webb	00-00-08
Two papers of Setts	00-01-00
One paper of small Setts	00-00-04
Tough Nails Bosses & Buckles	00-02-00
In Leather	00-06-00
In Working-Tools	00-05-00
Boxes drawers Shelves Chest & Desk	00-04-00
four saddle Trees ordinary ones	00-05-00
three pair of Bows for Padds	00-00-08
one Vice	00-03-06
	06-03-06
	13-05-01
Total	19-08-07

David Owen   Evan deer   Tho[s] Glascott
Exhibited at Llandaff by Anne Glascott, 15th October, 1733.

Administration Bond: Thomas Glascot, sadler: 16th October, 1733

In the Consistory Court at Llandaff, 16th October, 1733, administration of the goods of Thomas Glascott, sadler, deceased, was granted to his widow, Anne Glascott. Anne Glascott, Thomas Glascott of Cardiff, sadler, and John Sweet of Cardiff, innkeeper, were bound by the Court in the sum of £40 for Anne Glascott to make and exhibit a true inventory of the goods of her late husband at or before the 30th April next, to administer according to law, to give a true account of her administration at or before the 31st October, 1734, and to present to the Court any last will and testament that might appear. Anne Glascott recorded her mark on the administration bond: Thomas Glascott and John Sweet signed the bond.

[National Library of Wales Document Reference: LL/ 1733/ 22]

Inventory of all the household furniture and stock in trade the property of the late Mr. Nathaniel Young of the Town of Cowbridge in the County of Glamorgan who died on the 8 of March 1842 and appraised on the 12 May following by John Aubrey, Auctioneer

Beaufit	£01-15-00
Sofa	01-05-00
5 Chairs	00-12-06
Card table	00-07-00
tea Chest	00-04-00
fire Irons and fender	00-08-00
oak table	00-07-00
6 Green Chairs	00-12-00
Round table	00-02-00
Set of fire Irons	00-02-06
2 tea kettles and Coffee pot	00-03-00
Ironing box and 2 flat Irons	00-03-06
3 Brass Candlesticks 4 Common Candlesticks	00-04-00
deal table 3 Chairs	00-09-06
Clock and Case	00-07-00
night stool 2 looking Glasses	00-09-06
Chest of drawers	01-10-00
1 Chair Maho[gan]y tray	00-05-06
3 Chairs looking Glass	00-12-00
Maho[gan]y Card table	00-14-00
Maho[gan]y Bureau	02-04-00
6 Beech chairs wash hand stand and Ware	01-00-00
2 feather Beds	03-05-00
Bedstead and furniture Mill Puff Bed	02-05-00
2 Old Bedsteads 1 night stool	01-07-00
2 Pair of Old Blankets 4 Common Coverlids	00-18-00
carried over	£23-07-00
2 Old Quilts	00-07-00
feather Bed	02-00-00
Wash hand stand and ware	00-08-00

Small Quantity of earthenware and Glass	00-14-00
3 Saucepans 2 Iron Boilers	00-16-00
3 Pails 2 tubs and several Small Articles	00-10-00
Stock in Trade 46 Cart Saddle trees	02-14-00
2 Cart Saddle trees partly finished	00-08-00
24 white Hides 12 Saddle trees	10-02-00
Quantity of Harness Buckles 3lb of hemp	00-12-06
1 lb. of .....? 8 ..? of saddle tax?	00-07-00
3 ……? Slippers 1lb of whip Cord	00-17-00
4 lb of twine 6 Coller Chains lot of Patten Rings	00-08-04
lot of Patten Wood Set of Gig Harness	02-05-00
15 Sets of head and ……? 2 shot Belts	03-03-00
12 Harness Collers 20 lb of Barel? 1 Bridle	01-06-06
4 Martingales 3 Skins of Saddle leather	02-14-00
13 Pieces of Web 10 Horse Brushes	02-10-00
2 Water Brushes 6 spoke Brushes	00-11-00
5 shoe Brushes 11 hunting whips	02-09-00
4 Bottles of harness liquid 4 Bridles	00-16-00
60 Bridle bits 12 Pair of Spurs	11-08-00
6 Pair of Stirrup Irons 24 Bridle Curls?	01-00-00
4 Main drawers 1 piece woolen web	00-07-00
4 head Collers, 2 lb of Spunge	01-08-00
7 Saddles	17-10-00
18 whips 4 Horse Cloths	02-14-00
6 yds of Serge 12 shammy Leather	00-12-00
lot of Patten tyes 4 Pair of Girth	00-08-06
4 Rollers 30 thong whips	<u>01-10-00</u>
carried on	£<u>97-14-10</u>
18 Horse Collers	03-03-00
8 Cart Bridles 3 Saddle trees	02-09-00
2 lb twine 3 Pair of stirup Leather	00-09-00
2 pair of ....? 71lb of horse chains	01-05-06
Quantity of Harness Bits and Buckles	00-08-00
6 lb of Cord 18 whips 2 Cattle tubes	01-19-00
12 Coller Chains 12 Curry Combs	00-07-00
10 lb of Cart Rope	00-02-00
Quantity of Harness Leather	<u>01-10-00</u>
	£<u>109-07-04</u>
	John Aubrey, Auctioneer

An Account of Personal Property of the late Nathaniel Young

Money out at Interest	250-00-00
Household Furniture, Stock in Trade as per Inventory	109-07-04
Book Debts	339-09-05
	£698-16-05

[National Library of Wales Document Reference: LL/ 1842/ 39]

Glovers

Glam[or]gan   A true & p[er]fect Invitory of all the goods Cattles & Chattles of Samuell William of Cowbridg late deceased taken by the p[er]sons undernamed the three & twentieth day of March one thousand six hundred sixtie & eight valued & prized as followeth

	li - s - d
Imprimis his wearing apparel	03-00-00
Itt[em] his brass & pewters	04-10-00
Itt[em] all his ready ware in his shop	05-12-11
Itt[em] Six hundred pelts	09-15-00
Itt[em] in fine woole beinge Sixtie stone	36-00-00
Itt[em] in Course woole 3 stone	00-10-00
Itt[em] in black woole	00-05-00
Itt[em] one Cubboard one table two chests one standinge bedd two chaires & fower stooles lying in the hall	02-10-00
Itt[em] one featherbed with its clothes & appurt[enance]s in the s[ai]d roome	02-10-00
Itt[em] the featherbed with its appurt[enance]s in the parloure	01-10-00
Itt[em] one boord one leverie Cooboord one field bedd & one truckle bedd in the said parloure	01-04-00
Itt[em] one other featherbed with its clothes	01-00-00
Itt[em] all Iron implements	00-06-08
Itt[em] two horses	01-13-04
Itt[em] all the implements belonging to his craft beinge tubs & trendles	00-15-00
	Tot[al] 71-01-11

Prizers Lewis Evor Lodwick gronow sign[um]Phelipp + [his mark] Crooke sign[um] Thomas [his mark] Edward sign[um] John J M [his mark] Morgan

Sworn by Catherine William before David Price, surrogate, and grant of probate, 16th September, 1669.

[National Library of Wales Document Reference: LL/ 1669/ 39]

The Inventory of the goods and Chattles of Lodwick Gronow of the Towne of Cowbridge in the Countey of Glamorgan and within the diocesse of Landaffe late deceased; made and appraised, by the appraisors whose Names are hereunto subscribed the third day of Januarie in the three and twentieth yeare of the Reaigne of our Soveraigne Lord, King Charles the Second; Anno d[omi]ni 1671

	li - s - d
Impr[imi]s his Apparell appraised to	03-00-00
It[em] All his Brasse and pewter valued to	05-00-00
It[em] 1 featherbedd and the bedstead w[i]th ye Curtains vallions 1 feather boulster 1 w[hi]t[e] Rugg w[i]thall other appurten[an]ces belonging to the s[ai]d featherbed	03-00-00
It[em] 1 Table and frame w[i]th 6 Joint stoole and two lesser stooles 1 cupboord 1 old standing bed 2 chests 1 wooden coffer 1 box 2 chaires valued to	02-10-00
It[em] Thirty Bushells of barely & barely Mault valued to	07-10-00
It[em] 40 sheepe valued to	07-00-00
It[em] 2 horses and 1 Mare valued to	02-00-00
It[em] All his leather and pelts & Gloves and other ready wares & their working Instrum[en]ts valued at	11-00-00
It[em] 7 doz[en] q[uarte]r sheepskins w[i]th the wooll upon them valued att	05-00-00
It[em] 3 Trendles 1 Mault Seive valued at	01-00-00
It[em] all the Corn in his barne valued at	05-00-00
It[em] all his wooll both ffine and course valued at	11-00-00
It[em] Two acres of wheate in the ground appraised to	05-00-00
It[em] 12 planckes and two pigs valued at	01-00-00
	69-00-00

Appraisors Names John Moris? The mark of Thomas T R Richards Senior
                           William bassitt   the marke of Thomas T P phillip

[National Library of Wales Document Reference: LL/ 1671/ 23]

A true & p[er]fect Inventory of all ye goods, cattle & Chattle as well moveable as unmoveable of John Morgan of Lantwitt Major now lately deceased taken & appraised by us, whose names are hereunto subscribed the twenty Eighte day of this Instant July, in ye three & thirtieth yeare of ye reigne of o[u]r Soveraigne Lord Charles ye second by ye grace of god of England etc King defender of ye faith & in the yeare of o[u]r Lord god 1681, as followeth   li - s -d

Impr[imi]s His wearing Apparell	01-00-00
Itt[em] One horse	02-00-00
Itt[em] One acre & ½ of Barely	02-00-00
Itt[em] One acre of pease	00-13-04
Itt[em] One pigge	00-06-00
Itt[em] Leather and pelts	02-00-00
Itt[em] three feather beds with its apurten[an]ces	04-00-00
Itt[em] Brasse and Peuter	01-10-00
Itt[em] Two Table Board & Bedsteeds one presse cupboard two coffers & two Chayers and other small things	01-06-08
Itt[em] Three paire of Loomes & Slayes and other Implem[en]ts thereunto app[er]taining	<u>02-13-04</u>
Tot[al]	17-09-04

Appraisers names   Lewis Madocks   E T [his mark] Edward Thomas
John Tailor   Edw Maddocks [his marke]   David Morgan   Jon Philpott

Extract from the Will of John Morgan, glover: 22nd May, 1681

'I give and bequeath unto my son David Morgan the Too paire of loumes which is in the shop loft and one haulfe of the slaies after my decease Item I give and bequeath unto my son Jenkin Morgan one pair of lomes which is in Willia[m] Philpots shop and the other haulfe of the slaies as for the shuttles ……….. and …….. and other impliments thereunto belonging I doe give it equally betweene my too sons'

[National Library of Wales Reference Number LL/1681/ 113]

****

An Inventory of the Goods and Chattles of Mr Arthur Yeomans Alderman of Cardiffe lately deceased made the 26th day of November 1686

   li - s - d
His wearing apparel   10-00-00
In the great Chamber   i Bedsteed   2 Bedds   2 Boulsters

2 Pillows Curtains and Vallians 5 pair of Blanketts, 5 Ruggs, i Counterpan 1 Table Board, i Side Board with Chairs and other things vallued att	18-00-00
In the next Chamber i Bedsteed 2 Boulsters, 2 pillows, Curtains and Vallians 1 Table Board w[i]th Chairs and other apperteinances vallued att	i 0-00-00
In another Chamber and Cogloft a parsell of wool vallued att	10-00-00
In the Parlour i Bedsteed and a Truckle Bedstead, i Bed with all things thereunto belonging, i trunk, i Table Board, i Case of Drawers, i Desk, 6 Turkey-work-Chairs, 4 Turkey-leather Chairs, 4 musquetts with a Pole Ax, and other things vallued	10-00-00
In the 2 Kittchins Brass Peuter Irons Cubbs Dressers, a Table, a Wheel with other Necessarys vallued att	ii - 00-00
All the Linery vallued att	05-00-00
The Plate vallued att	12-00-00
The Shoppe and the Pelts in the Pill and the Worke house vallued att	i 0-00-00
In the House over the way 2 Bedsteeds, i Table-Board, i Cubbord with a Chair and a Joynt Stool vallued at	02-00-00
The Books vallued att	<u>02-10-00</u>
	i 00-10-00

George Pranch   Wm Richards

Sworn by Hanna Yeomans, widow, 7th December, 1686.

Administration Bond: Arthur Yeomans: 7th December, 1686

In the Consistory Court at Llandaff, 7th December 1686, administration of the goods etc. of Arthur Yeomans, deceased, was granted to his widow, Hanna Yeomans. Hanna Yeomans, George Pranch, vintiner, and William Richards, mercer, were sworn by the Court in the sum of £200 for Hanna Yeomans to make and exhibit a true inventory of the goods etc. of her late husband at or before the 6th December next, to administer according to law, to give a just account of her administration by 7th December, 1687, and to present to the Court any last will and testament of the deceased that might appear. George Pranch and William Richards signed the administration bond: Hanah Yeoman recorded her mark.

[National Library of Wales Document Reference: LL/ 1686/ 44]

A true and perfect Inventory of the goods and Chattells of Rees Llewellin of the parish of St Andrews in the County of Glamorgan and Diocesse of Llandaffe lately deceased   taken and prized by us whose names are hereunto subscribed   the seventeenth day of January in the year of our Lord 1699. viz

	li - s - d
Imp[rimis]: his wearing apparrell prized at	00-06-08
itt[em]: one dust bed and bedstead with its appurtenances at	00-06-08
itt[em]: one old table board and frame two old coffers and one old and decayed livery cubbured at	00-05-00
itt[em]: all the other poor lumber stuffe in his house at	00-02-06
itt[em]: the small quantity of wooll with some small peices of leather & his working tools	00-05-00
itt[em]: one iron crock and one little brasse posnett at	00-02-06
itt[em]: two ews and two yearling lambs at	00-12-00
itt[em]: one small pig and a small parcell of hey at	00-06-08
the sum is	02-07-00

prizers   ffrancis Richards   Phillip White

Exhibited at Llandaff, 19th January, 1699, before Phil: Maddocks, by Catherine Henry alias Llewelyn, relict and administratrix.

Administration Bond: Rees Llewellin: 19th January, 1699

In the Consistory Court of Llandaff, 19th January, 1699, administration of the goods etc. of Rees Llewellin, deceased, was granted to his widow, Catherine Henry alias Llewelyn. Catherine Henry and Francis Richards of St. Andrews parish, gentleman, were sworn by the Court in the sum of £10, for Catherine Henry to exhibit a true inventory of the goods etc. of her late husband at or before the 1st of April next, to administer according to law, to render a true account of her administration at or before the 19th January, 1700, and to present to the Court any last will and testament of the deceased that might be discovered. Catherine Henry recorded her mark on the administration bond, and Francis Richards signed the document.

[National Library of Wales Document Reference: LL/ 1699/ 153]

A true & perfect Inventory of all & Singular the goods ch[att]eles & creditts of Arthur Yeomans Late of the town of Cardiffe in the County of Glamorgan and Diocess of Landaffe Alderman dece[ase]d made valued & Appraised   the Seaventh day of January Anno D[omi]ni 1719   by

Nathaniell Wells Esq   William Lambert Alderman & David Owen Taylor Appraisers as followeth (viz^(t).)

	li - s - d
Imprimis the Decedents weareing Apparrell valued att	03-00-00
Item in the Kitchin one Square & one oval table one old elbow chair nine old Leather chairs one dresser & Shelves one Cupboard two hand guns one grate two Smoothing irons & boxes a tinning coffee pott one grater Candlebox one flower box some few earthen ware & glasses halfe a Dozen of knifes & forks two old brushes & a small picture att	02-17-06
Item in the brewhouse one old furnace one old broken table two old Cupboards one dog wheel one pair of old racks two fire iron bars one old tongs two Small old Chairs one joynt Stool 1 fat some few Small insignificant trumpery with two twiggin basketts and four tubbs att	01-05-00
Item in the Parlor one Oval table one Square table one tea table one Couch one Looking glass 14 old decayed Cane Chairs one Clocke & Case ffive Small maps Seaven pictures & three fire iron bars together with the window Curtains & valliants att	06-04-00
Item in the Cellar ffour old Casks & one old tubb att	00-06-00
Item in the Chamber over the shop one bed Stead one paire of Curtains and valliants one paire of window Curtains & valliants & a Counterpane att	01-10-00
Item one Looking glass one Square table Six black chairs & a picture and fire iron bars	01-04-00
Item in the Closet two Leather Chairs an old desk and a few books att	00-15-00
Item in the Chamber over the entry one bedstead Curtains and valliants one press bedstead one Case of drawers one old dressing box two quilts two pair of blanketts one old Cupboard and five ruggs att	02-10-00
Item in the passage two old Coffers & one old trunk att	00-07-00
Item in the room over the parlour two old Chests & an old box att	00-04-00
Item one bedsteed Curtains & valliants att	00-05-00
Item 53^(li) of brass at 8^d p[er] pound att	01-15-04

Item 179 pound of pewter at 7^d p[er] pound att	05-04-05
Item two paire of Andirons & a warming pan att	00-04-00
Item 58^{li} of iron ware at 1^d 2/1 p[er] pound att	00-07-03
Item 19^{li} of bell mettle ware at 5^d p[er] pound att	00-07-11
Item one pair of old blanketts in the Serv[an]ts bed att	00-04-00
Item a brass fender weighing 5 pound at 8^d per pound	00-03-04
Item three ffeather beds three ffeather bolsters ffour ffeather pillows ffour Small elbow pillows weighing in all 274^{li} at 6^d p[er] pound att	06-07-00
Item one ffeather bed and bolster weighing 72 ^{li} at 5^d p[er] pound att	01-10-00
Item the Deced[en]ts house furniture and hay att	03-10-00
Item one pair of holland Sheets & Eleaven pair of fflaxen Sheets	04-17-00
Item one Large Damask table Cloth & two Dozen Damask napkins	02-00-00
Item ffive other Course table Cloths & two Dozen & a halfe of Napkins	01-10-00
Item 62 ounces and one Eight penny weight of plate at 4^s & tenn pence p[er] ounce att	15-00-00
Item a Chattell from Sir Charles Kemeys for a house in Cardiffe att	09-12-00
Item **in the Shop** Eight Dozen of Lined Shammy gloves at 1^{li} 10^s p[er] Dozen att	12-00-00
Item two Dozen of black kid gloves at 1^{li} 5s p[er] Dozen att	02-10-00
Item tenn Dozen of mens mock Shammy unlined at 12^s p[er] Dozen	06-00-00
Item Seaven Dozen of mock Shammy gloves for women att	04-04-00
Item ffive Dozen of Inseam toped att	02-10-00
Item two Dozen of Drawn topped at	02-15-00
Item three Dozen of round Seam drawn topped att	02-00-00
Item one Dozen of Coloured Lamb topped att	00-10-00
Item Nine pair of white & coloured topped att	00-09-00
Item ffive pair of drawn mens topped gloves att	00-05-00
Item Eight Dozen of men's & womens Lambskin gloves att	02-12-00
Item one Dozen men's gloves white topped att	00-11-00
Item 18 pair of boys and girls gloves at	00-08-00
Item ffour Dozen of men & woemens dy'd Shammee gloves att	02-16-00

Item	Eighteen pair of Dyed Shammee att	01-00-00
Item	Two Dozen of glazed Lamb gloves woemens att	01-04-00
Item	Six pair of glazed Kid att	00-10-00
Item	One Dozen of Glazed Lamb att	00-12-00
Item	Nine pair of Glazed Mittens att	00-09-00
Item	thirteen pair of Coloured Lamb att	00-12-00
Item	tenn pair of Dy'd tann gloves att	00-13-04
Item	Eight pair of woemens dy'd Shammy gloves att	00-08-00
Item	Eighteen pair of ordinary Sheep Skin gloves att	00-12-00
Item	Eleaven pair of ordinary men's Sheep Skin gloves att	00-07-04
Item	ffourteen pair of mens Lambskin gloves att	00-09-04
Item	Eleaven pair of girls dyd Shammy gloves att	00-08-00
Item	Nine pair of mens dyd shammy gloves	00-09-00
Item	Eight pair of girls glazed Lamb att	00-06-00
Item	one Dozen of ordinary Sheep Skin gloves att	00-05-00
Item	Sixteen pair of mens ordinary Sheep Skin gloves att	00-07-00
Item	Six pair of ordinary wash Leather gloves att	00-05-00
Item	two Dozen of boys and Girls ordinary gloves att	00-06-00
Item	Nine pair of boys topped gloves att	00-05-06
Item	100 of white Leather at 8^d per Skin att	04-00-00
Item	7 Skins ditto	00-03-00
Item	two Dozen of wash Leather Skins att	01-05-00
Item	13 wash Leather skins more att	00-08-00
Item	One Dozen of black bazills half eaten and damnified by ratts att	00-02-00
Item	ffour buck Skins weighing in all 4^{li} & a quarter att	01-00-00
Item	7 pair of boys and mens shammy breeches at 4s p[er] pair	01-08-00
Item	three pair of ordinary Sheep Skin breeches att	00-04-06
Item	68 black and red bazill Leather Skins att	03-08-00
Item	Nine pair of Course gloves and a pair of Cuffs att	00-04-00
Item	60 Skins to be allomed at 6^d p[er] skin att	01-10-00
Item	in the Shop a table old Counter Cupboard and Shelves att	01-00-00
Item	200 & a halfe of Pelfs att	07-10-00
Item	desperate debts due on the Shop book	17-17-02
Item	Sperate debts due on the Shop book	45-08-02
Item	Eight Stone of Slipt? wooll att	05-06-08
Item	24 Stone of Short ffell att	14-00-00

Item 19 Stone of Short ffell more att	11-02-03
Item Twelve Stone of middle wooll att	04-00-00
Item Twelve pair of mens and womens wash att	00-09-00
Item two Stone of black wooll att	01-10-00
Item one Dozen & a halfe of dryd Skins att	<u>00-10-00</u>
sum total is	<u>234-04-00</u>

Zipporah yeomans

Sworn before William Morgan, surrogate, 7th March, 1719, by Zifforah Yeomans, widow and administratrix.

Administration Bond: Arthur Yeomans: 7th March, 1719

In the Consistory Court at Llandaff, 7th March, 1719, administration of the goods etc. of Arthur Yeomans of the parish of St. John's, alderman, deceased, was granted to his widow, Zipporah Yeomans. Zipporah Yeomans and David Owen, taylor of St. John's parish, were bound by the Court in the sum of £600 for Zipporah Yeomans to make and exhibit a true inventory of the goods etc. of her late husband at or before the last day of May next, to administer according to law, to render a true account of her administration at or before the 1st March 1720/21, and to present to the Court any last will and testament of the deceased that might appear. Zipporah Yeomans signed the administration bond, and David Owen recorded his mark..

[National Library of Wales Document Reference: LL/ 1719/ 29]

---

7. Wood Trades: Carpenters/Cooper/Sawyer/ Ship Builder/Builder

Novemb[e]r 15 1694   True Inventory of the goods & chattles of Tho. Smyth Late of Cardiff Carpenter deceased taken and apprais'd by Tho. Williams Alderman of Cardiffe and Hen. Rogers. Reece Davy. James Thomas Carpenters.

Imprimis At the Longcross 30 foot of half-inch elm board at 1d p[er] foot	00-02-06
72 foot of 3 qr elme at 1½d p[er] foot	00-09-00
124 foot of 1inch & quarter at 2d p[e]r foot	01-05-10
For other Timber & waste stuffe the Sum of	02-05-00

Inventories of Village Shopkeepers and Tradesmen: Wood Trades

In Mr Williams's Garden One peice of Oak Rafter 3ᵈ per foot 10 foot long	00-02-00
30 Rafters. 6 foot long each	00-15-00
In yᵉ Castle green One Long-Oak at	00-08-00
A short butt of an Oak at	00-05-00
8 other peices at	00-12-00
At yᵉ Shire-hall, one peice of Rafter 8 foot long	00-10-08
14 Rafters	00-05-00
Polls at the Millgate, Longcross & Churchyard	00-09-00
In Money, Rings, & buckles	01-16-00
Wearing Apparel	01-10-00
	09-15-06

Tho. Williams   Reece David
Sworn by William Andrews of the City of Gloucester.

Administration Bond: Thomas Smyth, carpenter: 31ˢᵗ December, 1694

In the Consistory Court of Llandaff, 31ˢᵗ December 1694, administration of the goods etc. of Thomas Smyth, carpenter, deceased, was granted to William Andrews of the City of Gloucester, Sadler. William Andrews and Thomas Andrews of the Town of Cardiff, were sworn by the Court for William Andrews to make and exhibit a true inventory of the goods etc. of the deceased at or before 1ˢᵗ April next, to administer according to law, to give a just account of his administration at or before 31ˢᵗ December, 1695, and to present to the Court any last will and testament of the deceased that might appear. William Andrewes recorded his mark on the administration bond: Thomas Andrews signed the document.

[National Library of Wales Document Reference: LL/1694/27]

A true and perfect Inventory of the Goods & Chattles of Thomas Powell late of the Town of Cardiff in the County of Glamorgan dece[ase]d taken and Appraized this fifteenth day of March Anno D[omi]ni 1732

	£ - s - d
Impr[imi]s His Wearing Apparell at	01-00-00
Kitching	
15 large Platters two Small Platters 5 dozen ½ of Plates 1 Cheese plate Seven pewter Porringers 1 pewter Quart 4 pewter Pints 4 half Pints 1 Tinn Coolinder & 2 Close Stool pans	01-10-00

155

2 old Brass Bottles one Brass Crock one Skillett 1 warming pan a Pestle & Mortar a Brass Slich? & Ring & 10 Candlesticks at	01-01-00
Two other old Brass Kettles at	00-05-00
2 Iron Potts 5 Spitts 2 ffrying panns 2 Grate Sliches? 1 pair of Tongs 1 Slich & Toasters 1 Grid Iron & 5 Iron Candlesticks	00-07-06
one Grate & a Smoothing Box at	00-02-06
one old long table ten old chairs & one small round table	00-03-00
one Dogg wheell at	00-01-00
7 earthen Platters at	00-01-00

Parlour

one ovall Table 10 old Leather chairs 1 old large Settle one old Square Table 2 Iron tongs 4 Barrs & 1 looking Glass	00-12-00

The Shop

4 large Ruff Coffins & 10 Small Childrens Coffins at	01-05-00
His Working Tools at	00-05-00

The Best Chamber

one Bedd Bedstead and Appurtenances at	01-10-00
one small Case of Drawers 10 Chairs 3 Square Tables one Close Stoll case & one old Grate at	01-00-00
one Small looking Glass at	00-01-00

The Chamber over the Shop

one Bedd Bedstead and Appurtenances at	01-10-00
one Chest one old Cobert & ovall Table at	00-06-00
4 Chairs & 1 old Trunk at	00-02-06

The Chamber over the Kitching

two old Beds Bedsteads etc	01-10-00
3 old Chests & 3 old Chairs at	00-03-06

The Little Chamber over the Buttry

2 old Beds Bedsteads etc at	00-15-00
one old Table & one old Chair at	00-00-06

The Garrett

4 old Bedds & fframes with the Appurt[enance]s etc	00-10-00

The Dineing Room

one presse Bedd one ovall Table 1 Dozen ½ of Chairs	00-15-00
one small Drinking Table & 4 small Barrs at	00-00-10

Cellar

Ale etc at	01-15-00

Two Silver Tankards & three Silver Spoons at	05-15-06
one Sow & eight Piggs 5 days old at	00-12-00
	22-09-10

Appraizers   George Lewis   George Evans
Exhibited at Llandaff, 16th March, 1732, by Cicill Clawdy, executrix.

[National Library of Wales Document Reference: LL/ 1732/ 29]

A True an Perfect Inventory of all and Singular the Goods Chattels and Credits of Edward Evans Late of the Town of Cardiffe in the County of Glamorgan and Diocess of Landaff   Carpenter Dece[ase]d   which was taken, Valued, and appraised the 12th Day of November in the year of our Lord 1751 by us who have hereunto subscribed our names as Appraisers

	£ - s - d
First of all His wearing apparel	01-10-00
In the Lower Room	
one Closet Bedstead feather bed bolster & appurtenances	02-00-00
one Clock and Case	01-00-00
Six small Tables	00-15-00
Seven chairs	00-05-00
one Dresser and shelves	00-06-00
Seven pewter platters & 29 plates wt. 40£ at 6d p[er] £	01-00-00
nine brass Candlesticks & other utensils	00-03-06
a parcell of Earthen ware and Glasses	00-05-00
a Corner Cupboard	00-02-06
ten pictures	00-10-08
The fire grate and fire Implements	00-05-00
a warming pan	00-02-00
Two iron Smoothing boxes stands and Clamps	00-02-00
one brass boiler, Kettles and small fire vessels	00-10-00
one standing Dog wheel	00-04-00
In the fore Chamber one bedstead, feather bed, bolster, Curtains Valiances and appurtenances	02-10-00
one buroe	00-15-00
one chest with a Drawer a square Dressing table a Looking glass and nine Chairs	00-10-00
In the Back Chamber one bedstead, feather bed, bolster, Curtains Valiances and appurtenances	01-15-00
Three old Chests	00-07-06

Two wooden Horses for Drying Cloths	00-02-00
one old skreen	00-01-06
a parcell of Table and bed Linen	02-00-00
In the Brewing House	
a Small boiler, Brewing vessels & ale Casks	00-15-00
In the Shop	
A parcell of Barnstaple Earthenware	04-00-00
Divers Other Goods of Sundry Sorts	40-00-00
In the Working Shop Twenty four Coffins	04-00-00
Twenty three Coffin Bottoms	00-12-00
Twelve Deal boards	00-10-00
A parcell of off fall Timber & Lumber	01-10-00
Implements and Tools for Trade	01-00-00
Sperate Book Debts	02-00-00
A House w[hi]ch he held by Lease under M[r] Tho[s] Lewis of Newhouse Esq.	01-00-00
In all	71-14-08

Valued and appraised by us   Thos. Seabrook   Hen: Lewis   appraisers

[National Library of Wales Document Reference: LL/1751/20]

An Inventory and Valuation of the Personal Property of the late Mr Thomas David of Ely in the Parish of Landaff in the County of Glamorgan deceased

	£ - s - d
Cash in the House	19-16-00
Mow of Hay sold	07-11-10
Two cows and one calf sold	14-14-00
Piece of Hay unsold	01-00-00
Cart, Harness, Chaffbox, three ladders, Tools of husbandry, Hurdles, Lot of Bricks etc.	08-09-00
Timber etc.	25-00-00
Carpenter's Tools	05-00-00
Household Furniture etc.	20-00-00
Wearing apparel	08-00-00
Rents & other debts due	29-00-07
Leasehold Property	16-00-00
Money out at Interest & Interest due thereon	275-04-07
Total	429-16-00

We the undersigned have made the above correct according to the best of our knowledge and belief. Dated this 6th day of May One thousand eight hundred and fifty   George Thomas, Ely Farm, Landaff   William Jenkins, Landaff

Extract from the Will of Thomas David of Ely, Yeoman and Carpenter, 11th February, 1840

'I give and bequeath to my Dearly beloved Wife Joan David if she continues to be my widow and not to be joined in Wedlock to any other person   I will for her to poses and enjoy the whole for her and her heirs and assignes for ever, But If whe will after my Decease Be married   Then and at that time I will that the whole of my Estate and Effects shall become the property of David David.   That is to say all the houses and gardens which are occupied by the following Tenants with all appurtenances belonging to the same namely Richard Prees Mr Oliver Jenkins The house which I occupy myself & family   Mr Wm Phillips Jno William   Edwd Morgan Mrs Elizabeth Miles Llewelin Williams Morgan David Richard Middleton David Rees Willm Griffiths And the house which is now being erected   All and singular of the house gardens & appurtenances belonging to the same at the time of my Wife Joan David's marriage to become the property of my son David David for him and his heirs and assignes to poses amd enjoy the same forever   And also at the same time I will that the Carpenter's shop adjoining the house in which Mr Oliver Jenkins now lives'

Administration Bond: Thomas David, carpenter: 4th June, 1850

In the Consistory Court of Llandaff, 4th June, 1850, administration of the estate of Thomas David, carpenter, who died on the 26th February, 1850, was granted to his widow, Joan David.. Joan David, John Evans of Ely, coal merchant, and George Thomas of Ely, farmer, were sworn by the Court in the sum of £1,200 for Joan David to make a true inventory of the goods etc. of her late husband on or before the December 31st next, to to pay his debts and legacies, and to give a true account of her administration when lawfully required. All three signed the administration bond. Joan David also swore that the Estate and Effects of her late husband were under the value of £600. George Thomas swore and signed a bond before Richard Prichard, surrogate, stating that the will of Thomas David had been written by William Thomas the Elder.

[National Library of Wales Document Reference: LL/ 18 50/ 88]

An Inventory of the Goods & Chattles of the Late John John of the Parish of St Andrews in the County of Glamorgan Carpenter Deceased Apprised by us whose names are here written this fifth Day of June one Thousand Eight Hundred & fifty Seven

	£ - s - d
in Dwelling House his as follows	
Wareing apparel	01-00-00
Furniture	
2 chest and Drawers	01-05-00
1 Mahogany Table	00-07-00
1 Deal Table	00-02-00
1 Square Oak Table (old)	00-02-00
1 Square Deal Table	00-04-00
5 Mahogany Chairs	00-10-00
4 Common Chairs	00-04-00
1 Oak Buffett	01-00-00
1 Oak Dresser	01-05-00
1 Looking Glass	00-01-06
2 Stools	00-01-00
1 American Clock	00-10-00
1 Steelyards	00-03-00
Fire Irons	00-02-00
2 Trays	00-01-06
3 Basketts	00-01-06
Casks etc	00-03-06
Knives, Forks etc	00-03-00
Salting Table, Scales & Weights etc	00-06-00
Old Fire Grates, Dutch ovens	00-05-00
Earthenware etc	00-03-00
3 Brass Candle Sticks	00-01-06
5 Beds, Bedsteads and Bedding	10-00-00
Bacon etc	01-00-00
Washing Tub, Pails, Pans etc.	00-06-00
Gardening Tools	00-05-00
Crop of a Small Garden lately set	<u>01-00-00</u>
	<u>20-12-00</u>
Crockery	00-05-00
To 1 Mare	15-00-00
1 Old Cart & Harness	03-00-00
Valuation of Articles in Carpenter's Shop	
1 Unfinished Cart	03-10-00

2 Working Benches	00-15-00
1 Screw Block	00-06-00
To Chest, Tools & Saws	04-05-00
Sawed Oak, Elm and Ash Timber	15-10-00
Turning Block	00-07-00
Lumber	00-12-00
Old Barrow	00-03-00
Sawpit-timber, and Scraps in the Yard	00-10-00
1 Grindstone	<u>00-05-00</u>
	65-00-00

Appraisers
Signed by Thomas David Denispowis   Edward Evans Michaelston le pit

A Cottage & Garden unfinished at Dynaspowis not freehould

[National Library of Wales Document Reference: LL/ 18 57/]

A true Invitorie of all yᵉ goods Chattells and Cattells of John Hammans of Cardiffe in yᵉ County of Glamorgan Cooper Lately deceased praysed by us whose names are herunto subscribed yᵉ 7ᵗʰ of July Anno dom[ini] 1684

	li - s - d
Imp[rimi]s for his wareing apparell	02-00-00
It[em] in yᵉ greate forestreete Chamber one feather bead one feather bollster one Rouge one paire of sheets and paire of blankets one paire of Curtains & vallians one pillow & pillow case one trockle beadsteede & one standing beadsteed 2 bead matts	04-10-00
It[em] more in the same Roome one chest one table boord one bench 4 Leather chaires one Looking glass one tinne Lamp	02-00-00
It[em] in yᵉ Little forestreete chamber one bead steede one coffer 4 Joynt stooles one wood chaire one strawe chaire	01-02-06
It[em] in yᵉ Chiching Chamber 2 flock beads two paire of blankets 2 paire of sheets 2 Rouges 2 bed matts	03-19-00
It[em] More in the same Roome one table boorde one old loafer 3 Joynt stooles one bench	00-06-08
It[em] in yᵉ garret one Rouge one dust bead one Lowe bead steede	00-09-08

It[em] in ye parlor one feather bead one feather bollster one pillow & pillow case one Rouge one paire of blanckets one paire of sheets one paire of curtians and vallians one bead matte one beadsteede	04-05-00
It[em] in ye same Roome one Livery coobert one table boorde 3 Joynt stooles 3 benches 2 greene chaires	01-09-06
It[em] ye chiching in pewter 8 platters halfe a doz[en] of plates 11 dishes 2 chamber potts 2 salts one doz[en] of spoones 4 tankets 4 flaggons one gune 2 pinnt potts two halfe pinnt potts 2 beakers 2 candlesticks one close toole potte	02-16-00
It[em] more in the chiching in brass 4 cittles two scimers one brass Ladle one candlesticke one pestle & Morter	02-07-06
It[em] more in Iron ware in the chiching one grate one crock 2 paire of tonges & 2 fier pans one pott hoockes 4 candlestickes one smouding Iron one spitte one frying pan one pellows	00-13-04
It[em] more in the chiching one case of knives one table boorde 3 benches 2 wood chaires 3 halfe stooles 6 shelves three doz[en] of trenchers one old silke sarch one baccon Rack one cubbert	01-02-00
It[em] a flech & halfe of baccon	01-00-00
It[em] in seller one barell & 2 doz[en] bottles of beare 3 steelings 5 doz[en] of emty bottles	01-01-00
It[em] in ye shoppe 27 pailes 3 h[ogs]h[ead]s	02-01-00
It[em] 4 small tubs 2 casks 3 gostralls	00-10-00
It[em] 3 doz[en] of Rine hoopes & 6 of white hoopes	00-13-00
It[em] in timber unwrought	00-05-00
It[em] ye workeing tooles	01-02-00
It[em] in the Stable 2 acceres of Hay	02-01-00
It[em] in table Lining 3 table clothes 2 doz & a halfe of table narpkins	01-05-00
It[em] in Live goods one pigge	<u>00-13-00</u>
The hole comes to	<u>38-12-02</u>

Prayseres names Hen Murton John Bennett Evan Jones Edward Rogers Sworn before David Price, surrogate, by Elinor Hammon, relict, 22 August, 1684.

Administration Bond: John Hammans, cooper: 22nd August, 1684

In the Consistory Court of Llandaff, 22nd August, 1684, administration of the goods etc. of John Hammans, cooper, was granted to his widow, Elinor. Elinor Hammans and John Bennett of Roath, husbandman, were sworn by the Court in the sum of £100 for Elinor Hammans to make and exhibit a true inventory of the goods etc. of her late husband at or before the 22nd September next, to administer according to law, to give a true account of her administration at or before the 22nd August, 1685, and to present to the Court any last will and testament of the deceased that might appear. John Bennett signed the administration bond: Elinor Hamman recorded her mark.

[National Library of Wales Document Reference: LL/ 1684/ 29]

A true & perfect Inventory of all & Singular the goods Chattells & creditts of William Owen   Late of the parish of Landaffe in the County of Glamorgan & Diocess of Landaffe   dece[ase]d   made valued & appraised the thirtieth day of January 1712 by Mr. William Turberville & Jenkin William   Appraisors as followeth (vizt)

	li - s - d
Impr[imi]s the Deced[en]ts waering apparell valued att	01-00-00
Item in the Lower Room one feather bed & bolster one feather pillow case a pair of blanketts two ruggs a bedsteed & curtains	02-00-00
A Long table & frame a Square table & frame an old Cupboard and old Chest a trunk & Coffer three benches two little chairs & four stools att	01-10-00
A platter a pewter fflagon a pewter tankard a pewer beaker two earthen dishes a brass Candlestick & an iron Candlestick	00-03-00
two brass kettles & two brass Skilletts att	00-10-00
Item two fflitches of bacon att	01-00-00
A pair of tongs a slice a ffrying pan a pair of Pothooks a Spitt & a pair of belows att	00-02-00
Item in the buttry One iron Crock & Some Lumber Stuffe att	00-05-00
Item in the Chamber One feather bed & bolster & bedsteed with the appurten[an]ces a Long table & frame a Square table three chairs a bench one Chest one Coffer	

a Straw whitch Case & Drawers three boxes & other Lumber att	02-10-00
a pair of fflaxen sheets & a pair of Callicoe sheets & a table cloth att	00-10-00
two pair of blanketts att	00-10-00
Item in the dark room An old bedsteed a dust bed & feather bolster one old rug two trindles & other trumpery at	00-10-00
The Decedent's shop valued att	06-00-00
300 Stakes & Severall Sorts of Lumber att	03-00-00
Three whip Saws att	00-15-00
A Small parcell of hey att	00-05-00
a pack sadle & a pad att	00-02-00
By bond & other Specialtyes the sum of	53-10-00
debts due by the shop book	14-09-00
a Lease of a house in reversion	
In ready money ab[ou]t	01-00-00
sum total is	89-11-00

Will: Turberville   the mark of Jenkin William

Administration Bond: William Owen, sawyer: 4th May, 1713

In the Consistory Court of Llandaff, 4th May, 1713, administration of the goods etc. of William Owen, deceased, was granted to his children, Edward, sawyer, and Catherine. Edward & Catherine Owen, and Morgan John, innholder, all of Llandaff parish, were sworn by the Court in the sum of £200 for Edward & Catherine Owen to make and exhibit a true inventory of the goods etc. of their late father at or before the 1st June next, to administer according to law, to give a true account of their administration at or before the 4th May 1714, and to present to the Court any last will and testament of the deceased that might appear. Edward and Catherine Owen signed the administration bond: Morgan John recorded his mark on the document.

[National Library of Wales Document Reference: LL/ 1713/ 60]

Ship Builder
The Estate of the late Mr Thomas Jenkins [Ship Builder]

Stock in Yard

Oak timber 445 ft at 1s 4d	29-13-04
2 ½ Oak plank 185 f[ee]t at 8d	06-03-03
2 in[ch] Oak plank 78 f[oo]t at 6¾	02-03-10

1 Cwt [hundredweight] of oakum	00-15-00
2 cwt of pitch	00-16-08
2 cwt of resin	00-16-08
30 f[oo]t yellow pine 1/-	01-10-00
500 Trenails	01-10-00
Unfinished boat	02-00-00
Pitch pots, Blocks and sheres? etc.	05-00-00
Household Furniture	
Glass	00-10-00
Chairs	03-00-00
Pembroke Table	00-05-00
Loo? Table	02-00-00
Dining table	00-15-00
Parlour Carpet	01-00-00
Fire irons & Fender	00-10-00
Kitchen Chairs	00-10-00
Sofa	01-00-00
Clock	02-10-00
Ware	00-05-00
Dresser	00-10-00
Dressing Table	00-02-00
Dressing Table	00-03-00
Washstand	00-02-00
Tent Bedstead	00-05-00
Bed	01-10-00
Chest of Drawers	01-00-00
Looking Glass	00-01-06
4 post bedstead	01-00-00
Bed	01-05-00
Drawers	01-10-00
Crib	00-05-00
Nightstool	00-02-00
Stump Bedstead	00-05-00
Bed	01-00-00
Bedding & Quilt	<u>03-00-00</u>
	<u>£75-14-04</u>

Lease of Premises called Dry Docks in the Town of Cardiff in the County of Glamorgan valued at £50   E. Leyshon   Cardiff June 16 1846

[National Library of Wales Document Reference: LL/ 1846/ 43]

Memorandum made this twenty second day of February One thousand eight hundred and Fifty five, by me Daniel Thomas of Cardiff in the County of Glamorgan Surveyor and Appraiser of the Property of Mr. Elias Jones, Builder, late deceased of No. 42 Caroline Street, in the Parish of St Mary in the Town of Cardiff, who died on the 19th day of November, One thousand, eight hundred and Fifty four a Schedule of which is as follows

	£ - s - d
1 Dwelling house, No. 42 Caroline Street & workshop behind Do. valued at	120-00-00
1 Dwelling house, No. 41 Caroline Street valued at	100-00-00
1 Cottage, No. 9 Bridge Street valued at	40-00-00
1 Cottage, No. 10 Bridge Street valued at	40-00-00
1 Cottage, No. 11 Bridge Street valued at	40-00-00
1 Cottage, No. 15 Union Street valued at	50-00-00
1 Cottage, No. 16 union Street valued at	40-00-00
1 Cottage, No. 17 Union Street valued a	40-00-00
1 Cottage, No. 18 Union Street valued at	40-00-00
1 House, No. 15 Rodney Street valued at	100-00-00
1 House, No. 16 Rodney Street valued at	100-00-00
Furniture and Goods in No. 42 Caroline Steet	
6 Mahogany Chairs £1-12-0 14 Common Chairs 14/-	02-06-00
4 Square Deal Tables 2 Round Tables	00-12-00
Corner Cupboard and tea things 10/- Sundry Pictures	00-12-00
2 Chests of Drawers £2-10-0 1 Clock £2 Looking Glass 2/6	04-12-06
Tea Caddy and Tray 2/- ½ Doz[en] old silver tea spoons 10/-	00-12-00
Sundry Plates, Dishes and Basons	00-01-06
2 Kettles, saucepan, and Frying-pan	00-04-00
2 Deal Dedsteads & 1 Tent Bedstead	00-12-00
3 Feather Beds £3 3 Quilts 9/- 7 Blankets & Sheets 12/-	04-01-00
1 Trunk & 1 Wasshstand 6/- Stair & Floor Drugget 2/-	00-08-00
1 Box of Carpenters tools	<u>03-10-00</u>
	727-19-06

signed   Daniel Thomas, Surveyor & Appraiser, 22nd February, 1855

Administration Bond: Elias Jones, builder: 16th March, 1855

In the Consistory Court of Llandaff, 16th March, 1855, administration of the goods, chattles and credits of Elias Jones, builder, who died on the 19th November, 1854, was granted to his widow, Mary Jones, of 42, Caroline Street, Cardiff. Mary Jones, Noah Jones of 41 Caroline Street, Cardiff, builder, and William Parry of Llandaff, builder, were sworn by the Court in the sum of £1,600 for Mary Jones to make and exhibit a true inventory of the goods etc. of her late husband on or before the last day of September next, to administer according to law, paying his debts and legacies, and to make a just account of her administration when lawfully required. Noah Jones and William Parry signed the administration bond: Mary Jones recorded her mark on the document. Mary Jones also swore that the value of her husband's estate was under the value of £800.

[National Library of Wales Document Reference: LL/ 1855/ 92]

8. Farmers with Commercial Interests/Gardener

An Inventorie made the second day of february of all the goods Cattles & Chattles of Richard John of the p[ar]ish of St Georges in the County of Glamorga[n] & dioces of Landaffe yeoma[n] late deceased and preised as ffolloweth/

	li - s - d
Imp[ri]mis all his weareing apparell preised at	1 - 0 - 0
Itte[m] eight milch Cowes preised att	20 - 0 - 0
Itte[m] two steers goeinge to three yere old preised att	4 - 0 - 0
Itte[m] five beast goeing to two yere old preised att	5 - 0 - 0
Itte[m] five yearling Calfes preised	2-10 - 0
Itte[m] seaven & twenty of all sortt of sheepe preised att	4 - 0 - 0
Itte[m] two horses one mare & one mare Colt preised att	4 - 0 - 0
Itte[m] three pigs preised att	0 - 15- 0
Itte[m] all the poultrie preised att	0 - 2 - 6
Itte[m] fowre acers of whet in the grownd preised att	8 - 0 - 0
Itte[m] all the Corn in the house & barn & a little Ricke of whet & barly by the house att	5 - 0 - 0
Itte[m] a packe of stockins preised att	10 - 0 - 0
Itte[m] provishon towards the house preised att	1 - 0 - 0

Itte[m] one standing bed with Curtaine and valions one
   boord w[i]th a ffram   five joint stooles & one press
   Cooboord   2 - 0 - 0
Itte[m] two feather beds & feather boulsters preised att   3 - 0 - 0
Itte[m] all the Ruggs Cov[er]leds blankets sheets doust
   beds and all the Rest that belongs to bedding preised att   2 - 0 - 0
Itte[m] all brasse and pewtyr preised at   2 - 0 - 0
Itte[m] all Chayrs Coffers binches & all sort of
   wood tincells att   1 - 0 - 0
Itte[m] all the impleme[n]ts of husbandry preised att   0 - 5 - 0
                                                              75-12 - 6

Preisors   the marke of Walter + Starke   John willia[m] his + mark
            Llison willia[m] his X mark   James Lewis

Debts due unto the decead[en]t   li - s - d
Andrew Mathew of Eley gent[leman] oweth me   3 - 15 - 0
Hugh Thomas of Eglwsila[n]   1 - 18 - 0
James Goyder of St Georges   1 - 8 - 0
Jenkin David of Eley   1 - 0 - 0
Willia[m] Thomas of Eley   0 - 10 - 0
Walter Starke of St Georges   3 - 6 - 0
John Pranch of Peterston being the sonne of Willia[m]
   Pranch deceased   4 - 16 - 8
Edmund Herbert of wenvoe   0 - 16 - 0
Edmund Thomas of wenvoe Castle Esq   0 - 10 - 0
                                                              17 - 19 - 8

                                           the marke of Richard John
wittnesses James Lewis   the marke of Walter + Starke
   the marke of Llison Willia[m]   15th February 1674/R Owen, surrogate.

[National Library of Wales Document Reference: LL/ 1674/ 89]

A true and p[er]fecte Inventory of the p[er]sonall estate, goods and chattels of William ffreame late of the Towne of Cowbridge w[i]thin the Diocese of Landaffe Alderman dece[ace]d taken valued and appraised by the p[er]sons hereunder named as followeth

                                                              li - s - d
His wearing apparel valued at   05-00-00

In plate one tankard two Spoons & one dish	05-00-00
Eight rewter platters, 24 pewter plates, 6 porringers, 3 quarts, 4 pints, 1 pestle? and 4 chamberpotts	02-00-00
Two brasse pans, 3 kettles, 1 crock, 5 candlesticks, 1 posnett and 1 paire of Andirons	03-00-00
Two Iron crocks, 2 paire of Andirons, 3 paire of tongs, 3 slices, 1 Jack, 3 iron hangings 1 dripping pan, three Spitts & other iron lumber	02-00-00
ffive featherbeds bedsteads and app[ur]ten[anc]es	20-00-00
One Dustbed w[i]th its app[ur]ten[anc]es	00-05-00
ffive tablecloaths 3 dozen of napkins 2 paires of Holland sheets & other Linnen	03-00-00
Six tables 12 joynt stools, 12 chairs, 3 chests 3 trunks 2 cupboards, 1 Settle, and other wooden lumber	03-00-00
One ffowling piece and two looking glasses	00-10-00
The goods in the Shopp	12-00-00
Wine in the Cellar	06-00-00
Six Bullocks goeing three years old	12-00-00
Three horses	06-00-00
Three Acres of wheat	07-00-00
Two acres of Oats	02-00-00
Six? acres of Hay	04-00-00
Pigs	03-00-00
provision in the house	02-00-00
Three Chattle Leases	<u>40-00-00</u>
Tot[al]	<u>151-15-00</u>

[total is £137-15-0 not as recorded in document]
Appraysors ffra: Coup?   Rich ff......   Thomas Philips   Edw Thomas

Exhibited at Cowbridge, 21 April, 1696, by Anna Fream, relict and executrix.
[National Library of Wales Document Reference: LL/ 1696/ 40]

A true and p[er]fect inventory of all and singular the Goodes Cattle Chattles & p[er]sonall Estate of Robert Bawdrey late of Place Turton in the p[ar]ish of St John the Baptist in the Town of Cardiff in ye County of Glam[or]gan dece[ease]d made and appraised by us whose names are hereunto subscribed the seaven and twentieth day of Aprill *in the fourth year of the reign of our Lady Anne Queen of England etc. in the year of our Lord [in latin]* **1705**

	li - s - d
Imp[rimi]s The dec[e]d[en]ts wearing Apparrell	05-00-00
In ready money	04-00-00
one Silver tankard one Silver Cup and six silver Spoons	04-00-00
In the parlor one presse Bedstead two feather Beds two feather Boulsters two Rugs three pair of Blanketts	03-00-00
two long tables & Eight joint stooles	01-00-00
Eight red Russia leather Chaires	00-10-00
In the Chamber over the parlour one low Bedstead one little feather Bed two Boulsters one Rug one paire of Blanketts & one hogshead	01-10-00
In the new Chamber over the Buttry one Bedstead and six Kane Chaires	01-00-00
In the Chamber over the Kitchin one Case of drawers one Chest one ovall table one great Chaire	02-00-00
In the Kitchin one Clock	00-05-00
one Brass pan one Brass Caldron one Brass morter peile & one Iron pistle	01-05-00
one warming pan two Brass Candlesticks one Brass Skimer & one brass basting spoone	00-10-00
twelve pewter platters two dozen & a halfe of pewter plates one small pewter Bason one pewter porringer Eight pewter spoons & one pewter Salt seller	01-05-00
two Iron Andirons two spitts two paire of tongs one slice one ffrying pan one dripping pan one toster three old Iron Candlesticks one fflesh fork one grate & twelve Iron Skewers	00-10-00
one Gun & pistoll	00-05-00
one small Iron Crock & one Brass skillet	00-08-00
all the tin appraised at	00-01-00
one large presse one ovall table one long table twelve old Chairs one Bench one dresser	01-10-00
In the dairy Roome	
one Poring?, the Tubs, Milk Vessells, & Earthen Ware	00-15-00
In the seller	
six halfe Barrells two three quarter Barrells one Cask	00-15-00

In the Brewhouse
one old ffurnace two vates and all other Brewing
    Vessells therein   02-00-00
                                                                                31 li 19s 0d

Linen
two holland sheets   02-15-00
one table cloth six diap[er] Napkins two Canvas sheets
    & four Calico sheets   00-15-00
one stone of wooll   00-10-00
Cattle   ffour Cows & ffour Calves   10-00-00
Eight dry Cowes   20-00-00
Eight steers and one heifer   20-00-00
one other Cow and one Calf   02-10-00
sold by Mr John Bawdrey since the deced[en]ts death
    Eight Cattle   28-11-06
Sheep   twenty Ewes and lambs   05-00-00
ffour & fforty weathers & dry sheep   10-00-00
sold by Mr John Bawdrey since Mr Robert Bawdreys death
    twenty weathers for   06-00-00
Horses   one old mare sold by the said John Bawdrey
    since the said Robert Bawdreys death for   01-09-06
one old horse and one old mare   02-00-00
three young horses and two Colts   05-00-00
Pigs   three pigs sold by the said John Bawdrey for   02-11-00
one sow and ten pigs   02-00-00
two other small pigs   00-16-00
one Lease granted by Sir John Aubrey & others to the said
    Robert Bawdrey in his life time for three lives one of ye lives
    bee dead and two are in being in a tenement of Land called
    place Turton valued to   150-00-00
Corn
one acre of Barley now in the barn   01-00-00
three acres of growing wheat in Landaff p[ar]ish   10-10-00
A stock of Mault consisting ab[ou]t Three hundred
    Welsh Bushells   90-00-00
all the implements of husbandry & one sadle   02-00-00
                                                                                378 li 08s 0d

Debts due to ye Deced[en]t Robert Bawdrey in his life time for Mault sold which are sperate

Mr Thomas Andrews of Cardiff	02-09-05
David Owen of Cardiff	01-01-03
Thomas Rees of Sully	00-05-00
Howell Harry of St Faggans	00-10-03
Mr Thomas Rice of Landaff	01-04-00
Mary Watkin of Lantrissant	05-17-00
Mr William Thomas late of Cardiff dece[ase]d	17-11-00
Mr Christopher Mathews of Cardiff	08-02-05
Edward Kew	00-00-10
David Spencer of Barry	01-06-06
Margery Smith	00-10-00
Robert Turner? of Landaff	01-19-06
Mrs Mary Corey	01-10-00
Mr Henry Lewis of Michaelstone	00-05-09
Mr Alex[ande]r pursell of Cardiff the younger	00-06-06
John Sweet of Cardiff	24-16-06
Mrs Alice Thomas of Cardiff	39-19-05 ½
Alice John of Landaff	01-06-04
Mr Thomas Maddocks of Landaff	01-00-00
David Rees of Cardiff	23-02-03
Morgan John of Keyrey	01-17-06
John Henson of Cardiff	11-00-03
William Scary of Sully	08-17-03
Thomas Cox of Lanharren	02-05-00
Grace ap John of Cardiff	00-18-00
Mr William Jones of Cardiff	13-12-09
Due the deded[en]t in his life time from one John Price for oxen sold	01-10-00
	136li05s3½
The Total sume of ye Goods & sperate debts	589-01-08 ½

Desperate debts that were due to ye Deced[en]t in his life time for Mault sold

John Thomas alias Kill? of Cardiff	12-11-03
phillip Thomas of St Nicholas	04-12-00
Barbara Lougher of flimstone	03-10-00
Thomas Lewis of Landaff	01-01-09
Richard ffreame? of Lantrissant	01-14-06
David Morgan of Lanharren	00-12-06
Cicill Murton of Cardiff	05-11-00

Arthur Roberts of Cardiff   02-08-00
Richard David …… of Coytre?   17-18-11
                                                                         49^li 19^s ii^d

Debts due to ye Deced[en]t in his life time by Bonds & other contracts which are desperate

Richard Williams of Cowbridge   06-02-00
Howell Pritchard late of Coychurch dece[ease]d by B[on]d   05-00-00
more due from him by Bond   08-00-00
Mathew Morgan of Stockland by B[on]d   05-00-00
William Hepley? of Cardiff by note   02-10-00
John William of Canton upon Acc[oun]t   12-16-00
William King late of Whitchurch dec[ease]d   20-10-00
                                                                         53^li 16^s 0^d
          The tot[al] of ye desperate debts   103-15-11
          The totall sume of the whole Inventory is   693-09-07½

Appraisers   Edward Vaughan   the marke of William Thomas
              the marke of Jenkin William   Wat Lloyd

Exhibited at Llandaff the 20th November, 1705, by John Bawdrey, brother and executor.

[National Library of Wales Document Reference: LL/ 1705/ 35]

A true & perfect Inventory of all & Singular ye goods, Ch[att]ells & Credits of Edward Rees, late of Ely within ye p[ar]ish of Landaffe, in ye County of Glamorgan, and Diocess of Landaffe dece[ase]d, made, valued, and appraised ye Last day of March in ye year of our Lord 1720 by Thomas Collins & James Philip appraisors as foll[ows] (vizt.)

                                                                         li - s - d
Inpr[imi]s   his wearing apparell valued at   01-00-00
It[em]   houshold stuffe at   02-00-00
It[em]   brass & Pewter at   01-00-00
It[em]   his beds & appurtenances at   01-10-00
It[em]   his Linnen at   00-05-00
It[em]   iron utensills belonging to ye fire   00-01-06
It[em]   Six oxen at   18-00-00
It[em]   four Cows at   08-00-00
It[em]   3 young Cattle of 2 years old at   03-00-00
It[em]   3 yearlings at   01-10-00
It[em]   2 Calves at   00-03-00

It[em]	four ordinary horses at	04-00-00
It[em]	7 sheep at	01-11-06
It[em]	his wheat at	10-00-00
It[em]	his barley at	07-00-00
It[em]	Beans at	06-00-00
It[em]	wheat in ye ground at	02-00-00
It[em]	Pease in ye ground at	01-10-00
It[em]	Beans in ye ground at	02-00-00
It[em]	Oats in ye ground at	00-10-00
It[em]	Due to ye s[ai]d deced[ent] for Pease sold in Bristoll & at home ye sume of	11-00-00
It[em]	Due to ye s[ai]d deced[ent] for Corn sold ye sume of	03-00-00
It[em]	implem[en]ts of husbandry at	02-00-00
It[em]	Pigs & poultrey at	02-00-00
It[em]	one Ch[att]ell Lease at	20-00-00
	Total	109-01-00

Exhibited at Llandaff, 6th February, 1720, by Jane Rees, widow and executrix.

[National Library of Wales Document Reference: LL/1720/74]

An Inventory of all & Singular ye Goods, Cattle & Ch[att]ells of Thomas Gronow late of ye p[ar]ish of St Andrews in ye County of Glamorgan & Diocess of Landaffe dece[ase]d ye 22th day of December Anno D[omi]ni 1720 made & appraised by ffrancis Richards & Reynold Thomas Appraisors

	£ - s - d
Inp[rimi]s his wearing apparell vallued att	02-00-00
It[em] in ye Hall one feather bed w[i]th its app[ur]tenances att	02-00-00
It[em] ye Pewter & Brass in ye Kitchin att	03-00-00
It[em] ye Shop goods att	40-00-00
It[em] one Ch[att]ell Lease under S[i]r Edm^d Thomas att	25-00-00
It[em] one Ch[att]ell Lease under Esqr Herbert of ye ffryars att	40-00-00
It[em] Six Cows & a heifer w[i]th their fodder att	13-00-00
It[em] Six feeding oxen w[i]th their fodder att	25-00-00
It[em] Six small workeing? Steers w[i]th their fodder att	12-00-00

It[em] Seaven Yearlings w[i]th their fodder att	07-00-00
It[em] Six Calves w[i]th their fodder att	03-00-00
It[em] one old Mare, one lame Mare & 2 Colts att	05-00-00
It[em] Seaven Sheep att	00-17-06
It[em] two Piggs & two small Slips att	02-00-00
Item 14 small Chicken att	00-02-04
It[em] Wheat & Beans att	03-00-00
It[em] two Acres of Wheat in ye ground att	03-00-00
It[em] due from Evan Rosser for a horse ye Sum of	02-00-00
It[em] Implem[en]ts of husbandry att	02-10-00
Sum total	182-09-10

Exhibited at Llandaff, 4th April, 1721, by Margery Gronow, widow and executrix.

[National Library of Wales Document Reference: LL/1721/150]

An Inventory of all and Singular the Goods Ch[at]ells & Creditts of Morgan Howell of the parish of Whittchurch in the County of Glamorgan and Diocess of Landaffe Yeoman dece[ase]d made valued and appraised the 12th day of November in the year of Our Lord 1722 by us Thomas Williams, Thomas John, and Edward Evan, Appraisers as followeth (Viz^t)

	£ - s - d
Imp[rimi]s Wearing Apparell att	02-00-00
It[em] his Houshold stuff to	00-12-00
It[em] Implements of husbandry	00-15-00
It[em] Two Cows att	03-00-00
It[em] four Oxen att	09-10-00
It[em] three steers att	03-00-00
It[em] five Horses att	04-00-00
It[em] Thirty sheep att	04-10-00
It[em] One Pig att	00-02-06
It[em] a Small p[ar]cell of Hay att	03-10-00
It[em] money due for Lime & Carrying Coals and stones to the furnace	06-00-00
Sum tot[al]	36-19-06

Exhibited at Llandaff, 15th November, 1722, by Thomas Morgan, son and administrator.

Administration Bond: Morgan Howell: 15th November, 1722

In the Consistory Court of Llandaff, 15th November, 1722, administration of the goods etc. of Morgan Howell, yeoman, deceased, was granted to his son, Thomas Morgan. Thomas Morgan and Thomas Williams, gentleman, were sworn by the Court in the sum of £100 for Thomas Morgan to make and exhibit a true inventory of his late father's goods etc. at or before the last day of May next, to administer according to law, to make a just account of his administration at or before the last day of November, 1723, and to present ot the Court any last will and testament of the deceased that might appear. Thomas Morgan recorded his mark on the bond, and Thomas William signed the document.

[National Library of Wales Reference Number LL/1722/ 174]

****

A True & perfect Inventory of the personal Estate goods Cattles & Chattle Moveable & immoveable of Edward Wattkin of Lannishan deceased the 2nd say of May 1729: Appraised the 7th day of the s[ai]d month the persons hereunder named

	£ - s - d
Imp[rim]is His wearing Apparell	01-00-00
Itt[e]m one fine feather bed & one fine bolster in the Esterne room	01-17-06
Itt[e]m one other feather bed & bolster in the same room	00-10-00
Itt[e]m one old dust bed in the same room	00-02-06
Itt[e]m 2 ruggs 2 blanketts one linnen Curtain & Vallions in the same room together with the beadstead	01-10-00
Itt[e]m one Cupboard 5s one oval table 15s one Long board w[i]th 3 benches 6s	01-06-00
Itt[e]m one Chest & one old Coffer 12s 2 boxes w[i]th 2 old Coffer all in ye same room	00-17-00
Itt[e]m 8 pewter dishes one tin coffine 2 pewter candlesticks 6 spoons two tankards & a pewter dish	01-00-00
Itt[e]m 4 Beadstead in ye Esterne room £1 6s 4 rugs 5 blanketts 3 Canvas Linnen £1 3 dust bed 3 dust bolster one feather pillow 8s	02-17-00
Itt[e]m one stone of wool 9s 6 corn sacks 15s one Coffer 1s 6d one pad 1s 6d	01-07-00
Itt[e]m two shovells 3s 6d one watter vessell 6d one spindle 1s 2d 2 pit saws 1 scive 10s	00-15-02

Itt[e]m one linnen Canvas 2 table Cloaths 2 pillowpers 3 table linen	00-10-00
Itt[e]m in midle room 2 Churns 2 benches 8 payles 2 milk tups 5 Cheese moulds 15 trenchers 5 cornoggins two trendalls one tub	00-15-00
Itt[e]m one brass Kettle one brass caldron one brass scales	01-15-00
Itt[e]m one Cheste £1 one oval table 8^s one table one bench 5^s in ye kitchin	01-13-00
Itt[e]m two Chairs 2 benches one trunk one box one joynt stool in ye kitchin	00-06-00
Itt[e]m Utensils for the dayry 5^s two iron Crocks one frying pan one iron skillet 10^s two spitts 2 flesh forks one brush one Curry comb	00-19-00
Itt[e]m one smoothing iron one pair of tongs & slice	00-02-00
Itt[e]m one plow 3 harrows 10^s other imployments of husbandry & trade	02-10-00
Itt[e]m six old coal sacks 7^s more utensils for trade 15^s	01-02-00
Itt[e]m four pack saddles with appurtenances 6^s wheelstraks? 10^s	00-10-00
Itt[e]m two riding saddles 2 bridles 12^s one reek of hay £1 10^s	02-02-00
Itt[e]m nine Cows £3 each £27 one heifer one bull £4	31-00-00
Itt[e]m three horses £5 four yearlings £2 three piggs £2 10^s	09-10-00
Itt[e]m Poultrey 2^s 8^d Coal £5 due for ..... £1 4^s	06-06-08
Itt[e]m Corn ready for thressing £3	03-00-00
Itt[e]m four yeaws twoo lambs £1 three Calves 10^s	<u>01-10-00</u>
	76-19-10

Appraised by us this 7th day of May 1729

Thomas William   Thomas Rees   Thomas James   Edward Lewis

Exhibited at Llandaff, 10th June, 1729, by Catherine Watkin, daughter and administratrix.

Administrtation Bond: Edward Wattkin: 10th June, 1729

In the Consistory Court of Llandaff, 10th June, 1729, administration of the goods etc. of Edward Watkin, deceased, was granted to his daughter, Catherine Watkin of the parish of Llanishen. Catherine Watkin and Edward Lewis, yeoman, also of Llanishen parish, were sworn by the Court for

Catherine Watkin to make and exhibit a true inventory of the goods etc. of her late father at or before the 10th December next, to administer according to law, to give a just account of her administration at or before the 10th June 1730, and to present ot the Court any last will and testament of the deceased that might appear. Both boundens recorded their mark on the administration bond.

[National Library of Wales Document Reference: LL/1729/]

An Inventory of all and Singular the Goods Chattles and Credits of William Lee late of the Parish of Cadoxton Near Barry in the County of Glamorgan and Diocese of Landaff deceased Made Valued and appraised on the twentieth Day of July in the year of Our Lord one thousand Seven hundred and Seventy five By Edward Jay and John Richards Appraisors as follows

	£ - s - d
His Wearing apparel valued at	5 - 0 - 0
An old watch at	2 - 2 - 0
One Cow and Calf and Small Quantity of Hay	7 - 0 - 0
Two yearlings £4-4 Sixteen sheep £8-8 & Eight Lambs £1-12	14- 4 - 0
One Mare at	4 -10- 0
In the Parlour One Feather Bed Boulster two Pillows Bedstead and appurtenances at	4 - 0 - 0
One Fire Grate & three Chairs one old Table, one Large Jug one Butcher's Steel	0 - 9 - 0
In the Hall One Bureau 18/- one Eight Days Clock £2-2-6 one Oak Round Table and two Houlds £1-1-0 one Less ditto 10s 6d and one small square ditto 3/-	5 - 5 - 0
One Oak Dresser 15s one Oak TeaTable 10s 6d and ffour Chairs at 5/-	1 -10- 6
Half a Dozen Pewter Dishes, half a Dozen of Pewter Plates, one Tinn Driping Pan, one Cheese Toaster and one Tinn Coffee Pott at	0 -18- 0
One Tea Board 5/- one set of Tea China 5/- Five Teaspoons 1s 6d and several other small Implements belonging to the Tea 9s	1 - 0 - 6
A few Earthen Plates Muggs & one Looking Glass and a few Bottles at	0 - 4 - 0
One fire Grate with its appurtenances two Spits four old Candlesticks a Warming Pan and one old Lanthorn at	0 -18- 0

Inventories of Village Shopkeepers and Tradesmen: Farmers with Commercial Interests/Gardener

One Pair of Stilliers and weights 5/- one meat fork 6^d and two old Saws 4^s	0 - 9 - 6
In the Kitchen One small Long Table and Frame 4/- One small old round Ditto 2/- one Brake 5/- One Large Chest for Corn 2/6 two Benches 2/- and one stool 6^d	0 -16- 0
One Bell Mettle Crock 5/- two small Iron Crocks, two Brass Kettles a Large Brass Pann one Pair of Iron Hangers & two Pott stooks and one Pair of Bellows	1 -10- 6
In the Hall Chamber One Feather Bed Bedstead and appurtenances	3 - 0 - 0
One Feather Bed old Bedstead and appurtenances	2 -10- 0
Three old Chests	0 - 3 - 0
In the Chamber over the Kitchen One old Bedstead and Cord at	0 - 2 - 0
Three old Casks 7/6 and one Cyder Bagg 1/-	0 - 8 - 6
Two Casks of Vinegar about 30 Gallons at 6^d ½ Gallon	0 -15- 0
A parcel of Lumber at	0 -15- 0
To a small Quantity of wooll to the Value of a stone at	0 -14- 0
To two sheep shears 2/- and a small saucepan at 6^d	0 - 2 - 6
In the Dairy One Cheese press 2/6 two milk Trundles at 2/6	<u>0 - 5 - 0</u>
	58 -12- 0
Two stils 2/6 two small Casks 6^d one Tundish 1/- and one meat Tub 3/-	0 -12- 6
In the Barn About two Welsh Bushels of wheat	1 - 6 - 0
A Wellsh Bushel of Beans at	0 - 9 - 0
One Wain & Cart wheels and Shaft	3 - 0 - 0
Two Pair of old Harrows & Togors etc	0 -10- 0
Some old Yoaks and Bows and some old Implements of Plow Tackling	0 - 5 - 0
Some Lumber & wherewith two Plow Tacking etc	2 - 0 - 0
An old Winnowing Sheet at	0 - 2 - 0
A Cyder Press and Mill at	2 - 2 - 0
Nine Cyder Casks at 5/- each	2 - 5 - 0
Two Ladders at 1/- each	0 - 2 - 0
One Horse Carr 1/6 a Grindstone 1/-	0 - 2 - 6
To 150 Gallons of Cyder sold at 6 p[er] [Gallon]	3 -15- 0
To one old Gunn 10/- and two Table Cloaths at 7/6	0 -17- 6

To Debts due to the deceased as appears by Notes £33-7-0	33 - 7- 0
To one small Tenement of Land Valued about £2-10 p[er] annum	30 - 0- 0
To another Ditto Valued about £3-0-0 p[er] annum	18- 0 - 0
To another Ditto Valued about £4-0-0 p[er] annum	16 - 0- 0
	173 -7- 6

The mark of Robert + [his mark] Morgan

Exhibited in the Consistory Court of Llandaff, 30th May, 1776, by Robert Morgan, the father of the deceased, and the Curator and Guardian lawfully assigned to his grand-daughter, Jane Morgan, a minor and infant, the sole executrix named in the last will and testament of her father, William Lee. Robert Morgan was sworn to the truth of the above inventory befor William Jenkins, surrogate.

[National Library of Wales Document Reference: LL/ 1776/]

A true an perfect Inventory of the Goods Chattels Rights and Credits of William Jones late of the Town of Cardiffe in the County of Glamorgan Gardener dece[ase]d taken and appraised the 20th day of June 1753 by us whose names are hereunto subscribed

His wearing Apparel at	01-10-00
In the Hall	
one oval Table	00-08-00
one Square Table	00-02-06
one Chest	00-02-06
5 wooden chairs & one leather chair	00-03-00
5 Pictures	00-00-06
2 Pails	00-01-00
1 old Saddle	00-02-06
12 Baskets	00-07-00
1 syder Hogshead and 3 small Casks	00-06-00
a parcel of old Seed Bags	00-01-00
In the Kitchin	
one settle	00-04-00
one Square Table and one round Table	00-02-06
one old Dresser	00-05-00
6 Chairs	00-03-00
5 pewter Dishes	00-08-00

4 earthen Platters	00-01-00
1 brass Candlestick	00-00-08
1 Tin Candlebox, one Coffee pot, one flour box and basting Stick	00-00-09
1 pudding Pan 1 skimmer and one dripping Pan	00-00-09
1 pudding Pan one strainer and one dripping Pan	00-00-09
2 pair of Iron Tongs, two Shovells, one Poker and one fire shovell	00-02-06
one frying Pan	00-01-00
Two AndIrons, two old Iron Pots, one Toaster and one Spit	00-02-06
In the best Chamber one feather Bed Bolster Bedstead Bedcloaths & Curtains	01-05-00
one Buroe	00-12-00
one Chest, one old Table	00-02-00
six old Chairs	00-04-06
In the Middle Room	
one feather Bed one Bolster one Bedstead 1pair of Blankets one pair of Sheets and one Rug	00-18-00
In the Chamber over the Kitchin	
one Bed one Bolster a pair of Blankets one Rug one Bedstead	01-00-00
one Closestool	00-02-00
one Cupboard	00-02-06
one old Chest	00-00-06
In the Court	
Two Benches and two Boards	00-04-00
Two pair of Panniers	00-01-00
In the Garden by the House	
12 Dozen Holes of Cucumber	00-03-00
a Bed of Onions	00-07-00
5 Beds of Carrots	00-04-00
another Bed of Onions	00-06-00
a Bed of Springe Seed	00-00-06
a piece of Cabbage	00-08-00
a piece of Collyflower	00-08-00
7 Rows of Kidney Beans	00-02-00
In the Fryers Garden	
a piece of Leeks and Onions	00-09-00
a Spot of Peas	00-02-06
The Cucumbers in the Cucumber Garden	00-14-00

a Border of Michaelmas Onions	00-01-06
a piece of Potatoes	00-10-00
11 Rows of Kidney Beans	00-02-06
Savoys	00-01-06
a piece of Parsnips	00-02-00
a small spot of Carots	00-00-06
a piece of Seed Onions	01-00-00
a Bed of Potatoes on the r^t hand	01-00-00
two Beds of Parsnip seeds	00-04-00
two Beds of Turnip seed	00-04-00
two Beds of Cabbage seed	00-04-00
a small spot of Potatoes	00-01-00
12 Rows of Peas	00-10-06
a piece of Potatoes	00-10-00
5 Rows of Peas	00-02-06
28 Holes of Cucumber	00-07-00
a piece of Leek seed	01-10-00
a piece of Potatoes	00-10-00
21 Rows of Peas	00-10-06
a piece of Cabbage	00-08-00
a piece of Beans	00-12-00
another piece of Beans	00-12-00
a piece of Onions	00-06-00
a piece of Beans	00-03-00
The cherry trees	00-08-00
Peach and nectarin Trees	01-02-00
Pear and Apple Trees	00-02-06
Goosberry and Curren Trees	00-12-00
one Horse	04-00-00
Part of a Rick of Hay	00-15-00
one old Cart and Wheels	01-00-00
30 square Glasses at 1^s 6^d	02-05-00
Frames and Lights	02-06-00
a Parcel of Dung	00-05-00
Ten more square Glasses	00-15-00
	£35-10-08

As witness our Hands
George Evans   John Minnitt   William Robert   John Watkin
Exhibited at Llandaff, 3rd July, 1753, by Trevor Jones, brother and administrator

Administration Bond: William Jones, gardener: 18th June, 1753

In the Consistory Court of Llandaff, 18th June, 1753, administration of the goods etc. of William Jones, bachelor, gardener, deceased, was granted to his brother, Trever Jones, tyler, of the parish of St. John. Trever Jones, Richard Jones, hatmaker, and George Williams, baker, both of the Town of Cardiff, were sworn by the Court in the sum of £200 for Trever Jones to exhibit a true inventory of the goods etc. of his late brother at or before the 18th September next, to administer according to law, to render a just account of his administration at or before the 18th June, 1754, and to present ot the Court any last will and testament of the deceased that might appear. Trevor Jones recorded his mark on the administration bond, and both Richard Jones and George Williams signed the bond.

[National Library of Wales Document Reference: LL/1753/30]

---

9. Salters

An Invaitorie of all the Goods Cattles & Chattles of John Wollrin of Cardiff in the Counnty of Glamorgan Ald[erman]: deceased the third of Aprill 1673: appraised by us whose names are hereunto Subscribed the 23rd day of Aprill 1673

	li : s : d
Imp[rimi]s In the Kitchin & Buttrie in peuter, brass, & Iron	40:00:00
It[em] In the Hall, two table boards twelve Joynt stooles three leather Chaires two wooden Chaires, one Suttle, one paire of virginalls, one Chest, one paire of brass Augers paire of Grates, w[i]th brass heads & foure green Carpets	06:11:00
Nyne paire of Dowlas sheets, five paire of flaxing sheets, six diaper table Cloathes, five Dowlas table Cloathes, three dozen Diaper Napkins, six dozen of Dowlas Napkins, ten towells, one paire of Cotten Blanketts; & ten Holland Pillowcases	27:10:00
It[em] In the Brewhouse, one Copper & head, one mashfatt two small fatts, two ffloats, one tunn, two Coolers, two head fatts, foure Laske? of barrells, & all the other appurtenances belonging to the Brewhouse	50:00:00
It[em] In the Parlour, three feather bedds five feather boulsters, three Ruggs, one Cov[er]lett, foure paire of blanketts, one bedsteed, one truckle bed, two Chests, one Deske & two paire of sheets	10:11:00

It[em] In the Chamber over the porch,   one bedsteed
   one Suite of wrought Curtaines & vallians, one feather bed
   three bolsters, one pillow, one rugg, & a Counterpanne,
   one Cotten blankett, one wrought Cubert Cloth, five Leather
   Chaires, two wrought, one twigging Chaire, one Cubbert,
   one table board, one truckle bed & one Lookeing Glass,
   & the hangings for ye Chamber   14:00:00
It[em] In the forestreet Chamber,   one standing bedsteed
   one feather bed, three bolsters, one pillow, one paire of
   cotten blanketts, one red rugg, one wrought Suite of
   Curtains & vallians   one wrought Cubbert Cloth,
   two wrought Curtains, five wrought Chaires, one table
   & Carbett, one Looking Glass, one paire of brass Augers,
   one Cubbert, & one Close Stoole   20:00:00
It[em] In the Chamber over the kitchin,   two feather
   bedds   two feather bolsters, one pillow, two Greene ruggs;
   wo paire of wrought vallians, one paire of Curtaines, one
   wrought Cushion, one Cubbert, one Chest, two trunkes;
   one Close Stoole, one Carbett, one truckle bed, six Joynt
   stooles, one paire of Augers & Grates, & one paire
   of planketts   15:00:00
                                                            183:17:00
It[em] In Judge Lloyds Chamber;   his wearing aparell   30:00:00
It[em] in plate   21:00:00
It[em] one bedsteed   one feather bed, two bolsters
   one red worsteed Rugg, one paire of Cotten planketts,
   one paire of Red Curtaines & vallians, one pillow,
   one press bed, five red Cloth Chaires & three Leather
   Chaires, one table board, & red table Cloth   one paire of
   brass Augers, one paire of Grates, the Hangings for the
   Chamber   one Looking Glass & six Joynt stooles   20:00:00
It[em] In ye dining roome   Seaven tables, one Cubbert &
   Cloth Seaventeene Chaires   eight Cushions   one Lardge
   thrum Carbett, two other Carbetts, one paire of brass
   Augers, & one paire of Grates   13:06:00
It[em] In the Chamber w[i]thin the Dineing roome,   two
   feather beds, two bolsters, one pillow, one red rugg, two
   Leather Chaires   one bedsteed   06:00:00
It[em] In the Painted Chamber;   two feather beds, three

Inventories of Village Shopkeepers and Tradesmen: Salters

bolsters, two pillows one Cotten plankett, two Chaires & two ruggs	05:00:00
It[em] In the Little chamber at the head of the staires, one feather bed, two bolsters one pillow, one rugg, two Leather Chaires & one great red Chaire, one small table & carpett, & one paire of Curtaines & vallians	06:00:00
It[em] ffifty eight tonns of french & Spanish Salt	200:00:00
It[em] Sixty Stone of wooll	034:00:00
It[em] in Mault	050:00:00
It[em] thirty oxen three Cowes & two yearlings	158:00:00
It[em] two Salt panns & Materialls	030:00:00
It[em] Six hundred sheepe,	200:00:00
It[em] Seaventeene Swyne	010:00:00
It[em] in good Debts	150:00:00
	933:06:00
The hole some is	1117:03:00

John sheere   Jonath: Jones   George Evans   William: Jones
R.. Davies   Tho: Wrenn   David Howell   Christopher Wells

xxth day of October Anno d[omi]ni 1676   This Writing or Inventory was p[ro]duced to Thomas Prichard Geo: Evans & Christopher Wells at the time of their sev[er]all Exa[min]acons on ye behalf of Mary Wollrin Catherine Wollrin Anne Wollrin Marg[are]t Wollrin & Geo[rge] Wollrin sev[er]ally   pl[ain]t[iff]s ag[ain]st David Morgan and Marg[are]t his wife def[enden]ts   By & before us   Edw Williams   W Thomas

[National Library of Wales Document Reference:LL/ 1673/]

———————

An Inventory of all the goods Cattle Chattles and personall Estate of John Stanmore of Cardiff in the County of Glamorgan, Saltmaker dece[ase]d made and appraysed by the persons whose names are hereunto subscribed the Thirtieth day of January *in the thirty fifth year of the reign of our Lord Charles the second by grace of God King of England etc. in the year of our Lord (in latin)* **1682/3 as followeth vizt**

	li - s - d
Imp[rimi]s the deced[en]ts Wearing Apparell	05 -00 - 0
Item the deced[en]ts Pewter & Brasse in all	20 -00 - 0
Item the Iron Implem[en]ts in the deced[en]ts house	02 -00 - 0

185

Item the Tables Bedsteeds Joynt Stooles Cupboards Chests Trunkes Coffers & other ye deced[en]ts woodden Implem[en]ts	10 -00 - 0
Item five feather Bedds five feather Boulsters 10 pillowes five Ruggs five paire of Blanketts three paire of Curtaines & Valiants three Carpetts six wrought Cushions and two Cupboard Cloathes	20 -00 - 0
Item three paire of holland sheets, three paire of dowlas sheets two paire of Cotton sheets ffour paire of Canvas sheets, two dozen of diaper and two dozen of dowlas Napkins Twelve Canvas Napkins, two diap[er] & two Holland Table Cloathes	10 -00 - 0
Item the deced[en]ts Plate	10 -00 - 0
Item the deced[en]ts two Gold Rings	01 -00 - 0
Item his Salt Panne & Implem[en]ts of Salteing	05 -00 - 0
Item the deced[en]ts Chattle Leases	32 -10 - 0
Item the deced[en]ts sperate debts	60 -00 - 0
Item the deced[en]ts ready money	50 -00 - 0
Item the deced[en]ts stock of Salte Earthen Wares and Glasse Wares	100 -00 - 0
	325 -10 - 0

Appraisers Names   Ben: Browne   Chr. Wells   Henry Morten
ye marke of Edward   E   Lewis   W Thomas

[National Library of Wales Document Reference: LL/ 1682/ 25]

A true Inventory of the goods cattells and chattles of Rowland Davies of Cardiffe in the County of Glamorgan Salter   Lately deceased praysed by us whose names are hereunto subscribed this one and twentith day of Aprill anno dom[ini] 1686

	li - s - d
Imp[rimis] his wearing apparell	02-10-00
It[em] in the dwelling Roome one feather bead two feather bollsters on bead steed on paire of curtians and vallians on pillow and pillowcase on Rugg on paire of sheetes on paire of blankets	00-10-00
It[em] in the same Roome foure pewter platters six pewter plates two pewter tankats seaven pewter porage dishes on blood dish two tin candlestickes two sacers on tin lamp on flower box on coffin two tonges on fier shoufels	

on frying pan on grid Iron on paire of cheekes and bares on smoothing Iron on Iron crock on Iron Marma two tin sawce panes on tin kittle on tin grater	00-16-00
It[em] in the same Roome on old trunk on old coffer seaven old chairs on old table board on paile on three Leged stoole six trenchers 19 peces of earthing ware	00-10-00
It[em] in the store house in salt	01-00-00
It[em] more in the store house two old basketts two old tubs on old trunk two old seeves two earthing pans	00-01-00
It[em] in the shop in salt	00-03-00
It[em] more in the shop three basketts three old Joynt stooles three earthing steanes? on peck two small measures and a small parcell of bark	00-05-00
It[em] in the salt house on Iron salt furnace and its appurtenances and in salt	10-00-00
some totall is	16-15-00

Prayseres names

Will Miles   The marke of Evan E Evans   Richo: Davies   Jo[h] Wollrin

Sworn, 22nd April, 1686, by Priscilla Davies, widow.

Administration Bond: Rowland Davies, salter: 26th April, 1686

In the Consistory Court of Llandaff, 26th April, 1686, administration of the goods etc. of Rowland Davies, salter, deceased, was granted to his widow, Priscilla Davies. Priscilla Davies and John Wollrin of Cardiff, salter, were sworn by the Court in the sum of £100, for Priscilla Davies to make and exhibit a true inventory of the goods etc. of her late husband at or before the 26th August next, to administer according to law, to give a just account of her administration at or before the 26[th] April, 1687, and to present to the Court any last will and testament of the deceased that might appear. Both signed the administration bond.

[National Library of Wales Document Reference: LL/ 1686/ 33]

An Inventory of y[e] Goods & ch[att]ells of Mary Murton of y[e] p[ar]ish of St. Mary's in Cardiffe in y[e] County of Glam[or]gan wid[ow] dece[ase]d taken & prized by y[e] p[er]sons under named y[e] 26[th] day of September Anno D[omi]ni 1699 as followeth (vizt)

Imp[rimi]s her purse & wearing apparell prized to	01-00-00
Item her beds & beddings with their appurtenances to	03-00-00

Item her peawter & brass to	01-00-00
Item her Iron utensils to	00-10-00
Item her household Stuffe to	03-00-00
Item in Salt & goods belonging to ye Salt house valued to	05-00-00
Item a little horse to	01-00-00
Item small things forgotten (if any)	00-05-00
Tot[al]	14-15-00

pryzers   John ffox   John Thomas

Exhibited at Llandaff, 28th September, 1699, by Mary Murton, daughter and executrix.

[National Library of Wales Document Reference: LL/ 1699/ 29]

10. Gentlemen with Commercial Interests/ Priest owning a Bookbinders Press

A true and perfect Inventory of all and Singular the goods cattells chattells debts and Credits of Henry Hill late of St. Athan in the countie of Glamorgan and diocesse of Landaff gent[leman] deceased had taken and appraized by James Turbervill gent[leman], John Walter Cler[k] and Evan Thomas yeoman the sixteenth day of January in the year of our lord god one thousand Sixe hundred Sixty Sixe as followeth.

	li - s - d
Imprimis the testator's wearing apparrell	50-00-00
It[em] in ready money	100-00-00
It[em] in plate	20-00-00
It[em] debts due to the testator	500-00-00
It[em] three severall leases held under the Lo[rd] B[isho]p and Chapter of Landaff aforesaid, of lands and tithes within the countie of Monmouth all	150-00-00
It[em] a lease with an assignm[en]t thereon of lands in the parish of Colwinston in the county of Glamorgan called Claypit determinable upon one life yet in being	30-00-00
It[em] two severall annuities all	80-00-00
It[em] 4 Cows and 2 oxen all	12-00-00
It[em] 2 calves	01-00-00
It[em] one Mare and two Nags all	06-00-00
It[em] corn in barn and three Reeks all	10-00-00
It[em] wheat in blade	15-00-00

It[em] hay	04-00-00
It[em] swine and poultrey all	01-00-00
It[em] brasse and pewter all	05-00-00
It[em] household stuff and implements of household	50-00-00
It[em] barque or vessel called the Speedwell	100-00-00
It[em] omitted and unseen things	01-00-00
	1135-10-00

James Turbervill   John Walter   Evan Thomas
Exhibited at Llandaff, 22nd January, 1666, by George Hill.
[National Library of Wales Document Reference: LL/ 1666/ 96]

A true and perfect Inventory of All the Howshold stuffe and Implements of Mr Rice Lewis of Landaffe   late deceased, taken and apprized by John Mathew of Landaffe gent[leman]   Mathew Joseph of Cayre Joyner and John Edward of Ely the six and Twentieth day of January in the 36 yeare of his ma[jes]ties Raigne An[no] 1684

	li - s - d
Imp[rimi]s His Wearing Apparell prized to	01-06-08
It[em] One Standing Bedsteed w[i]th Curtaines and Vallians	00-07-00
It[em] One ffeather Bed, One ffeather Bolster, One Rudd-Rugg and one payre of Sheetes prized to	01-10-00
It[em] Two ffowling pices, one Brass Burding pice and Two pockett pistolls to	01-15-00
It[em] ffifteen pieces for Stocks Gunns prized to	00-11-03
It[em] His ffishing implements of all sorte	00-02-00
It[em] fforeteen pieces of pistoll stocks	00-03-00
It[em] ffive planks ready sawed	00-10-00
It[em] three new Bulk-Harpes	00-15-00
It[em] Two Tunnell netts	00-10-00
It[em] His workeing Tooles and Implements of all Sort prized	01-10-00
It[em] Two old Truncks three small Boxes and one payre of Tables prized to	00-05-00
It[em] All other small Trumperies prized to	00-02-06
Sume tot[al] is	09-07-05

Prizers names   John Mathews   the marke of Mathew M Joseph   the marke of John Edwards
Sworn before David Price, surrogate, by William Jenkin, nephew, 28th March, 1685.

Administration Bond: Rice Lewis, gentleman: 28th March, 1685

In the Consistory Court of Llandaff, 28th March, 1685, administration of the goods etc. of Rice Lewis, gentleman, was granted to his nephew, William Jenkin. William Jenkin and Morgan David of the city of Llandaff, yeoman, were sworn for William Jenkin to make and exhibit a true inventory of the goods of his late uncle at or before the 24th June next, to administer according to law, to render an account of his administration at or before the 28th January, 1685/6, and to present to the Court any last will and testament of the deceased that might appear. Both William Jenkin and Morgan David recorded their mark on the administration bond.

[National Library of Wales Document Reference: LL/1685/80]

A True and Perfect Inventory of all and sing[u]lar ye goods, Cattle, ch[att]ells and Credits of Richard Jenkins late of the Parish of Lanishen in the County of Glamorgan Cl[erk] dec[ease]d priz'd the 16th day of May 1698 by ye p[er]sons undernam'd as foll[ows] vizt

	li - s - d
Inprimis his wearing Apparrell priz'd to	06-00-00
Item his Books priz'd to	01-00-00
Item one Truncke to	00-05-00
Item Book binders Presse to	00-02-06
Item one Table Board to	00-10-00
Item a quantity of feathers to	00-10-00
Item Desperate debts due to ye dec[ease]d	15-05-04
[total should be 23-05-10] Total	25-12-10

Prizers   Samuell Powell   sig[num] David Evan   Tho: William

Exhibited at Llandaff, 7th September, 1698, by Jenkins Lewis, administrator.

Administration Bond: Richard Jenkins, clerk: 7th September, 1698

In the Consistory Court of Llandaff, 7th September, 1698, administration of the goods etc. of Richard Jenkins, clerk, deceased, was granted to his father, Jenkin Lewis. Jekin Lewis and William Morgan of the parish of Llandaff, were sworn by the Court in the sum of £50 for Jenkin Lewis to make and exhibit a true inventory of the goods etc. of his late son at or before the 1st December next, to administer according to law, to give a just account of his administration at or before the 7th September, 1698, and to present to the Court any last will and testament of the deceased that might appear. Jenkin Lewis recorded his mark on the administration bond: William Morgan signed the document.

[National Library of Wales Document Reference: LL/ 1698/ 72]

11. Mariners

A true and perfect Inventory of all the goods, cattle chattells and creditts of Thomas Spencer late of the parish of Penmark in the Diocesse of Landaffe, Mariner, dec[ease]d, made and taken the seaventh day of March, in the year of our Lord 1681 as followeth. Vizt.

	li - s - d
Imprimis His wearing apparell and horse furniture	03-00-00
Item fifteen pieces of plate and one bowle weighing 64 ounces att four shillings the ounce	12-16-00
In the Hall att Penmark	
Item one table board, frame, nine Joynt stooles and a carpett cloth	01-00-00
Item one Cupboard, one chest and three wooden Chaires	01-06-08
Item one clock	01-05-00
In ye Entry one old chest and settle	00-06-00
In the Parlor	
Item one cedar chest, two octher small chests, one desk, one Livery cupboard, one sea-chest, two great joint stooles, three wooden chaires and two small Joynt stooles	03-10-00
Item one bedsteed with curtains, vallions, two feather beds, two bolsters, one rugge and one coverlett	05-05-00
Item one citterne	00-03-04
Item Three fowling pieces, two muskett barrells, two pistolls, one whereof brasse, two box smoothing Irons, one sword, one pair of andirons, one pair of pott hooks, tongs and slice, one Iron bar, one Iron beame with scales and weights, and one iron sledge	02-11-06
In the Kitchin	
Item Eight fleeches of Bacon and Pork	01-10-00
Item The salting trow and haircloth	00-10-00
Item Two large brasse pans, two lesser pans, two brasse potts, one brasse sea kettle, one bell mettle skillett, two brasse kettles, one frying pan, one great brasse kettle, one large	

brasse brewing kettle, one dripping pan, three brandirons, one bakestone, one brasse chafing dlsh, one iron grate, one morter, one candlestick, and one brasse ladle	08-06-00
Item Pewter in the Kitchin	02-16-00
Item The Iron things	00-15-00
Item One brewing vat and all other wooden vessells, two side table boards, and planks in the Kitchin and milkhouse, and ten casks of all sizes	01-03-04

In the cellar Chamber

Item one great trunck of Drawers, one liver cupboard, one round table, four green chairs, one bedsteed, one feather bed and boulster, two pillowes, one desk, one case of bottles, one rug, one coverlett & two blanketts	06-15-00

In the hall Chamber

Item In the settle bed, two feather beds, two feather boulsters, one rug and blankett	03-00-00
Item one bedsteed, one feather bed, two feather bolsters, two pillows, one coverlett, and one blankett	02-15-00
Item one pallett bed, one feather bed and bolster, one rugge and three blanketts, one coverlett, one turne and the rest of the wooden things.	01-00-00

In the Parler Loft

Item Nineteen cheeses, one pot of butter, 30 pounds; one board and two Joynt stooles	01-06-00
Item Halfe a stone of coarse wooll	00-05-00

In the Kitchin Chamber

Item one French bedsteed, one dust bed, and one feather bolster and two Coverletts	00-16-00

In the hall att Aberthaw

one standing bedsteed, one table, one chair, one dust bed, one feather boulster, two blanketts, two Ruggs and two pecks and a half of mixt pease	01-06-08

In the Parlor

Iten one old standing bedsteed	00-08-00
In the Kitchin one old bedsteed, one presse cupboard, six & twenty Deale boards and one little brasse crock	01-15-00

In the Hall Chamber

Item A parcell of old iron about 20 pounds	00-01-06

In the Cellar

Item one barrell, one kilderkin and six white earthen dishes	00-06-00

In the shop
Item one table board and a parcell of lime	00-08-00

Other goods att Penmark
Item Three oxen	09-00-00
Item Five cowes and two calves	12-00-00
Item one steer and one heifer of two years old	03-00-00
Item one horse and two mares	06-00-00
Item thirty eight ewes and lambs and one weather	14-00-00
Item Four acres of wheat	09-00-00
Item Two pieces of reeks of Hay	03-00-00
Item Five loads of barley in sheaves	09-02-00
Item Fifteen bushells of oates	02-12-06

other goods In Aberthaw
Item One long wayne with its appurtenances, one pair of wheeles, one plough, two pair of harrowes two pair of tresses and batkins, 3 yoakes and five strings	05-10-00
Item Two shovells, two spades, one pickaxe, two picks, one mattock, one dungfork, one billhook and one hatchett	00-08-00
Item Wheat theshed and unthreshed	20-00-00
Item 38 yearling sheep and one ram	08-15-06
Item Nine acres of wheat and one of pease	21-10-00
Item Six bushells of salt in the store house	00-18-00
Item The deced[en]ts share of two barks	100-00-00
Item Three quarters of an old Hull called the Mary	00-15-00

Att Penmark
Item Ten pair of sheets, whereof some are cotton, Ten bolster cases, ten pillow cases, five table cloaths, Two douzen of napkins, and two towells	07-08-00
Item Ten yards of searge, thirteen yards of half cloth, and six yards and a half of kersey	03-00-06
Item One old pair of red curtains and vallions	00-03-00
Item one pair of wrought vallions	00-07-00
Item One rugge, three pair of blanketts, one Irish Rugge and one old carpett	01-08-00
Item His Pigs and poultrey	04-00-00

Debts due
Item Due to the deceased from Mr. Matthew Giles	20-00-00
Item Due from Mr. Eward Thomas of Rudry	33-11-00

Iteem Lying in the hands of Arthur Sweet for the deceased's part of the profits and returnes of a bark called The Blessing of Aberthaw	01-06-06
Item In ready monies	06-01-00
Item Three twelve month old bullocks, one two year old colte, one twelve month old Colte, and one Hide	05-15-00
Item Unpaid of the decedent's part of the profitts & returnes of the said bark called the Blessing	06-00-00
Item Unpaid of the decedents part of the returnes of another bark called the Elizabeth	<u>03-00-00</u>
	<u>381-17-00</u>
Desperate debts due to the deceased	30-10-00

Apprisers   Richard Lucus   Rynold Giles   Richard Lison
      Hugh Mathews   John Spencer   Evan Thomas

[National Library of Wales Document Reference: LL/ 1681/ 147]

A true and perfect Inventory of all and singular the goods and Chattles of John Brewer late of Cardiff in the County of Glamorgan Mariner deceased made and appraised by the persons whose names are hereunto subscribed the second day of December *in the first year of the reign of our Lord James the second by grace of God King of England etc. in the year of our Lord (in latin)* **1685 as followeth vizt.**

	li - s - d
Imp[rimi]s in ready money	00-05-00
His wearing apparell appraised to	01-00-00
In the kitchin	
ffifteene Pewter Platters appraised to	01-10-00
Twelve Pewter Plates appraised to	00-04-00
Two Pewter Candlesticks one Pewter Chamber Pott Two Pewter Tanketts one Pewter Pott & one Pewter Beger	00-06-06
One Warming Pan Two Bras Candlesticks Two Bras spones att	00-03-06
Two Iron Crocks Two andirons Three Brakes one paire of Docks one Gridiron Tormentors & a Pottox one Tongs appraised att	00-08-00
Pewter Potts & one Pewter Tankett att	00-03-00
ffour joynt stooles ffour halfe joynt stooles one leatheren chaire one wooden chaire att	00-04-00

an old dresser appraised att	00-00-08

In ye Parlor

one table Board three joynt stooles one Bench three wooden chaires and one Press Cubbord appraised att	01-04-00
One standing Bedsteed two ffeather Bedds one Rugg one paire of Blanketts two Boulsters one paire of Curtaines and valians appraised att	04-10-00
Two Bras Candlesticks two Chussions seaven Earthen Platters three small Earthen Muggs att	00-04-08
one paire of Iron andirons appraised att	00-02-06

fforestreet Chamber

One standing Bedsteed one ffeather Bed one Bowlster two Pillows one Rugg one paire of Sheetes	03-10-00
one Table Board one fframe one side Cobboard one wooden chaire one chest one chaire table one Picture fframe appraised att	01-10-00
one ffrying panne appraised att	00-01-00

Higher Chamber

one standing Bedsteed one ffeather Bed one Boulster one Rug one paire of Sheetes one Blankett	03-00-00
one Round table one little Red Cubboard tenne leatherin chaires and one old trunk att	01-01-00

ye other Higher Chamber

one old Bed steede one old Table Board & one old joynt stoole att	00-07-00
In the Study one old chest appraised att	<u>00-02-06</u>
	19-15-10
ffive diaper Napkins one diaper Board cloath att	00-05-00
The Lease of his dwelling house att	60-00-00
His Barke called the Speedwell of Cardiff with the small Boate riggins furniture and appurtenances appraised att	80-00-00
In Desperatt Debts	<u>01-00-00</u>
	161-02-10

Appraisors Names Will Richards   Jonathan Greenfield   Thomas James the marke of George G R [his mark] Rees   Richard Davis Mathew Edwards

Administration Bond: John Brewer, mariner: 15th March, 1685/6

In the Consistory Court of Llandaff, 15th March 1685/6, administration of the goods etc. of John Brewer, mariner, deceased, was granted to his principal creditors, Wm. Morgan of Coed y Gores, gentlemen, and Cradock Nowell of the town of Cardiff, glover, the estate having been left unadministered by Mary Brewer, widow of the deceased, herself now deceased. William Morgan, Cradock Nowell and Robert Hodds of the City of Llandaff, innkeeper, were sworn by the Court for Wm. Morgan and Cradock Nowell to make an inventory of the goods etc. of the deceased, to pay his debts and legacies so far as the goods etc. will allow, and to render an account when lawfully required. All three boundens signed the administration bond.

[National Library of Wales Document Reference: LL/ 1685/ 29]

The Inventory of the goods and Chattles of Richard Davis late of Cardiffe in ye County of Glamorgan Marriner who departed this life ye 6 of January 1693

	li - s - d
Imp[rimi]s for his whering Apparell	02-00-00
It[em] in the Citching and parlor	02-10-00
It[em] in the great Chamber Lynen and wolling bead and beadsteed	01-10-00
It[em] in the Little Chamber bead and beadsteed Lynen and woolling	01-00-00
It[em] The share in the barque Called the Lyon	40-00-00
It[em] The share of the barque Called the speedwell	40-00-00
It[em] the share of the Grindstones	01-01-00
It[em] The share in the barque Called the two brothers	10-00-00
It[em] The share of the salt	10-00-00
It[em] The share of A stone boate	02-00-00
It[em] halfe A dozen planks and a mast to share	00-10-00
It[em] As for debts uncertaine	
It[em] sum other lose things About ye house	00-05-00
	110-15-00

The praysers names Will Richards senior Emanuel Miles
  Will Richards William Williams Edw: Want

Administration Bond: Richard Davies, mariner: 25th January, 1693/4
In the Consistory Court of Llandaff, 25th January, 1693/4, administration of the goods etc. of Richard Davies, mariner, deceased, was granted to his widow, Thamasina Davies. Thamasina Davies and William Richards,

gentleman, both ot the Town of Cardiff, were sworn by the Court in the sum of £300 for Thamsina Davies to make and exhibit a true inventory of her late husband's goods etc. at or before 1st May next, to administer according to law, to give a just account of her administration at or before 25th January, 1694/5, and to present to the Court any last will and testament of the deceased that might appear. William Richards signed the administration bond: Thamasin Davies recorded her mark.

[National Library of Wales Document Reference: LL/ 1693/]

An inventory of all the Goods Cattle Chattles and personall Estate of Nicholas Stidman late of the Towne of Cardiff in the County of Glamorgan Marriner deceased made and approved by the persons whose Names are hereunto subscribed ye ffirst day of Aprill *in the seventh year of the reign of our Lord William the third King of England etc. in the year of our Lord (in latin)* **1695 as followeth viz**

	li - s - d
Imp[rimi]s the deced[en]ts wearing Apparell	02-00-00
One Bedstead two feather Bedds two ffeather Boulsters two feather pillowes two Paire of Canvas Sheets one pair of Blanketts two Ruggs and one paire of Curtaines and valiants Appraised at	05-00-00
One Chest one Cuppboard, one small Table Board and one box w[i]th drawer	01-00-00
Ten pewter platters Six pewter plates Six pewter Porrigners ffour pewter Candlesticks, one pewter Gunne or pott appraised	01-10-00
Two small Brasse Kettles, one small Brasse Skillet, and a small Iron Crock	00-08-00
One Iron ffire Slice, one paire of Tongs and one paire of Andirons	00-02-00
The Moyety or one halfe parte of the Barke or Vessell called ye Speedwell w[i]th the Tackle and ffurniture thereto belonging, and the half p[ar]t of two .... Boates belonging to the s[ai]d Barke	40-00-00
Sperate debts due to the deced[en]t	08-00-00
Tot[al]	58-00-00

Appraisors William Lambert Joseph Sheltenham John? Jenkins Exhibited at Llandaff, 7th May, 1695, by Blanch Stidman, relict and administratrix.

Administration Bond: Nicholas Stidman, mariner: 7th May, 1695
In the Consistory Court at Llandaff, 7th May 1695, administration of the goods etc. of Nicholas Stidman, mariner, deceased, was granted to his widow, Blanch Stidman. Blanch Stidman and Thomas Jenkins of Cardiff, innholder, were sworn by the Court in the sum of £200 for Blanch Stidman to make and exhibit a true inventory of the goods etc. of her late husband at or before the 1st September next, to administer according to law, to give a just account of her administration at or before the 7th May, 1696, and to present to the Court any last will and testement of the deceased that might appear. Blanch Stidman recorded her mark on the administration bond: Thomas Jenkins signed the document.

[National Library of Wales Document Reference: LL/1695/25]

A True and perfect Inventory of all the goods and Chattles Rights and Creditts of John Greenfield late of the Town of Cardiffe in the County of Glamorgan Marriner Deceased taken and Appraized the twelvth day of November 1736 by us whose names are hereunto Subscribed as followeth

In the Kitchin
Imprimis   one Pewter Dish or platter marked W: C:
   Eight marked J: L: three marked J: O   four marked J: H Cl
   three marked J: CL   three marked J: G: Seven small platters
   marked G: L J   one marked R: J D: two marked W CL: M
   and one Pye plate,   Two Doz[e]n Pewter plates J CL: H
   two Doz[e]n Marked J: L   three Doz[e]n Marked J: A
   six pewter Porringers marked G: L: one pewter Cheese
   plate two pewter Rings   1 pewter bed pan   two warming
   pans and fourteen brass Candlesticks   02-10-00
Six Wainscott Chairs   one Elbow Chair   one oval Table
   two Dressers   one Dog Wheel   one Copper Pott   one brass
   Kettle   one Tea Kettle   one Grate   Tongs   ffire shovel
   Poker   ffender & andirons   & one brass Ring   & a brass
   Spoon   a plate warmer   one joint stool at   01-10-00
In the Brewhouse
Item   four large brass Pans   two small Do.   One ffurnace
   one Boiler   two brass Skilletts   two Saucepans and one
   other pan   a Brass Pestle and mortar   two ffats & three
   Tubs at   05-00-00
In the Hall
Item   one Clock and Case   two Ovall Tables   Eight Cane

Chairs   one Round about Chair   one easy Chair   one Grate
  one pair of Tongs and ffire shovel   and a pair of brass
  Andirons   twenty Pictures   one large Map   17 alabaster
  Images & two Brushes   07-00-00
In the Parlour
Item   one ovall Table   one Buroe   six Cane Chairs
  one Grate   tongs   Slice   ffender and a pair of Andirons
  one China Punch Bowle   a Map and one and twenty
  pictures   02-00-00
In the Best Chamber
Item   one Bedstead with Curtains and Vallance   one ffeather
  Bed and Bolster   one Press Bedstead   twelve Cane Chairs
  one Square table   one Dressing Box   two Stands
  one powder Box and a Brush   one large looking Glass
  six Pictures   a Glass of fflowers   a Chimney Glass and two
  Sconces   one large Chest   one Stone Grate   ffire Shovel
  and Tongs   one ffender   two Brass Andirons   one Brush
  and one large earthen Punch Bowl at   10-00-00
In the Chamber over the Parlour
Item   one Bed and Bedstead with Curtains & Vallance
  one Bolster   one Desk or Buroe   one Swinging Glass
  one Trunk   one small oval table   two old Cane Chairs
  one Close Stool Case   six old Pictures   a pair of Iron
  Andirons & some Barrs in the Wall instead of a grate at   02-00-00
In the Captain's Chamber
Item   one Case of Drawers   one ovall table   four joint stools
  one Elbow Chair   & an old leather Chair and a looking
  Glass at   00-12-00
In the Chamber over the Kitchen
Item   one Bedstead with Curtains and Valliance   one Bed
  and Bolster   one Case of Drawers   one oval Table   one
  Swinging Glass   ffour Chairs   five Pictures   one Close
  Stool Case   window Curtains   ffender at   03-00-00
In the Garrett
Item   one Bedstead with Curtains and Valliance   one Bed
  and Bolster   and three old Trunks at   01-00-00
two half peeces of Gambrick   two half peeces of Holland
  two half peeces of Muslin   two half peeces of ffringe
  three whole peeces of Lace marked K: J: and a remnant
  of a Scollup Lace   20-00-00

His wearing apparell	10-00-00
one Horse	05-05-00
one Silver Watch	03-03-00
In the Cellar	
Empty Casks and Bottles	01-00-00
Six Gold Rings one Silver Tankard ten Silver Spoons two Silver plates two silver Salts two Silver Porringers two Silver Cupps one Silver Sugar Dish at	10-00-00
Sperate Debts By Bond & Mortages	4124-00-00
By Notes	83-00-00
Desperate Debts	205-00-00
His ready money	03-00-00
His Linnen	
eight pair of Sheets and one and five ffine Holland Sheets 10 Diaper and Damask Table Cloths Eight pillow Cases ffour lace Cloths for a small Table 2 Doz[e]n Damask Napkins 1 Doz[e]n Daiper Do. 12 Holland Napkins with Lace & 3 with Layd Work	05-00-00
Item The ffurniture of the Testator's own Chamber given as a Specifick Legacy to Miss Hannah Howels consisting of the particulars following one Clock and Case one Case of Drawers one Table one Dressing Box one Weather Glass twelve leather Chairs one Cane Chair one large Chest one old Desk one Trunk covered with Leather six pictures a Grate tongs ffire shovell ffender and Poker one Close Stool Case and a pan one Bedstead with Teaster Curtains and Vallance Window Curtains a large looking Glass a ffeather Bed & Bolster Glasses & Wax work on the Mantle Piece	10-00-00
Item Plate given to Miss Hannah Howell as a Specifick Legacy six Silver Spoons six Silver Tea Spoons one Silver pair of Tea Tongs one Silver Tankard and a Silver plate at	06-00-00
Item two pair of Gold Sleave Buttons six diaper Napkins and one Diaper Table Cloth given to Miss Hannah Howell at	01-00-00
Item A Silver Cupp containing about a Pint given to Miss fflorence Howell as a legacy	<u>04-00-00</u>
	4121-00-00

                                                           21-00-00
                                                         4142-00-00
                                                          383-00-00
                                                         4525-00-00

Appraisors   George Evans   George Williams
Exhibited at Cardiffe, 27th November, 1736, by Mr. Llewelin Trehern and Richard Jenkins, two of the Executors for a true and perfect Inventory.

[National Library of Wales Document Reference: LL/ 1736/ 20]

A true and perfect Inventory of all the Goods and Chattles Rights and Credits of Robert Priest the Younger of Cardiff in the County of Glamorgan Marriner deceased taken and appraised the tenth day of May 1742 by us whose Names are hereunto Subscribed as followeth

Imprimis His wearing Apparel	8 : 0 : 0
In the Kitchen	
Item three oval tables	0 :15: 0
Item six Chairs	0 : 4 : 0
Item one Tea Table	0 : 1 : 0
Item one small Dresser	0 : 4 : 0
Item one Skreen	0 : 2 : 6
Item one pair of Andirons	0 : 4 : 6
Item one Grate one Grid Iron two Toasters one Fender one Cleaver one frying pan one pair of Bellows one pair of Tongs one Slice one other pair of Tongs one other frying pan	0 :17: 0
Item one Dog Wheel & three Spits	0 : 4 : 0
Item one plate Warmer	0 : 2 : 6
Item one looking Glass	0 : 4 : 0
Item one Smoothing Box & Standard	0 : 2 : 6
Item The Crane and Hangings	0 : 2 : 0
Item one warming pan	0 : 3 : 0
Item one Corner Cupboard	0 : 0 : 6
In the Parlour	
Item one Mohogony Buroe	1 :10: 0
Item two Mohogony Tables	1 : 1 : 0
Item one small Table	0 : 1 : 6
Item two Elbow Chairs	1 : 0 : 0

Item	four Chairs	0 :10: 0
Item	one gilt looking glass and one Tea Chest	1 : 0 : 0
Item	one grate one Slice 1 poker and one pair of Tongs	1 : 5 : 0
Item	one Map and one Brush	0 : 1 : 0
Item	two Sets of China	1 :10: 0
Item	three Cloathes Brushes	0 : 1 : 0
Item	two Grates and other Tin Ware	0 : 3 : 0
In the best chamber		
Item	one Bedstead and Curtains	3 :10: 0
Item	one Quilt one Rug one pair of Blankets	1 : 1 : 0
		24: 0 : 0
Item	one ……..	1 : 0 : 0
Item	one Close Stool Case	0 : 6 : 0
Iten	Seven Chairs	1 :10: 0
Item	one Tea Table	0 : 2 : 6
Item	one looking Glass and two small Pictures	1 : 0 : 0
Item	one Grate and Fender	1 : 0 : 0
Item	one Cradle	0 : 1 : 0
Item	one Cradle	0 : 1 : 0
In the little Chamber		
Item	one looking Glass	0 : 17 : 0
Item	one Case of Drawers	0 : 10: 0
Item	one Sea Chest	0 : 5 : 0
Item	The Window Curtains & Vallience	0 : 3 : 0
Item	Two small Boxes and one Chair	0 : 2 : 6
In the blue Chamber		
Item	Two Bedsteads and Curtains	4 : 0 :0
Item	one Rug and one Blanket	0 :10:0
Item	one other Rug and one Blanket	1 : 0 : 0
Item	Nine leathern Chairs	1 : 0 : 0
Item	two Maps	0 : 1 : 6
Item	one small Grate	0 : 2 : 6
Item	all the EarthenWare at	0 :10: 0
Item	The Window Curatins	0 : 2 : 6
Item	one Fire & Skreen	0 :10: 0
In the back Chamber		
Item	Eight Chairs	0 : 8 : 0
Item	two old Bedsteads	0 : 5 : 0
Item	Curtains Vallience and Rug	0 :10: 0

Item	Bars and Fender	0 : 1 : 6
Item	two old Boxes	0 : 1 : 0
Item	a Parcell of Books	0 :10: 0
Item	Three Quilts	2 : 0 : 0
Item	four pairs of Blankets	2 : 0 : 0
Item	five pair of Sheets	3 : 0 : 0
Item	two other pair of Sheets	0 :10: 0
Item	a Cradle Quilt and Rug a pair of Blankets	
	a pair of Child's Blankets and a smoothing blanket	0 :10: 0
		48:10: 0
Item	The Table Linnen	3 : 0 : 0

The Bedding

Item	one Feather bed and Bolster in the Boat w[eigh]t 37^{lb} at 5^d	0:15:11
Item	one feather Bed and Bolster in the best Chamber w[eigh]t 84^{lb} at 6^d	2 : 2 : 0
Item	one other Bed and Bolster in the same Room w[eigh]t 71^{lb} ½ at 6^d	1 :15: 9
Item	a bed and bolster in the blue Room w[eigh]t 82^{lb} ½ at 6^d	2 : 1 : 3
Item	In the back Chamber one Bed and Bolster w[eigh]t 60^{lb} at 4^d	1 : 0 : 0
Item	13 pillows w[eigh]t 38^{lb} at 6^d	0 :19: 0

The Brass

Item	sev[era]l Brass Candlesticks and other brass w[eigh]t 41^{lb} at 10^d	0 :17: 6
Item	Three small Kettles and one small Coffee pot weight 14^{lb} at 8^d	0 : 9 : 4
Item	a brass Door Knocker	0 : 6 : 0

The pewter

Item	sev[era]l Dishes and Plates weighing 116^{lb} at 6^d	2 :18: 0

In the Brewhouse

Item	three Cloaths Basket and one Chest	0 : 4 : 0
Item	four Chairs	0 : 6 : 0
Item	two Tea Kettles & one Copper Saucepan	0 :15: 0
Item	one Iron Crock	0 : 2: 6
Item	one old small brass Pan	0 : 3 : 4
Item	one Furnace	2 :10: 0
Item	one Vat	0 :10: 0
Item	two Pails & one wooden Bowl	0 : 2 : 6

Item two brewing Tubs & two washing Tubs	0 : 10 : 0
Item some Lumber ab[ou]t the House	0 : 5 : 0
In the Cellar	
Item one Bottle Rack	0 : 5 : 0
Item one Iron Bar one Sledge one other Bar one Pickax two wedges & other old Iron	1 : 0 : 0
	72 : 10 : 1
In the Store house	
Item one Large oval Table	0 : 10 : 0
Item a Spinet and Frame at Mr William Richard's	2 : 2 : 0
Item Several parcels of Deal Boards in sev[era]l Storehouses	30 : 0 : 0
Item the Jaine Sloop and long Boat	166 : 0 : 0
Item his Watch	4 : 0 : 0
Item one double handed Silver Candle Cup one half Pint Mug three Silver Spoons two Silver Salts six Tea Spoons one Tea Tongs w[eigh]t 30 ounces and a half at 5ˢ	7 : 12 : 6
His ready money	50 : 0 : 0
His sperate Debts	250 : 0 : 0
Book Debts	25 : 0 : 0
Desperate Debts	2 : 0 : 0
Item one Gun at	0 : 10 : 0
	610-05-07

Nicholas Jayne   George Evans   Jane Priest

Exhibited at Llandaff, 15th June 1742, by Jane Priest, widow and administratix, and sworn before William Harry, surrogate.

Administration Bond: Robert Priest, mariner: 19th April, 1742

In the Consistory Court at Llandaff, 19th April, 1742, administration of the goods etc. of Robert Priest, mariner, deceased, was granted to his widow, Jane Priest. Jane Priest and Robert Priest of the Town of Cardiff, gentleman, were sworn by the Court in the sum of £500, for Jane Priest to make and exhibit a true inventory of the goods etc. of her late husband at or before the 19th July next, to administer according to law, to render a true account of her administration at or before the 20th April, 1743, and to present to the Court any last will and testament of the deceased that might appear. Both boundens signed the administration bond.

[National Library of Wales Document Reference: LL/ 1742/34]

An inventory of the Real Estate chattels and personal effects of the late John Williams, of the town of Cardiff, Master Mariner as taken 9th day of June 1847.

	£ - s - d
A Freehold Cottage in the Parish of St. Dogmells in the County of Pembroke	30-00-00
A leasehold cottage situate at Millicent Street Cardiff	60-00-00
Two sixty[th] of the schooner Emma of the Port of Cardiff	15-00-00
Due from the Ancient Briton Benefit Society London	35-00-00
Due from the Ancient Briton Society St Dogmells	05-00-00
Received from the Ivorites Society Cardiff	08-06-00
Household Furniture Book etc	12-14-06
Wearing apparel	05-00-00
	170-14-06

Elias Jones   Eli Evans

A list of the debts and liabilities of John Williams of the town of Cardiff Master Mariner at the time of his death, April 7, 1847

	£ - s - d
Ground rent of Cottage in Millicent Street	01-14-00
Rates and taxes on Cottage in Millicent Street	01-02-06
Mr Edward Evans Surgeon's bill	10-15-00
Bread for Ship	01-17-00
For meat	00-12-00
Funeral Expenses	24-00-00
In debt to the owners of the schooner Celerity of which he was Master	00-14-00
Mortgage on house in Millicent Street	10-10-00
Coals for house	00-15-09
Debt incurred by Repairs of the schooner Emma	22-00-00
	74-00-03

[National Library of Wales Document Reference: LL/ 1848/ 43]

---

12. Innkeepers/Maltsters/Vintner

A true and perfeckt Inventorie of the Goods and Chattells of Richard Sheers Alderman of the towne of Cardiff deceased Seaventh daye of Januarie one thousand six hundred fiftie and nyne And beinge taken the nynteeth daye of the same Instant Januarie Anno 1659

In the wine seller   li - s - d

Item Three Hogseds of Malligo sacke at £18 p[er] hog.	54-00-00
one Hogsed of Sherre sacke at £15	15-00-00
One Hogsed of white wind at	06-10-00
One Tearse of white wined at	04-00-00
One Hogsed of Clarret at	05-00-00
Halfe a Hogsed of Methiglene at	03-00-00
One Renlet of Malligo sacke and One Ronlet of sherre sacke Both	08-00-00
some is	95-10-00

In the Beare Seller

Three Hogsedes And ffower Barrells of Beare Beinge 11 Barrells in all at Twelfeshillings the Barrel is Just	06-12-00
some is	06-12-00
Iteme More for Beames And other Sorte of Timber for Buildinge Beinge valued to the Some of	20-00-00
some is	20-00-00
Iteme for Brasse And pewter Beinge All valued to the some of	24-00-00
some is	24-00-00
Iteme ffor Sixtie three ounces of Silver plate at iiii^s vi^d the ounce is just	14-03-06
More for Tenn Silver spoones at iiii^s vi^d p[er]	02-05-00
some is	16-08-06

In the Belle Chamber

Iteme One Fether Bead two ffether Boulsters one fether Pillow And one Greene Rouge vallued at	03-10-00
One Round Board one Liverie Cubert six Chayers and two Carpets vallued at	01-04-06
some is	04-14-06

In the Angell Chamber

Iteme One downe Bead Two downe Boulsters and one downe Pillows andtwo Rougs	10-00-00
one paire of Greene Sarge Cortains	02-00-00
one Nedell worke Carpet And to paire of nedell worke valliens with silk frenge	10-00-00
In the truckell Bead one ffether Beade and ffether Boulster And one Small Rouge	02-00-00
To old Geene Broad Cloth Carpettes	00-13-04
To Tabell Boards one Side Cubert	00-15-00

one standinge Beadsteede one Truckell bead	01-00-00
ffoure chayers at ii^s the Peace	00-08-00
One Neadel worke quishinge at	00-10-00
One pair of Brasse Andiers w[i]th Slices and Tongs of Brasse And An Iron Backe	04-00-00
some is	<u>31-16-04</u>
Total of this side	<u>199-02-02</u>

In the White Harte Chamber

Iteme To ffether Beads, three ffeather Boulsters one downe pillow two Rougs and one Coverled beinge vallued at	07-10-00
one Pair of Blew Sarge Curtains and valliens ffoure Chayers Sutabell one nest of Boxes one tabell Board one old Carpet to quishings with one old Truncke beinge to	<u>04-00-00</u>
some is	<u>11-10-00</u>

In the Rosse Chamber

Iteme Two fether Beads Three ffether Boulsters one Pillow and Three old Rougs beinge vallued to	07-10-00
one standinge Bead one Truckell Bead Coarde mates one pair of old Carpetine Curtaines and valliens one Tabell Board and one old carpet beinge vallued to	<u>01-06-08</u>
some is	<u>08-16-08</u>

In the Parlour

Iteme One Tabell Board one Presse Cubert one Chest sixe Joynt stolles one old Carpet to quishings sixe Pickturs and one pewter stille beinge vallued to	<u>01-06-08</u>
some is	<u>01-06-08</u>

In the kitchinge

Iteme One dresser one Cubb one doge wheele for all sorte of Trininge goods three turnd Chayers one paire of Rackes one pair of Iron doggs seaven Iron spitts w[i]th other Iron goodes Belonging to the Kitchinge	<u>02-00-00</u>
some is	<u>02-00-00</u>

In: the Luce: Chamber

Iteme One downe Bead one Boulster	07-00-00
Three ffether Beades five fether Boulsters and two old Rouges beinge vallued to	10-10-00
three standinge Beadsteeds one truckell Bead one tabell	

Board three Benches foure Chayers one Spruce Chest one old truncke one old Chest 2 paire of dornix Curtains and valliens much worne beinge vallued at	02-10-00
One paire of Nedell worke Curtains valliens Counterpane one Carpett Cubert Cloth Covers for sixe Chayers	15-00-00
One Iron Backe and one pair of Iron doggs	00-05-00
Twentie dossen of Diaper and dowlas Napkins at 10s. the dossen is	10-00-00
Tenn Pair of Flaxen and Canvas Sheets	03-00-00
one pair of Bombebast sheets at	00-08-00
Eight pair of dowlas sheets at 15^s p[er] pair	06-00-00
eight Pair of Holland Sheets at 20^s	08-00-00
To dozen of diaper towels at	01-00-00
one dossen of Coarse Canvas towells	00-04-00
Six Pair of much woren Blanketts	00-15-00
ffoureteene Pillow Casses of holland and Callicko	00-14-00
some is	65-06-00

More in the Luce Chamber

Item Eight Diaper Tabell Clothes at 20^s	08-00-00
Fourteene dowlas and Canvas Tabell Clothes	03-10-00
some is	11-10-00

In the Dragon Chamber

Item One Downe Bead and to Boulsters	07-00-00
Two ffether Beads and foure fether Boulsters	07-10-00
To old beadsteeds mates Coards and three paire of Curtains and valliens much woren To tabell Boards one old Chest	03-06-00
Eight Bushells of malte and to old Chests	03-04-00
some is	21-00-00

In the Backer Kitchinge

Item One Beadsteede one Cubbe one old Chest one Cheese presse 3 Tabell Boards	01-00-00
Thirtie Cheeses at xii the peace is	01-10-00
some is	02-10-00

In the house at Roth:

One Beadsteed one pair of old Curtains and valliens	01-00-00
One Tabell Board & one Livery Cubert	00-06-00
One floxe Bead & one doust Bead & ii Boulsters	01-00-00
some is	02-06-00

In the stabell

ffor haye the Some of	20-00-00

ffor Racks and mangers	01-00-00
Tenn Cowes vallued at 50ˢ the p[ea]s[e]	25-00-00
ffoure hayfars at 30ˢ the peace	06-00-00
ffoure yearelings at 10ˢ the peace	02-00-00
ffive Horses Beinge vallued at	08-00-00
some is	62-00-00
More	
ffor three Ackers of wheate vallued to	10-00-00
In Hopefull Debts 35:	35-00-00
Money Desperate debts	00-00-00
ffor a peace of Land to ackers three quarters more or less Suppos[e]d	24-00-00
Adventured In goods sent to sea to the Su[m] of	08-00-00
more for the profit of A Chattell Lease held by the deceadent by the grant of Edward Stradling Esqʳ of Certaine Landes in the parish of Roth In the Countie of Glamorgan at the yearly Racke Rent of xvˡⁱ p[er] Annu[m] the yearly profite of which Lease being vallued to	01-05-00
ffor his Gowne and for all sorte of his wearing Apparrell beinge vallued to the some of	10-00-00
some is	88-05-00
In the room next to yᵉ Bell chamber	
i fether bead ii boulsters one old Rouge one old Coverled one old Chest one Round Tabell Beinge all vallued to the some of	03-10-00
The Tottall Some is	479-01-08

The praisers: names   Elix [his mark] Fox   Rice Davis   John Sheere
                      William Williams   John Greene uphoulster

[National Library of Wales Document Reference: LL/ 1662/ 23]

A true and perfect Inventory made the seventeenth day of November in the year of our Lord one thousand six hundred seventy and three of all the goods cattles and chattles of Richard Hawkins Alderman in the towne of Cardiffe in the Count[y] of Glamorgan and Diocesse of Landaffe who deceased the tenth day of the s[ai]d month in the said yeare, Prised by the persons who have hereunto subscribed, as followeth

	Lib-Sol-d
Imprimis His wearing Apparell	11-00-00

It[em] Four bibles and other books	00-10-00
It[em] His money in his owne possession and debts due to him	60-00-00
It[em] Two Cubboard one table board five joint stooles three chaires and all the rest of the houshold stuffe in the roome called the Beares head	05-10-00
It[em] One standing bedstead one feather bed w[i]th theire appurtenances in the roome called the lambs	04-10-00
It[em] In the s[ai]d roome one table w[i]th its frame one joint stoole one chaire two chests two truncks one back? and three boxes	01-00-00
It[em] In the Chamber called the crowne one standing bedstead one featherbed one Aras Coverlett w[i]th Curtaines and valians belonging to the standing bed and the rest of its appurtenances	05-00-00
It[em] In the s[ai]d Chamber one table and its frame six Joint stooles one chest one livery cubboard one bason one ewer two cushins and one cubboard cloath	02-10-00
It[em] In the s[ai]d Chamber one truckle bedstead one feather bed w[i]th their apputenances	01-10-00
It[em] In the s[ai]d chamber one table carpett two small joint stooles four great joint stooles three chaires four Cushins	00-13-04
It[em] In the chamber called the George one standing bedstead one truckle bedstead one feather bed w[i]th their appurtenances and all other houshold stuffe in that chamber	04-13-04
It[em] In the Chamber called the Ross two standing bedsteads two feather beds w[i]th their appurtenances one table one chest and all other houshold stuffe in the s[ai]d chamber	04-06-08
It[em] In the Chamber called the Faulken, one bedstead one feather bed one settle one chaire and all other houshold stuffe in the s[ai]d chamber	02-10-00
It[em] In the two upper chambers two bedsteads two feather beds w[i]th their appurtenances	03-00-00
It[em] All the pewter platters pewter plates and all other pewter vessells being in number about one hundred and ten	05-00-00

It[em] All the Silver Plates	03-00-00
It[em] Eight bras pots six kettells or Cauldrons two Skilletts two bras pans six bras candlesticks one bras ring one bras cup three bras spoones one chaffron dish one bras warming pan	10-00-00
It[em] Two Iron potts eight pair of Anndiers, five pot hooks four pair of tongues, five fire slices two frying pans three Iron grates one dropping pan and all he rest of Iron instruments and implements	02-10-00
It[em] All other wooden vessells and stuffe in the kitching	00-05-00
It[em] two truncks, one coffer, three boxes one table	00-10-00
It[em] the furnace and all the other vessells belonging to the brewhouse	10-00-00
It[em] ten paire of sheets six table cloath ten diaper napkins eighteen course napkins	02-00-00
It[em] All the salt in the shop	08-00-00
It[em] All the deal boards	01-00-00
It[em] the crests bricks and latts	02-00-00
It[em] The new Iron unworked	01-00-00
It[em] the velies? yoakes and bows	01-00-00
It[em] the Hay	02-10-00
It[em] the wheat sowen and unsowen	09-00-00
It[em] the barley	01-00-00
It[em] one chattle lease on two acres of land in Canton	08-00-00
It[em] the profit of five Acres of Land in Canton	03-00-00
It[em] the profit of a lease on a house in the parish of St Maries in Cardiff	05-00-00
It[em] All the woodden implements in the stable	00-05-00
It[em] One mare	02-00-00
It[em] All the swine	01-10-00
It[em] All his houshold stuffe in Mr Miles Morgan's house	00-05-00
It[em] All desperate debts	<u>10-00-00</u>
The totall sume is	<u>196-08-04</u>

Prisers   Robert Jones Cl[er]k   Thomas Taylor signu[m]
          Wm Lle[elli]n of Elly   Math: Evans

[National Library of Wales Document Reference: LL/ 1673/ 26]

A true and perfect Inventory of all the goods Cattle and Chattles of Wenllian James of Landaffe in the County of Glamorgan widd[ow] late deceased as well moveable and Inmoveable taken and Apprized by us the persons herein named the ninth Day of December in the ffirst yeare of the Raigne of our Soveraigne Lord King James the second Annoqe D[omi]ni 1685

	li - s - d
Imp[rimi]s her Wearing Apparell prized to	03-00-00
Itt[em] In the Haule One Standing Bedsteed w[i]th Curtaines and valians, one ffeather Bed and one dust Bed, one ffeather Bolster, one dust Bolster, one ffeather pillober, one greene Rugg two payre of Sheets and two payre of Blanketts One Table Boord and fframe, ffive Joynt stooles one press Coupbord, one Chest three Chayres one fframe Binch, ffower three Leged stooles one Iron grate, one Cast Iron Back, two Gridirons, one Backestone, one ffrying pan one tongs, one Iron fforck, one ffrying pan, two spitts one Iron Candlestick, one Iron Box one ffowleing piece one Loocking Glass and one Cage w[i]th Earthen Ware prized to	10-00-00
Itt[em] In the Little Chamber one ffrench Bedsteed one ffeather Bed, one ffeather Bolster, one dust Bed, one dust Bolster and theyr appurtenances one Cupboord one Chest and severall other houshold stuff in the sayd Chamber to	08-00-00
Itt[em] In the Chamber over the sayd roome, Two ffeather Beds, two ffeather Bolsters, Two dust Beds and two dust Bolsters and theyr appurtenances Two Baggs of Hops, one Chest and other appurtenances belonging to the sayd Roome prized to	15-00-00
Itt[em] In the Roome in the Entry one Cupboord & other small Trumperty to	00-10-00
Itt[em] In another small Roome one Table and few small Trumpery	00-10-00
Itt[em] All her Linnen prized to	00-10-00
Itt[em] All her Brass and pewter prized to	07-00-00
Itt[em] In the upper house soe called, one standing Bedsteed, one Great Table, one Coupboord w[i]th a parcell of Cheese and other houshold stuff in the sayd house prized to	08-00-00

Itt[em] her Brewhouse and all the Implements in the sayd Brewhouse prized to	15-00-00
Itt[em] Abouts Twenty ffower Empty Barrells of all sortes prized to	02-08-00
Itt[em] Abouts Twenty Bushells of Barely in the storehouse	04-10-00
Itt[em] more in the storehouse of Mault ffifty Bushells prized	11-05-00
Itt[em] Stone Cole prized to	05-00-00
Itt[em] All sorte of Grayne in Reeks and in the Barne prized to	34-05-00
Itt[em] Wheat in the Ground prized to	16-00-00
Itt[em] Six Oxen prized w[i]th theyr fodder to	20-00-00
Itt[em] Six Milch kine prized w[i]th theyr fodder to	12-00-00
Itt[em] ffoure yearlings w[i]th theyr fodder prized to	05-00-00
Itt[em] Two steeres w[i]th theyr fodder prized to	03-00-00
Itt[em] Two Calves w[i]th theyr ffodder prized to	01-00-00
Itt[em] Three Horses w[i]th theyr ffodder prized to	10-00-00
Itt[em] ffower and Twenty sheepe of all sorte prized	04-00-00
Itt[em] Swine and poultrey about the House	06-00-00
Itt[em] One Waine and all sortes of Implem[en]ts belonging to Husbandry to	06-00-00
Itt[em] depts due to the decedent from the p[er]sons in the Codicill hereunto annexed	56-05-03
It[em] one acre and a halfe of oates	01-00-00
Sum tot[al]	265-03-03

Prizers names
John Mathews   Morgan Williams de ….   Andrew Mathew   David James

debts due from the p[er]sons undernamed to Wenllian James at the time of her decease

due for 4 Barrells of Ale from John Robbert	03-04-00
Wm. Vuckles for 4 Barrells	03-00-00
Wm. Llewelin 4 Barrells	03-00-00
Mary Williams 2 Barrells	01-10-00
Walter Baker and Wm. Howells	03-04-00
Thomas Morgan of Ely	03-02-00
Phillipp David of Lantwitt Vairdre	02-05-00
due from Morgan David	13-02-03

due from Morgan John Morrice	05-00-00
from David William of Pentirch	05-00-00
from Katherin Harry of Landaffe	03-00-00
due from Edward Lewis of Landaffe	04-00-00
from David Jones of Peterstone Sup-Ely	02-00-00
John Thomas of Walsterton	00-14-00
William Saunders of Whitechurch	<u>04-04-00</u>
Sum due	<u>56-05-03</u>

Exhibited at Llandaff by Anthony and Margarett Phillipp, 10th December 1685.

[National Library of Wales Document Reference: LL/ 1685/ 79]

An Invetary of the goods of William Rowbotham who departed this Life ye 12 day of february 1686,

	li - s - d
Item two suits and Coats and all his Apparell	05-00-00
In the forestreet chamber 2 fether beads 2 feather boulsters & 2 pillows 2 pair of blanketts 2 Ruggs on paire of Curtains and valliant with all ye furniture belonging to ye Chamber	15-00-00
In the middle Chamber one feather bed 1 bolster 1 pillow 1 paire of Curtains and vallience one Rugg on paire of blanketts with ye rest of the goods belonging to ye Chamber	07-00-00
In the back Chamber 2 feather beads 4 boulsters 2 pillows 2 Ruggs 2 pare of blanketts 1 paire of Curtains and vallience one Truckle bead steede & ye rest of ye goods belonging to ye Chamber	09-00-00
In ye upper Chamber 3 feather beads 6 fether boulsters 4 pillows 3 ruggs 3 paire of blanketts 3 paire of Curtains and valliences 1 standing bead with ye Rest of ye furniture belonging to ye Chamber	12-00-00
The goods in the gallery	00-10-00
In ye Gallery 2 beads & 2 beadsteeds & furniture belonging to them	02-00-00
In the parlor 1 feather bed 2 boulsters 1 pillow 1 pair of blanketts 1 Rugg 1 pare of Curtains and vallience with the appurtenances	08-00-00

In the buttry 1 feather bead 2 bolsters 1 pillow one Rugg with ye rest of ye Appurtenances belonging	03-00-00
In the shop one old press Cubbert & all ye Appurtenances belonging	01-00-00
One Chamber in the little house 3 feather beads & 3 bead steeds 5 boulsters 1 pillow 3 Ruggs 1 pare of Curtains and vallience 3 standing bead steeds	08-00-00
Linning belonging to ye house	
25 paire of sheets w[i]th pillow cases boards Clothes & napkins 1 new peese of demitti with other Lynen	20-00-00
	90-10-00
In the kichin pewter brass and Iron and all the furniture belonging to ye kichin	20-00-00
In ye Seller 14 barells of Ale one hogsetts of sider six dozen bottles of sider	15-00-00
It[em] 4 piggs	02-00-00
It[em] in the stable in hay and Corne	02-00-00
	39-00-00
	90-10-00
	129-10-00

Cradock Nowell   Lewis Cox   Edward Deron?   Edward Sant

Sworn before David Price, surrogate, 28th April, 1686, by Mary Robotham, widow.

Administration Bond: William Rowbotham: 28th April, 1686

In the Consistory Court of Llandaff, 28th April, 1686, administration of the goods etc. of William Robotham, deceased, was granted to his widow, Mary Robotham. Mary Robotham, John Robotham, barber, and Anth. Philpott, gentleman, all of the town of Cardiff, were sworn by the Court in the sum of £200 for Mary Robotham to make and exhibit a true inventory of her late husband's goods etc. at or before the 28th August next, to administer according to law, to give a true account of her administration at or before the 12th February, 1686/7, and to present ot the Court any last will and testament of the deceased that might appear. Mary Robotham recorded her mark on the administration bond. John Rowbotham and Anth. Philpott signed the document.

[National Library of Wales Document Reference: LL/ 1686/]

A true Inventory of the goods, Ch[att]ells and creditts of Robert Hodds late of Landaffe in the County of Glamorgan Inkeeper, deceased, made valued and apprized the ffifteenth Day of Aprill, one Thousand six hundred Eight Seaven by the p[er]sons whose names are heereunto subscribed.

	li - s - d
Imprimis the sayd deceadents wearing Apparell	03-00-00
Itt[em] In the parlor, One ffeather Bed and Bolster, one payre of Blanketts, one payre of sheets, one Clock, one Cupboord, one small case of Drawers, Two Brass Candlesticks, one Iron Toster, one Brasse skonce, Eight Earthen porrengers, three Earthen dishes, Eight Earthen plates, fforteen drinking Glasses, two Crewets, one Brass fframe and Wax Candle, Three paper picktures, one small Bird Cage, & some other small earthen ware prized to	04-00-00
It[em] In the Butterry one powdering Tubb, one Napkin press, one Tining Coffin, and two silkin sines prized to	00-08-00
It[em] In the Hall One Ovall Table, one Cage, one Earthen Bason and three Glasses valued to	00-12-00
It[em] In the Kitchin one Iron Crane, one Iron slise one Iron ffork, one large Iron spitt, three Iron speares nine Iron skewers, one Copper Kettle, Two Brass Kettles, one little Brasse Crock and pott-lid, One Brass Chaffin Dish one Brasse sawce panne three Brass Candlesticks one Iron Candlestick, Two pewter Candlesticks, ffower Tining Candlesticks, One Brass Skonce, seaven pewter dishes small and great, one Cheese plate, one pewter pie-plate, ffower pewter Chamber potts, one pewter saltseller, One pewter muster-pott, ffive pewter fflaggons, two pewter pintes, one halfe pinte, one quarter pewter pott Two dozen of pewter plates, one Copper Tankett one Tining watering-pott, one Tining Candlestick, and one Rack to	04-03-00
It[em] In the great Chamber, one payre of Greene Curtaines and Vallions, one Greene Rugg, one payre of Brasse Andiarnes and a ffender, two Coushins and six Leatherin Chayres prized to	01-19-00
It[em] In the Little Chamber, one ffeather Bed and ffeather Bolster, Curtaines and Vallions belonging to ye sayd Bed Two ffeather pillows and one Greene Rugg	02-12-00

216

It[em]   More in the sayd Chamber   one payre of Holland sheets   one payre of Canvas sheetes, Two diaper Table Cloathes   three Dozen and Eight diaper Napkins, one Course Table cloath, one Course Towell prized to   02-04-00

It[em]   In the Clossett   Two Boxes of Candles, Two Loaves and a halfe of sugar, Two Boxes of sugar prized to   00-15-08

It[em]   In the Coglofts   one ffeather Bed, one ffeather Bolster   two ffeather pillows   one dust Bed; one Rugg   one payre of Blanketts, Three sheetes, and Two Turnes prized to   03-00-00

It[em]   Two suites of Callico Curtaines and Vallions, one painted and one plaine,   Two sarge Curtaines prized to   01-05-00

It[em]   In the seller   one Hoghead of decayed Clarrett   01-10-00
It[em]   one Remnant of decayed Clarrett   00-02-06
It[em]   more one Hogshead of Clarrett   04-00-00
It[em]   more one Remnant of good Clarrett   00-03-00
It[em]   One Hogsh[ea]d of Whitewine   05-00-00
It[em]   more one Hogsh[ea]d of Whitewine prized to   05-00-00
It[em]   A Remnant of a Hogsh[ea]d of Whitewine   01-05-00
It[em]   more one Remnant of Hogsh[ea]d of Whitewine   00-05-00
It[em]   a Remnant of Sherry prized to   01-00-00
It[em]   Two Gallons of Clarrett Vinegar   00-01-06
It[em[Halfe a Hogsh[ea]d of Sherry prized to   05-10-00
It[em]   part of a Butt of sack prized to   07-00-00
It[em]   Halfe a Hogsh[ea]d of Canary prized to   05-00-00
It[em]   A Remnant of Malligo prized to   00-18-00
It[em]   A Remnant of Brandy prized to   00-02-00
It[em]   A Remnant of Tent prized to   01-00-00
It[em]   Some Bottles of decayed Wine and Syder prized to   01-00-00
It[em]   In the House over the way a Remnant of Lees prized to   00-02-06
It[em]   About 1 Hoggs[hea]d of sider vinegar prized to   00-08-00
It[em]   Two dozen of Bottles prized to   00-03-00
It[em]   six empty Wine Hogsh[ea]ds   00-12-00
It[em]   one melted ffurnes prized to   03-00-00
It[em]   one Burnt Mault mill prized to   01-00-00
It[em]   one great Cooler prized to   00-10-00
It[em]   one great Vate   01-00-00
It[em]   ffower Tubbs prized to   00-08-00

It[em]	ffower empty Barrells prized to	00-08-00
It[em]	ffive Empty Hoggs[heads] prized to	00-10-00
It[em]	Twenty Bushells of Mault prized to	05-00-00
It[em]	One still at	00-12-00
It[em]	ffower empty Barrells prized to	00-08-00
It[em]	ffive Barrells of Ale	03-15-00
It[em]	Reed? for Wine	05-00-00
It[em]	Three fflitches & a halfe of Backon & a side of porke	01-10-00
It[em]	One silver Cupp and silver spoone	02-03-00
It[em]	One Horse and Hey Reeck	04-00-00
It[em]	Nine piggs prized to	04-12-00
It[em]	depts desperate due to the deceadent	189-10-00
	sume tot[al] is	287-07-00

Prizers names
Phil Maddocks Clerk   Geo: Pranch   Wm. Richards   Will Deare
Exhibited by Martha Hodds, widow and administratrix, 8th April, 1687

Administration Bond: Robert Hodds, innkeeper: 11th April, 1687
In the Consistory Court of Llandaff, 11th April, 1687, administration of the goods etc. of Robert Hodds, innkeeper of the City of Llandaff, deceased, was granted to his widow Martha Hodds. Martha Hodds, John Mathews of the City of Llandaff, gentleman, and George Little of Tewksbury, were bound by the Court for Martha Hodds to make and exhibit a true inventory of the goods of her late husband at or before 11th July next, to administer according to law, to give a just account of her administration at or before 7th March next, and to present to the Court any last will and testament of the deceased that might appear. All three boundens signed the administration bond.

[National Library of Wales Document Reference: LL/ 1687/ 45]

A true and perfect Inventory of all the Goods Cattles, Ch[att]ells and personall Estate of Anstance Wells of Cardiffe in the County of Glam[or]gan widd[ow] dec[ease]d made valued and appraysed ye Eight & Twentieth day of June 1705 by us ye p[er]sons undernamed as followeth vizt

	li - s - d
Imp[ri]mis all her wearing Apparell valued att	02-00-00

Inventories of Village Shopkeepers and Tradesmen: Innkeepers/Maltsers/Vintner

In the fforestreet Chamber
One bed & Bedstead One Boulster, One pillow, One
   Rugg, One pair of Curtains & Vallions, One pair of window
   Curtains, One Case of drawers   Two Stands, One Side Table,
   four leathear'd Chairs and one Smale lookeing Glasse   02-10-00
In the Gallery
Two old Chests and a Trunck valued att   00-03-00
In ye Back Chamber
   One Bed & Bedstead, One pair of Curtains & vallions,
   One Boulster & Rugg, two pillowes, Two old Cubbards
   One Side Table, One Small Looking Glasse, Eleaven Chairs
   & a joint stole, Six pair of Sheets, three pair of blanketts,
   three table Cloths, six pillow Cases & a dozern & a halfe of
   napkins & four Iron Barrs in ye Grate   12-00-00
In ye outward Shopp
A Beam and pair of Scales & old led waits valued att   00-07-00
In ye Inner Shopp
In plague Water   03-00-00
In ye Parler
Two tables, One Settle, Tenn Chairs, three Silver Spoones &
   a Taster, four barrs & a Grate   01-15-00
In ye Sellar
Three barrells of Ale, three empty Oxetts and two empty
   barrells   02-16-00
In ye Kitchin
Two Beds, two ruggs, one pair of blanketts, two Boulsters,
   One Sheete, thirete one Platters & three dosen of plates,
   One Cheese plate, one pair of brasse AndIrons, Two pair
   of Iron AndIrons, One warmeing pan, two hand Candlesticks,
   One small Slice, two Iron potts and a Skillett, One Small
   brasse pott, two old frying pans, three pair of tongs & Slices,
   One Crane, Potthookes, and one dogg wheele   06-00-00
In ye Brewhouse
Two furneists, Two vates, One Cooler, Nine Tubbs & one
   empty halfe barrell, One head vate and two small vates and
   a Shoote   12-00-00
In ye washing Roome
One Small Boyler & a Lymbick & Pott & Iron marmett   00-15-06
In ye Shevell Board Roome
One flock bed & dustbed and Bedsteade, three feather

pollowes, two Ruggs, One pair of Curtains, One large tubb,
One empty Barrell, One table board One Cubbard,
One Chair, One side Cubbard & one Mault Mill   04-00-00
In yᵉ Summer house
One Case of Drawers feather bed and Boulster One pillow
One pair of Blanketts, One rugg three Chairs and One
Side Table   02-00-00
                                        Tot[al] is   49-06-06
Apprais[er]s names
Richard Gibbon   Geo. Mower   ....   Henry Meredith
Exhibited at Landaff, 5ᵗʰ July, 1705, by Mary Jones, daughter and executrix.

[National Library of Wales Document Reference: LL/1705/32]

A true & perfect Inventory of all & singular yᵉ Goods & Chattells, Creditts & Personall Estate of Katherine Hammond, late of yᵉ Town of Cardiffe in the County of Glamorgan widdow, & Administratrix of the Goods & Chattells of John Hammond of yᵉ s[ai]d Town of Cardiffe & County afores[ai]d Maltster deceased: Made valued and appraized by us whose names are hereunto subscribed this 25ᵗʰ day of Aprill An[n]o D[omi]ni 1720

Inp[rimi]s Her wearing Apparrell	3 - 0 - 0
2 Gold Rings	1 - 2 - 0
In yᵉ forestreet Chamber & Closet	
Item 1 Bedstead, Curtains & Vallians, a white Quilt & window Curtains A Chest of Drawers a Square table A looking glass 3 stands & a Close Stool Case	4 -10- 0
It[em] 10 Cane Chairs & a Picture	0 -18- 0
It[em] An old Grate in the s[ai]d chamber	0 - 3 - 6
In the Blew Chamber A bedstead a Quilt, a Set of Curtains & vallians, & window Curtaines	1 -15- 0
It[em] A Case of Drawers a Square table, a Looking glass, an Ovall table a Close stoole Case	1 -12- 0
It[em] 7 old worm eaten chairs & 2 small pictures	0 - 4 - 0
It[em] One fire grate a pair of tongs & slice	0 - 2 - 6
In yᵉ Chamber over yᵉ Kitchen 1 Bedstead & Curtains & vallians 1 Quilt, window Curtains & hangings	2 -12- 6

Inventories of Village Shopkeepers and Tradesmen: Innkeepers/Maltsers/Vintner

It[em] A Case of Drawers a little square table an Ovall table & a looking glass	1 -10- 0
It[em] 4 Cane Chairs & a fire grate	0 -18- 6
In the Back Garrett A sloap bedstead, Curtains & vallians a little square table 3 old chairs a small iron grate an old Close Stool case	0 -16- 0
In ye forestreet garretts 2 small bedsteads, 2 old Quilts 1 little grate a Set of old Curtains & vallians	0 -10- 0
In ye Room above ye Cellar & Closet within 6 old Sedge chairs, a bedstead, a little square table	0 - 5 - 0
It[em] Beds, bolsters & pillows at 6d p[er] p[ound]	12- 0 - 0
In ye Parler	
3 Ovall tables, 7 Cane Chairs, a looking glass & an old Carpet	3 - 0 - 0
It[em] A fire grate, a ffender, tongs Slice & poker	0 - 8 - 0
In ye Hall	
One bedstead & Curtains, a Press, 1 Desk with Drawers	0 -18- 0
It[em] 4 old leather chairs & a grate	0 - 7 - 6
It[em] 2 old birding pieces & a Sconce	0 - 5 - 6
It[em] A Rack	0 - 5 - 0
It[em] an old looking glass	0 - 5 - 0
In ye Kitchen 1 Grate, A Dogwheel, 1 old table, 4 leather chairs 2 twig chairs & a Screen	1 - 0 - 0
It[em] 1 ffurnace	1 -15- 0
It[em] 1 vate 5 small casks & tubs & other brewing vessells	0 -16- 0
It[em] A Cheese press, an old table & sheets in the Sellar	0 - 8 - 0
It[em] Tin & earthen ware & glasses	0 - 2 - 0
It[em] An old shockalate? pot & little table	0 - 2 - 0
It[em] Linnen	5 - 0 - 0
It[em] Ruggs & Blankets	2 - 0 - 0
It[em] 112 ounces of Plate at 4^s 10^d p[er] ounce	27- 1 - 4
It[em] 12 p[oun]d of cast brass at 6^d p[er] p[oun]d	0 - 6 - 0
It[em] 230 p[oun]ds of pewter at 6^d p[er] p[oun]d	5 -15- 0
It[em] 27 p[oun]ds of pan brass at 9^d	1 - 0 - 3
Pott brass at 4 ½	0 - 7 - 6
wrought brass at 7^d	1 - 0 - 0
An old warming pan	0 - 2 - 0
It[em] A pair of brass tongs & Slice	0 - 4 - 6
Irons belonging to y fire	0 -10- 0

An old pott	0 - 2 - 0
Old iron	0 - 1 - 0
In Alice Stedmans house An old Coffer & Cupbord	0 - 3 - 0
In ye Malt house 2 fflitches of Bacon	0 -14- 0
9 welsh bushells of barley at 5^s 3^d	2 - 7 - 3
304 Bushells of Malt & 4 strikes at 8 shill[ing]^s p[er] bushell	121-18- 0
It[em] A Quern & steel mill much worn	0 -16- 0
It[em] 5 barrells of coal	0 -11- 8
It[em] In ready Cash	236 -7 - 6
A Chattle Lease of Lands at Whitmore	49- 0 - 0
A Chattle Lease from Richard Lewis Esq	2 -12- 6
A Chattle Lease of ye Town Ditch	1 - 0 - 0
A small parcell of Hay	0 - 6 - 0
Sperate Debts	170-19- 01 ¼
Desperate Debts	195-13- 09 ½
Tot[al]	878- 9-10 ¾
Another Debt to ye Decedant	7-14- 0
Tot[al]	885-17-10 ¾

Apprizers   Th: Edwards Cl[erk]   David Owen [his mark]

Exhibited at Llandaff, 28th April, 1720, by Anne and Joan Thomas, sisters and administratrixes.

Administration Bond: Katherine Hammond: 28th April, 1720

In the Consistory Court of Llandaff, 28th April, 1720, administration of the goods, chattells and credits of Katherine Hammond, deceased, was granted to her sisters, Anne and Joan Thomas, spinsters. Anne and Joan Thomas, and John Thomas of the town of Cardiff, malster, were sworn by the Court in the sum of £2,000 for Anne and Joan Thomas to exhibit a true inventory of the goods etc. of their late sister at or before the last day of October next, to administer according to law, to render a true account of their administration before the 28th April, 1721, and to present to the Court any last will and testament of the deceased that might appear. John Thomas and Joan Thomas signed the administration bond: Anne Thomas recorded her mark on the document.

[National Library of Wales Document Reference: LL/ 1720/ 37]

An Inventory of all the goods Chattells and Creditts of Hopkin Williams late of the Town of Cardiffe in the County of Glamorgan and Diocess of

Inventories of Village Shopkeepers and Tradesmen: Innkeepers/Maltsers/Vintner

Landaffe Maltster deceased valued and appraized by William Howells amd William Edmund and Exhibited into the Consistory Court of Landaffe by Martha Williams the Relict of the said deceased on her Corporal Oath do follow, that is to say.

First	the Deced[en]ts wearing apparel valued at	03-00-00
Also	In the Kitchin Two Oval Tables at	00-12-00
Also	5 Leathern Chairs at	00-05-00
Also	6 wooden Chairs at	00-09-00
Also	4 Small Chairs at	00-02-06
Also	a Case of Drawers at	00-18-00
Also	a Jack at	00-05-00
Also	an Iron Grate	00-09-00
Also	a Spitt at	00-00-09
Also	a Crane at	00-01-06
Also	two fire tongs and two fire Shovels at	00-02-00
Also	a Gridiron and Cliver at	00-00-08
Also	8 iron Sciwers at	00-00-08
Also	2 Brass Candlesticks & a Brush at	00-02-00
Also	an iron Candlestick, peper box & flesh fork	00-00-06
Also	a parcell of earthen Ware, Glasses and a Weather glass at	00-08-08
Also	a Parcell of old Books at	01-17-00
Also	a pair of Bellows, and a Salt box at	00-01-07
Also	a Pestle & mortar and a Brush at	00-02-06
Also	a pair of Andirons at	00-02-04
Also	an easy Chair with one Hussu? at	00-03-06
Also	7 pillow Cases, and 8 Towells	00-11-00
Also	one pair of Blanketts, one Quilt, two pillow Cases, and a Bedstead at	00-14-06
Also	Two Coverlids and window Curtains at	00-02-06
Also	one Close Stool at	00-02-00
Also	In the Room within the Kitchin 5 pewter platters, 13 plates, and funnel weighing 26^{li} at 6^d p[er] pound	00-13-00
Also	a parcell of Tin Ware at	00-04-00
Also	a Lanthorn, a small brass Spoon with a few earthen Ware at	00-01-10
Also	in ye Cellar a dozen and half of Empty Bottles at	00-01-06
Also	3 dozen of Coal at	00-12-00

Also	2 Stillings and a Costrel at	00-01-04
Also	one Horse Swab & a lime Brush	00-02-00
Also	a Furnace at	00-10-08
Also	Two old Tables at	00-02-00
Also	2 small vates, 3 Tubs, 4 Quarter Casks at	00-18-04
Also	one ffrying pan, one Range & a few earthen Ware at	00-02-06
Also	3 small iron potts, one brass Kettle at	00-08-00
Also	in the forestreet Chamber, Two feather Beds weighing 156 at 6^d p[er] pound	03-18-00
Also	Ditto weighing 171 at 4^d p[er] pound	02-17-00
Also	4 bolsters, 7 pillows weighing 94 at 6^d p[er] pound	02-07-00
Also	3 pair of sheets at	00-15-06
Also	one Bedstead Curtains & Vallians	00-12-00
Also	2 small Tables, 2 Stands & an old Trunk	00-11-00
Also	one old Truckle Bedstead at	00-01-06
Also	Two pair of Blanketts, a pair of sheets, Two pillow Cases & a few course Towells	00-14-00
Also	one Quilt and 3 Rugs at	00-14-00
Also	2 old black Chairs at	00-00-06
Also	in the back Chamber One Bedstead 2 table cloths, one Blankett, one Sheet, one pair of Curtains, Rods, Cords & Mattras 01-01-02 Also one Ream of brown paper, one old Cupboard an old Trunk and an old Chair at	00-05-00
Also	in the Malthouse, 33 welsh bushels of Malt at 8^s p[er] Bushel	13-04-00
Also	52 bushels of Barley at 5^s p[er] bushel	13-00-00
Also	60 Barrells of Stone Coal at	07-15-00
Also	50^{li} of Hops at 10^d p[er] pound	02-01-08
Also	1000 of Tile Stones at	00-07-06
Also	500 Lathes at	00-06-00
Also	an old malt hand mill & two Kipes at	01-01-00
Also	15 old Sacks at	00-15-00
Also	an old hair Cloth and a few Rafters at	00-11-03
Also	2 old Scubs with ye measure Vessels at	00-02-00
Also	one Silver Watch at	02-12-06
Also	one Silver Cup weighing 5 ounces at 5^s an Ounce	01-05-00
Also	the Lease of ye Malthouse at	25-00-00
Also	the Lease of ye decedent's dwelling house	12-00-00
Also	ready money in ye house ye sume of	41-12-00

Also due to the deceased from John Thomas of St Faggans by Bond bearing date 6th April 1734	20-00-00
Also due from Wm Deer of St Georges by Bond bearing the date 14th June 1735	20-00-00
Also due to the deceased from George Williams of Cardiffe by Bond bearing date the 29th day of July 1734 the sume of	04-00-00
Also from Henry Williams of Kellygare remainder by Bond bearing date 8th April 1734	02-00-00
Also from Mr. Edward Herbert by mortgage	100-00-00
Also from John Powell of Pantreig? by note	10-00-00
Also from William John Lewis of St Brides by note	02-00-00
Also from Wm Pedwardine? of Whitchurch by note	04-08-06
Also from John Cary of Cardiffe by note	01-11-00
Also from William Davies Coytre by note	05-08-00
Also from Lewis William of Kellygare by note	03-05-00
Also from James Williams Esquire the remainder by note	03-03-00

Also   Book Debts due to the deceased from the severall persons following

Ann Nicholas of Sully	00-10-00
Alice John of Ruddry	00-19-01
Christopher Price of Cardiff	00-17-00
Mrs Elizabeth Burrow of Cardiffe	00-15-09
Morgan Griffith of Cardiff	02-13-06
John Thomas of Caerphilly	00-18-05 ½
John Howard of Halfird	00-03-06
Jenkin Howard of Roath	00-07-07 ½
The Widow Gibbon of Whichurch	00-04-00
John Morgan Shingrig Carrwck Eglws Ilan	00-07-07
William Edwards of Kellygare	00-08-06
Mrs Jones of Lanederne	04-04-02
Jennett Butler of Cadoxton	00-10-00
Jennett Morgan of Maindu	00-12-01
Morgan Griffith Minister	00-08-05
James Williams Esquire	04-16-00
Ann Jones of Michaelston le pitt	01-04-03
William the Miller of Whitchurch	00-04-00
James Jones of Cardiffe	05-08-00
John William of Penylan	00-01-09
John Jervis of Whitchurch	00-05-05

David Lewis of Kevrn coed Weaun?	00-08-03
David Thomas of Rumney	00-04-00
David Lewis of Fairwater	00-06-04½
David Davies of Canton	00-01-05
Daniel Morgan Griffith yᵉ old Furnace	00-06-03
David Griffiths of Carphilly	01-11-06
Edward Hughes of Radyr	00-02-02
Edward Woods of Cardiffe	00-04-00
Edward William David of Rumney	00-03-07½
Edward Hughes of Radyr more	00-01-06
Evan Morgan of Lanwonno	00-08-00
Evan Morgan of Pentirch	00-07-00
Edward William of Lisvane lent to his wife	00-05-00
Edward Morgan, Park in Eglws Ilan	00-04-03
Edmund Harry of Whitchurch	00-01-09½
Evan Thos Howell Whitchurch	00-03-00
Edward Robins of Penarth	00-16-00½
Evan Harman of Whitchurch	01-11-00
Edward Morgan Lewis of Carphilly	00-09-02
Edmund Lewis of Lanvabon	00-05-00
Edmund Williams of Kellygare Hopnwick?	00-07-00
Evan Howell of Chapel	00-07-00
Francis William of Wrinston	00-08-07½
Edmund David of Lisvaen	00-02-00
Elizabeth Thomas of Cadoxton	01-12-06
Evan William his brother	00-13-06
Edward Lewis of Waun Treoda	04-00-00
Evan William of Lancross	01-04-00
Evan Thomas of Aber in Eglws Ilan	02-03-00
Mʳ Lloyd of Cardiffe	00-14-02
Edward William Howel of Rumpney	00-17-00
Griffith Price of Lidmor Miller	00-07-00
George Prury of Cardiffe	01-01-06
Margarett John of Hensol widow	00-03-10
George Watkin Carpenter at yᵉ great Bridge	00-01-09
widow Hamerston of Lanederne	02-00-09
George William's widow Pantmawr	00-19-00
George Hassill of Cardiffe	00-07-03
George Rosser of Cadoxton	00-03-06

Howell William of Carphilly	00-17-00
Thos Harry Thomas of Whitchurch	00-19-00
Henry John Edward of Lisvaen	00-04-10
Joseph the Racer of Eglws Ilan	00-01-01
John Lewis of Landaffe	01-09-00
John Morgan of Cardiffe	00-13-06
Catherine Lewis of Pentirch	00-08-00
widow Lloyd of St Mellans	00-04-05
Lewis Thos Miller of Energlyn	01-04-00
Lewis Evan of Castletown	00-02-00
Mrs Morgan of Greenway	00-10-06
Lewis David the Dyer	00-02-00
Lewis Gibbs of Pencottry	01-14-00
Lewis Gibbs of Pencottry more	00-12-04
William Jones of Penypeel	00-01-03
Mr Nathaniel Wells of Cardiffe	01-04-00
Miles Thomas of Cardiffe	01-12-00
Morgan Evan John of Eglws Ilan	00-13-03
William Thomas of ye five Bells	05-09-00
William Thomas Besom maker Whitchurch	00-03-06
William Thomas of Nantgarw	00-01-06
Mary Miller of Pentirch	00-02-00
Mary William of Porthkerry	01-01-00
William Evan of Bedwas Tanner	00-13-01 ½
Owen David of Whitchurch	00-01-00
Widdow Morgans of Lanishen	01-16-01
John William Prythrch of Bedwas	00-03-06
Morgan John was Nantgarw in Eglws Ilan	00-05-03
Morgan Powell of Lecquith	00-02-00
William Lewis of Michaelston le pitt	00-07-00
William Jenkin of Barry	00-04-06
William Evan Rosser of Wedal	00-10-00 ½
William Elbrid of Lanilltern	00-16-00
Philip Jones of Cardiffe	00-02-00
Mr Philips the Keeper	02-03-11
Mr Wilson	01-00-00
Henry Jones Tyler	00-08-00
Rosser Jeremiah of St Mellans	00-06-01
Rowland Thomas of ye Cathays	00-04-04

Rees Howell of Roath	02-02-00
Rees William Water of Lanishen	00-16-00
Richard Evan Morgan of Ynis y Bool	00-08-00
Rowland Lewis of Bedwas	00-06-00
Rees Howell of Kellygare	01-06-06
Richard Morgan of Pentirch	00-05-00
William Stephen of Whitchurch	01-02-09
Rowland Christopher of Nantgarw	00-10-05
Roger Morgan of Llwyn in Lantrissant	00-17-06
Sarah Jones of ye weighouse	00-03-00
Thomas Llewellyn his brother in law	11-10-00
Thomas Miles Penylan in Roath	00-04-00
Thomas David of St Mary parish	01-04-02
Thomas Richard of Whitchurch	00-02-07
Thomas Anthony of Kruecarne?	00-06-03
Thomas Evan of St Georges	00-04-03
Thomas Jones of St Mellans	00-01-00
Thomas Harry Peterston sup Ely	00-04-00
Thomas Evan of Lantwitt vaidre Butcher	00-17-00
Thomas Hopkin of Porthkerry	00-08-00
Thomas Glascott	00-13-06
Thomas Webb of Swanbridge	00-01-09
William Rowland of Lisvaen	00-07-00
William Philips of Cardiffe shoemaker	00-05-06
William Jenkin of Cardiffe shoemaker	04-01-00
William Llewellyn of Lanedern	00-08-03
William Thomas of Lancarvan	02-11-00
Mr Williams ye parson Penarth	00-10-00
William Gabriel of Whitchurch	00-06-00
William Evan of Caephilly	01-04-08
Gwenllian Hedges widow	00-09-04 ½
Henry William of Caerphilly	00-11-11
Morgan Howell of Lancross	00-06-02
Margarett William widow of Wm Thomas of Eglws Ilan	00-03-06
William Pedwardine Whitchurch Whitchurch	04-02-00
William Edward of Park in EglwsIlan	00-04-06
John Sweet jun[ior] on account of Mr Smith ye parson of Eglws Ilan	00-03-09
John Jones of Cadoxton's widow	00-12-09

his Sister Ann	02-05-00
James William of Penywain	04-14-06
Eleanor Griffith of Cardiffe	02-02-00
John Cary Taylor	01-07-00
William Lewis Skrivner?	02-04-00
George Lewis perriwigg maker lent	01-01-00

Desperate Debts due to ye Deceased from the severall persons following that is to say

From Anthony William Eglws Ilan by by note	01-16-06
Howell William of Carphilly remainder by note	02-11-06
James Jones of Cardiffe by note	02-00-00
James Philip of Landaffe by note	00-19-00
John Rees of St Nicholas by note	01-14-00
By another note	01-00-02
Sarah Jones of Cardiffe by note	04-00-00
William Lewis by note	03-14-00
John Richard late of Canton by note	00-15-07
Sum total	482-05-10

December 2nd 1735   Sworn by Martha Williams, widow, before Wm. Morgan, surrogate

Administration Bond: Hopkin William, innkeeper: 2nd December, 1735

In the Consistory Court of Llandaff, 2nd December, 1735, administration of the goods of Hopkin William, innkeeper, deceased, was granted to his widow, Martha Williams. Martha Williams, William Edmonds of the parish of Baslegg, Monmouthshire, yeoman, and Evan William of the parish of Cadoxton juxta Barry, yeoman, were bound by the Court in the sum of £900 for Martha Williams to make and exhibit a true inventory of the goods and credits of her late husband before the last day of February next, to administer according to law, to render a true account of her administration at or before the 2nd December, 1736, and to present to the Court any last will and testament of the deceased that might appear. Evan William signed the administration bond, and both Martha Williams and William Edmonds recorded their mark.

[National Library of Wales Document Reference: LL/ 1735/ 25]

Inventory and Valuation of the Goods & Chattels of Catherine Powell deceased, late of the "Cefn Mabley Arms" in the Town of Cardiff

	£ - s - d
Bar-Parlour	
1 Dining Table	01-00-00
1 Small Card Table	00-08-00
7 Common Chairs	00-10-00
1 Tray	00-02-00
Fender and Fire Irons	00-03-00
Old Sofa	00-12-00
4 Common prints	00-02-00
Sitting Room	
2 Tables	02-10-00
Sofa	00-10-06
6 Chairs	00-12-00
1 Round Table	00-10-00
Old Chimney Glass	00-12-00
Sundry small prints	00-03-00
Old Carpet & Rug	00-10-00
Fender and Fire Irons	00-03-06
Little Sitting Room	
Six Common Chairs	00-06-00
Deal Round Table	00-01-06
Fender and fire Irons	00-02-06
Small glass	00-02-00
The Bar	
Bar Fixtures	00-10-06
Beer Engine	01-10-00
Sundry Glass etc.	01-00-00
Sundry Jugs	00-04-00
Sundry Jars etc.	01-00-00
Small Deal Table and 2 Common Rush Chairs	<u>00-03-00</u>
	<u>13-07-06</u>
Bed Room No 1	
Feather Bed, Bolster and 2 pillows	02-10-00
Tent Bedstead and Common Furniture	00-10-00
Round Table	00-08-00
2 Side Ends	00-16-00
Night Commode	00-06-00
Deal Table	00-02-00

Small Swing Glass	00-02-06
Side Deal Cupboard	00-07-06
Common Straight Washstand	00-02-00
One picture	00-03-00
2 Chairs	00-05-00
1 Small Table	00-05-00
Bed Room No 2	
Feather Bed Bolster and pillows, same as in No 1	02-10-00
Tent Bedstead & Furniture	00-10-00
Old Chest of Drawers	00-10-00
Deal Table and Small Glass	00-06-00
4 Common Chairs & upright wash Stand	00-04-00
Bed Room No 3	
Inferior Feather Bed & 2 pillows	02-00-00
Tent Bedstead	00-05-06
Small Deal Table	00-02-00
Bed Room No 4	
Two inferior Beds	02-10-00
Two Bedsteads	00-08-00
Old Deal Drawers	00-07-00
Lumber	<u>00-01-06</u>
	<u>28-18-06</u>
Bed Room No 5	
Two old Beds	01-00-00
Two old Bedsteads	00-07-06
Two old Chests of Drawers	00-15-00
Turnup Bedstead	00-10-00
Three old Chairs	00-04-06
Night Chair, old Fender etc	00-04-00
Kitchen	
Common Settle, deal furn? and Table	01-00-00
Small Cuckoo Clock	00-05-00
Kitchen Requisites	01-10-00
4 Tea Trays	00-07-00
Back Kitchen	
Crockery and Earthen Ware	00-12-06
Culinary Articles	00-14-06
Sundry articles	00-08-00
Brew House	
Sundry Brewing Utensils, with an Iron Boiler	05-10-00

Out door lumber	01-10-00
Bed and Table Linen	07-00-00
Wearing Apparrel	06-00-00
Lease of Ground Recently taken	05-00-00
	61-16-06
Cellar and Stock in Trade	
1 B[arre]l of porter	02-00-00
5 B[arre]l Beer	10-00-00
10 Gallons Rum	07-10-00
4 Gallons Gin	02-02-00
2 Gallons Brandy	03-00-00
1 Gallon Peppermint	00-10-00
1 Gallon Shrub?	00-10-00
2 Gallons Raspberry Brandy	01-00-00
3 Gallons Whisky	02-08-00
Store Casks, together	05-00-00
	95-16-06

I hereby Certify that the above is a correct Inventory & Valuation of the Goods and Chattels of Catherine Powell Deceased, to the best of my judgement and belief, taken this 28th day of November 1838. Charles Sawyer Appraiser   Cardiff

[National Library of Wales Document Reference: LL/ 1839/ 29]

An Inventory and Valuation of the Effects of the late Mr James Morgan of Hills Arms in the parish of St Johns in the Town of Cardiff in the County of Glamorgan Innkeeper who died on the 8th day of June 1845 appraised and valued this 19th day of August 1845 by us Thomas Edwards and Isaac Roberts

In the Parlour 1 Clock	01-10-00
Glasses Jugs & Earthenware in 2 Cupboards	00-10-00
1 Round Table	00-04-00
1 Unig? table	00-10-00
9 chairs	00-18-00
1 Elbow chair	00-02-00
1 old desk	00-02-06
1 Looking Glass	00-05-00
Sundry Small pictures	00-08-00
Fender & Fire Irons	00-05-00

In the Kitchen 2 Settles	00-15-00
2 Chairs	00-04-00
Dresser and Shelves & Plate thereon	00-10-00
Sundries on Mantlepiece	00-09-00
Toaster	00-02-00
Lot of pints Jugs etc	00-06-00
In the Brewhouse 1 Iron Copper	00-15-00
Coolers	01-00-00
1 Brewing Vat	01-13-00
2 Small Casks	00-05-00
1 old Barrel	00-03-00
1 Bucket	00-01-00
1 Sieve	00-01-00
1 Small Boiler	00-04-00
In the Brewing Passage 2 Ha[lf]? Casks	00-05-06
1 Wash Tub	00-01-00
1 Pail	00-00-06
Carried forward	11-11-06
First Room upstairs 1 Bedstead Bed Clothes and furniture	02-00-00
1 Case of Drawers	01-00-00
2 old Boxes	00-02-00
Washing Stand Basin & Ure	00-05-00
1 Bureau	00-05-00
Sundry small articles	00-02-06
1 Looking Glass	00-02-06
Night Commode	00-04-00
3 old Chairs	00 04 00
Second Room upstairs 6 Elbow chairs	00-18-00
5 Tables	01-15-00
Pipe Holder	00-01-06
6 Benches	01-10-00
1 Looking Glass	00-05-00
Third Bed Room Upstairs 1 washhand Stand Basin & Ure	00-05-00
1 Bedstead	00-10-00
1 Tray	00-01-06
2 Chairs	00-02-00
Fourth Bed Room Upstairs 1 Bedstead Bed & Clothes	02-00-00
5 Chairs	00-10-00
Chest upon Chest	00-04-00

1 old Bureau	00-03-00
2 old Pictures	00-04-00
1 old Looking Glass	00-06-00
Carried forward	24-02-04
In the Store room 1 Stump Bedstead & Flock Bed	00-15-00
1 Bedstead and feather Bed etc.	01-10-00
1 Malt Mill	00-18-00
2 old Chairs	00-01-06
1 Bushel measure	00-05-00
Sundry Rakes etc.	00-08-00
In the Cellar 3 Barrels of Beer	04-10-00
5 Barrel Casks	00-18-00
2 Half Barrel Casks	00-06-00
3 Stillings	00-06-00
In the Yard 1 Water Cask	00-06-00
2 Carts	08-00-00
2 Pails & Lumber	00-02-00
1 Waggon	05-00-00
1 Drawl Cart	01-15-00
In the Stable 1 old Barrel	00-01-06
Shovels etc.	00-01-06
3 Horses	18-00-00
3 Sets of Harness	05-00-00
Spirits in the House	06-00-00
Wearing Apparel	02-00-00
	80-05-10

Witness

The mark of Thomas X Edwards   Isaac Roberts   Jnº Williams Cardiff

[National Library of Wales Document Reference: LL/ 1845/ 42]

Valuation of the Household Goods and Furniture Plate Linen and China Wearing Apparel   Jewels   Trinkets and Stock in Trade of the late Mʳ John Nisbett who died at Cardiff in the county of Glamorgan on the Sixteenth day of August 1846.

Household Goods and Furniture   Dresser, 7 Candlesticks, Tub,
   Fender & Fire Irons, Tea Urn, Arm Chair, Table, Coffee Pot &
   Toast rack Windsor Blinds, 14 Chairs, Fender & Fire Irons, Sofa,
   3Mah[ogan]y Tables, 4 Cane Chairs, 8 Birch Chairs, Fender &

Fire Irons Mah[ogan]y Table, Fender, 11 Chairs, Settle, Oak
Table, Curtains,3 Settles, 3 L. Tables, Fender & fire irons,
4 Chairs, 1 Table and 2 Benches, Board & Gun, Shutter,
6 Chairs, Table, Bedstead, Chest of Drawers, Swing glass, Wash
Stand & Ware, Blind, Clock, Drugget   Bedstead & Do.
Dressing Table, Washing Stand & Ware, 2 Chairs, Pier Glass,
2 Bedsteads, 2 Milpuff Beds, 2 Bolsters, 1 Milpuff Bed,
2 Pillows, Bedstead, Milpuff Bed, Feather Bed & Bolster,
Glass Table, Wash Stand & Ware, 1 Chair, Bedstead &
Furniture, Feather Bed, Table, 2 Bedsteads bed Table.   £31-08-08
Plate Linen & China   6 Teaspoons, 2 Table Spoons,
8 Sheets, 10 Towells   £2-08-00
Wearing Apparel   2 Coats   2 trousers   3 P[ai]rs Shoes
3 Vests   2 hats, 3 neckerchiefs, 6 Pocket Do
2 P[ai]rs drawers, 6 Shirts   £2-10-00
                               Carried forward   £36-06-08
Jewells and Trinkets   1 watch   £1-05-00
Stock in trade   3 motion Beer Engine, 30 pints & ½ Pints,
6 Quart Jugs, 7 Pint Jugs, 15 Glasses, 8 Decanters, 10 ales,
10 wines, Set of Pewter Measures, 4 Spirit Casks, 11 Spittoons,
Tobacco Box, 9 Barrel Casks, 1 ½ barrel Cask, 1 9 Gallon
Cask, 3 Jars, Mashing Vat, Sieve   Shutes   Tundish, 2 Buckets
2 Coolers 5 Tubs 1 Pail   Iron Boiler Bench Skittles &
Bowl Boiler   2 Tubs & Bench Skittle Boards Sundries
4 Spirit Casks 3 Spirit Casks   7 Stillings   20 Gallons Gin,
6 Gallons Rum   4 Gallons Whiskey, 2 Gallons Peppermint,
6 Barrels Beer   1? Gall[on] Brandy   £45-04-08
                                             Total £82-16-04
Thomas Watkins, Appraisor, 19th September, 1846

Schedule of debts due from the Estate of the late Mr John Nisbett at the time of his decease.

Vallance & Co. Brewers	61-00-00
George Pinchin & Co. Brewers	22-00-00
H Grey Bath Brewers	17-05-00
Hens & Sons Spirit Merchants	42-18-09
David Evans & Sons	05-08-00
Pardoe – Pipes	01-06-00
Coleman – Lemonade	01-14-00

Bryant - Ginger Beer	01-06-00
Thos Evans surgeon	10-00-00
Wm Bird – Acct. papers	00-15-00
Servants Wages	03-00-00
Assessed taxes	03-10-00
Gas Co.	03 00 00
John Biggs ¼ rent of house	10-00-00
Total amount	183-16-09

Administration Bond: John Nisbett, victualler: 16th August, 1846
In the Consistory Court of Llandaff, before Richard Prichard, surrogate, 1st October, 1846, administration of the goods etc. of John Nisbett, victualler, deceased, who died on the 16th August, 1846, was granted to his widow, Charlotte Nisbett. Charlotte Nisbett, John Biggs, sprit dealer, and John Edwards, accountant, both of the Town of Cardiff, were sworn by the Court in the sum of £600 for Charlotte Nisbett to exhibit a true inventory of the goods etc. of her late husband on or before the last day of April next, to administer according to law, to give a just account of her administration on or before the last day of October, 1847, and to present to the Court any last will and testament of the deceased that might appear. The administration bond was signed by all three boundens.
[National Library of Wales Document Reference: LL/ 1846/ 45]

Will of Richard Powell, vintner, proved 12th September, 1661
In the name of god amen. I Richard Powell of the towne of Cowbridge vintner weake of bodie butt of p[er]fect memorie doe make this my last will and testament bequeathing my soule into the handes of god my Creator through the only merits of Jesus Christ my blessed Redeemer and my body to the earth from whence if Came to bee buried in xtian burial and my goodes to bee disposed of in forme following Always reserving first that my whole debts bee payed by my welbeloved wife
Impr[rimis] I give and bequeath forty shillings to Thomas Yorath the sonn of John Yorath. Item one pound Eight shillings to Thomas Jenkins the sonne of Jane Wear Item fowere pounds to Johan Hyett the daughter of Griffith Hyett of Siginston.
Item to the Church of Landaph two shillings Item to the Church of Cowbridge five shillings and Mr. Davies minister of the said towne ten shillings

Item to the poore of the said towne twelve shillings in bread to be payed by 12^d monthly yearly for ever to be payed by the house of the Crosse of the said town of Commonly called the oake penthouse.

Item I leave and bequeath my mothers main ten acres to my wife in case shee survives her husband   Item I give and bequeath to my Nephew Richard Powell after my wifes death the said house by the Crosse and my Nephew Roger Powell after my wifes life all my right and title w[i]thin the Lordship of Tallavan to my Lands and house there.

Item I give and bequeath to my Nephew Miles Powell after my wifes death the two houses w[i]thout the westorne-gate of this said towne of Cowbridge moreover I hereby order that my wife pay my brother Lewis Powell twelve pounds in Consideration of the Lands in the parishe att the first parting and her the said Lewis and twenty pounds more to bee payed the same Lewis by my said wife the same tyme of parting for hime to enjoy the benedfitt of the due life? thereof only provided the premises remaine and returned to his daughter Anne Powell after his death.

Item I further give and bequeath to the s[ai]d Anne …[lost].. poundes money to be payed by my nephew Richard Powell or ye Survivor in possession of the house by the Cross

Item I give and bequeath to Thomas Hyett sonne of Sixio Hyett two pounds to be payed by Richard Powell my Nephew or the Survivor of him in possession of the said house by the Cross when the s[ai]d Thomas Hyett shall arrive to the age of twelve yeares.

Item it is hereby my last will and testam[en]t that my wife Anne Powell & Richard Powell my nephew bee Cooperated of this my Last will & testament in forme aforesaid; (my debts first payed & satisfied)

Item I give and bequeath to my stepfather Howell Evan the remainder of the Lease w[i]thin and by the westerne gate of the said towne in Case hee Survive my mother & if hee and my mother should not live to weare out the terme of the Remainder of the said yeares I give the enjoym[en]t to my brother Lewis.

Item I leave and bequeath to my brother in law Griffith Hyett all my wearing apparel (excepting my best suite and coate and two shirts w[hi]ch I leave to my brother Lewis Powell

Lastly I ordain Robert Thomas of Lanmihangell Esq[uire] John Broadway of Bristoll vintner and Evan Jenkin of Treganllaw to be overseers of this my Last will

Proved 12th September, 1661, before Jenkins Williams, surrogate.

[National Library of Wales Document Reference: LL/ 1661/ 26]

Appendices

1. The Inventory of James Harries of the Town of Usk, mercer/chandler/general shopkeeper, 1692.

2. The Inventory, List of Debts and Administration Bond of Jennet John of the parish of Llancarvan, 1733.

3. A Record in Tabular Form of the Information from each Inventory relating to the seven major categories of wealth – Clothing: Household Goods: Farm Crops/Livestock/Farm Machinery: Trade Goods: Debt: Ready Money: Leases: – converted into a Cash Value and into a percentage of total estate.

4 Charts Exploring the Relationship Between Total Value of Estate and (i) Value of Clothing; (ii) Value of Household Goods; and (iii) Debt.

Appendix 1

A true & Perfect Inventory of all & Singular ye goods chattels rights & Creditts of James Harries late of the Town of Usk in ye County of Monmouth Dece[ase]d appraised by us ye persons Subscribing ye Appraisors named and sworn for ye appraisem[en]t of ye same by virtue of a Comicon forth of ye Consistory Court of ye Diocesse of Landaffe ye Sixteenth Day of August Anno Domini 1692: as followeth

	li - s - d
Inp[ri]mis the said Decead[en]ts wearing apparell valued att	03-00-00
Item 28 ounces & ¼ Silver plate att 4s.8d.per oz [ounce]	06-11-10
Item 11: yards of Iron Gray broad Cloth att 4s. p[er] y[ar]d	02-04-00
Item 10: y[ar]ds. & ½ broad Cloth att 8s. p[er] yard	04-04-00
Item 4: yards of red broad Cloth att 3s.9d. p[er] yard	00-15-00
Item 4: yards of black Cloth in 2 remnants att 7s. p[er] y[ar]d	01-08-00
Item 7: yards of black Cloth att 4s. p[er] y[ar]d. in 2 Remnants	01-08-00
Item a remnant of black Broad cloth containing 5: yards att 2s.6d. p[er] yard	00-12-06
Item 12: yards of broad Cloth att 4s.6d. p[er] yard	02-14-00
Item 12: yards of black Cloth att 5s. p[er] yard	03-00-00
Item in ready money	01-10-00
Item 6: yards of Grey Broad Cloth att 6s. p[er] yard	01-16-00
Item 10: yards of dark Cloth att 4s 6d. p[er] yard	02-05-00
Item 7: yards of Cloth att 5s. p[er] yard	01-15-00
Item 3: yards ¾ of Light Coloured Cloth att 4s.6d. p[er] [yard]	00-16-10½
Item 8: yards of Broad Cloth att 4s. p[er] y[ar]d	01-12-00
Item 8: yards of Broad Cloth att 4s. p[er] y[ar]d	01-12-00
Item 2: yards of cloth in two remnants att 4s. p[er] y[ar]d	00-08-00
Item a remnant of Cloth of 2: yards & ½ att 3s.4d. p[er] [yard]	00-08-04
Item 7: yards of Cloth in two remnants att 4s. 6d. p[er] [yard]	01-11-06

Appendix 1

Item 4: y[ar]ds. ½ of fine Grey Cloth att 7s. p[er] y[ar]d	01-11-06
Item 4: y[ar]ds. of Grey Cloth att 5s. p[er] y[ar]d	01-00-00
Item 3: yards of Cloth in 2 remnants att 4s. p[er] y[ar]d	00-12-00
Item one piece of Druggett at	01-00-00
Item 11: yards of Shalloone in 5: remnants att 10d. p[er] y[ar]d	00-09-02
Item 22: yards of Shalloone att 14d. p[er] y[ar]d	01-05-08
Item 22: yards of shalloone att 15d. p[er] yard	01-07-06
Item 8: yards of Shalloone in 2 remnants att 10d. p[er] y[ar]d	00-06-08
Item 6: yards ¾ of Serge att 18d. p[er] y[ar]d	00-10-01½
Item 17: yards Serge att 14d. p[er] y[ar]d	00-19-10
Item 6: yards of Serge in 3: remnants att 1s. p[er] y[ar]d	00-06-00
Item 33: y[ar]ds ½ of Serge att 15d. p[er] yard	02-01-10½
Item 16: yards of black Serge att 16d. p[er] y[ar]d	01-01-04
Item 14: y[ar]ds ½ of Serge att 15d. p[er] y[ar]d	00-18-01½
Item 15: yards of Serge in 2 remnants att 13d. p[er] y[ar]d	00-16-03
Item 16: yards ½ of Serge att 15d. p[er] y[ar]d	01-00-07½
Item 16: y[ar]ds ½ of Serge att 18d. p[er] y[ar]d	01-04-09
Item 8: yards & ½ of Cheyney att 1s. p[er] y[ar]d	00-08-06
Item 10: yards & ½ of Serge att 15d. p[er] yard	00-13-01½
Item 9: y[ar]ds of Serge att 14d. p[er] y[ar]d	00-10-06
Item 14: y[ar]ds of Serge att 2s. 2d. p[er] y[ar]d	01-10-04
Item 16: yds. of Serge att 14d. p[er] yard	00-15-08
Item 10: yds. ½ of Serge att 2s. p[er] y[ar]d	01-01-00
Item 7: yards & ½ of Serge att 16d. p[er] y[ar]d	00-10-00
Item 15: yards & ½ of Serge att 18d. p[er] y[ar]d	01-03-03
Item 6: yards & ½ of Serge att 18d. p[er] yard	00-09-09
Item 3: yards ¾ of Serge att 1s. 8d. p[er] y[ar]d	00-06-03
Item 20: yards of Cloth Serge att 20d. p[er] y[ar]d	02-00-00
Item 7: yards of Pennystone? att 1s. 2d. p[er] y[ar]d	00-08-02
Item 18: yards & ½ of worsteed Farrandine att 11d. p[er] y[ar]d	00-16-11½
Item 13: yards of Grey Serge att 1s. 9d. p[er] yard	01-02-09
Item 4: yards & ½ of Serge att 15d. p[er] y[ar]d	00-05-07½
Item 2: yards of Lempiterneim? att 9d. p[er] y[ar]d	<u>00-01-06</u>
	68-09-10
Item 2: remnants of Cloth att	00-04-00
Item 7: y[ar]ds ¾ of Haire Camlett att 3s. p[er] yard	01-03-03

241

Item 8: yards of haire Camelett att 2s.4d. p[er] yard	00-18-08
Item 4: yards & ½ Serge att 14d. p[er] yard	00-05-03
Item 8: yards of haire Camelett att 3s. p[er] yard	01-04-00
Item 5: yards of Serge in remnants att 15d.	00-06-03
Item 4: yards of Serge in 2 remnants att 1s. p[er] y[ar]d	00-04-00
Item 47: yards of worsted Camlett att 10d. p[er] y[ar]d	01-19-02
Item 38: yards of Camlett att 8d. p[er] y[ar]d	01-05-04
Item 16: yards & ½ of black Camlett att 1s.2d. p[er] y[ar]d	00-19-03
Item 8: yards of Camlett att 10d. p[er] yard	00-06-08
Item 5: yards of black Primella? att 1s. 6d. p[er] y[ar]d	00-07-06
Item 2: yards ¾ of Barrenetto att 14d. p[er] yard	00-03-02½
Item 16: yards & ½ of Stuffe att 8d. y[ar]d	00-11-00
Item 8: yards of Parragon att 1s. p[er] yard	00-08-00
Item 2: remnants of Camelett att	00-03-00
Item 14: y[ar]ds ½ Silk & worsteed Stuffe att 1s. p[er] y[ar]d	00-14-06
Item 19: y[ar]ds ½ Stript. Silk & woollen Crape att 10d. p[er] y[ar]d	00-16-03
Item 17: y[ar]ds Striped Silk Crape att 10d. p[er] y[ar]d	00-14-02
Item 14: y[ar]ds ½ of silk & worsted Diamond att 1s.2d. p[er] y[ar]d	00-16-11
Item 19: y[ar]ds ½ striped Nectorella att 1s. p[er] y[ar]d	00-19-06
Item 15: y[ar]ds Silk & worsteed Diamond att 13d. p[er] [yard]	00-16-03
Item 4: y[ar]ds of Silk & worsteed Stuffe att 14d. p[er] [yard]	00-04-08
Item 18: y[ar]ds ¼ Strip't Crisp? att 1s. 6d. p[er] [yard]	01-07-04½
Item 3: y[ar]ds ¼ of y[e] same in two remnants att 14d p[er] [yard]	00-03-09½
Item 6: yards Silke & worsteed Ware att 1s.4d p[er] [yard]	00-08-00
Item 17: y[ar]ds black & white Silk Stuffe att 1s.6d p[er] y[ar]d	01-05-06
Item 9: y[ar]ds Barrenetto att 1s. p[er] yard	00-09-00
Item 11: y{ar}ds strip't Silk Crape att 9d. p[er] yard	00-08-03
Item 20: y[ar]ds strip't Stuffe att 10d. p[er] y[ar]d	00-16-08
Item 7: y[ar]ds & ¼ strip't Silk Crape att 9d p[er] y[ar]d	00-05-05½
Item 9: y[ar]ds Silke & worsteed Stuffe att 1s. 2d. p[er] yd.	00-10-06
Item 8: y[ar]ds ¾ of silk Barrenetto att 1s. 2d. p[er] [yard]	00-10-02½
Item ? yds. of worsteed Toy? att ….. [crease in original]	00-12-06
Item 17: y[ar]ds ½ of Damask Stuffe att 1s. 2d. p[er] y[ar]d	01-00-05

Appendix 1

Item 22: y[ar]ds ½ of Druggett att 11d. p[er] y[ar]d	01-00-07½
Item 7: y[ar]ds of Pranella att 1s. 3d. p[er] y[ar]d	00-08-09
Item 9: y[ar]ds of Druggett att 10d. p[er] y[ar]d	00-07-06
Item 11: y[ar]ds of worsted Stuffe att 9d. p[er] y[ar]d	00-08-03
Item 14: y[ar]ds of Stuffe att 7d. p[er] y[ar]d	00-08-02
Item 9: y[ar]ds of Stuffe att 9d. p[er] y[ar]d	00-06-09
Item 27: y[ar]ds of Crape att 10d. p[er] y[ar]d	01-02-06
Item 7: Ells of Flannen att 1s. p[er] Ell	00-07-00
Item 6: y[ar]ds of flannen att 10d. p[er] y[ar]d	00-05-00
Item 5: y[ar]ds ½ of Tammy att 11d. p[er] y[ar]d	00-05-00½
Item 14: y[ar]ds & ½ of worsteed Toy at 6d. p[er] y[ar]d	00-07-03
Item 1 y[ar]d ⅞ of Braided Guernsay att 12d. p[er] y[ar]d	00-01-10½
Item 13 y[ar]ds ½ of Stuffe att 7d. p[er] y[ar]d	00-07-10½
Item 23: y[ar]ds ½ Strip't Tamarine att 13d. p[er] y[ar]d	01-05-05½
Item in remnants of Stuffe shalloome & serge 8 y[ar]ds att 10d.	00-06-08
Item 4: y[ar]ds of red Serge att 2s. 2d. p[er] y[ar]d	00-08-08
Item 17: y[ar]ds of Tammy att 10d.	00-14-02
Item 29: y[ar]ds & ½ Black Crape att 8d. p[er] y[ar]d	00-19-08
Item 36: y[ar]ds Coloured Fustian att 8d. p[er] y[ar]d	01-04-00
Item 10: y[ar]ds of Fustian att 5d.	00-04-02
Item 7: y[ar]ds ½ of fustian Buff coloured att 8d. p[er] y[ar]d	00-05-00
Item 20: y[ar]ds ¼ of fine Jeane? att 1s. p[er] y[ar]d	01-00-03
Item 13 y[ar]ds of white fustian att 7d. p[er] y[ar]d	00-07-07
Item 11 y[ar]ds of Tufted Fustian att 6d. p[er] y[ar]d	00-05-06
Item 4: y[ar]ds of Tufted holland att 1s. p[er] y[ar]d	00-04-00
Item 43 y[ar]ds of blew harford att 6½d. p[er] y[ar]d	01-03-03
Item 18 y[ar]ds ½ of Strip't Linen att 7d. p[er] y[ar]d	00-10-09
Item 11 y[ar]ds narrow Coloured Linnen att 6d. p[er] y[ar]d	00-05-06
Item 19 y[ar]ds ¾ of Callico att 10d. p[er] y[ar]d	00-16-05
Item in remnants of Coloured Linnen and fustian	00-11-00
Item 12: y[ar]ds ½ of Scotch Lawne att 11d. p[er] y[ar]d	00-11-05
Item 3: y[ar]ds of Camerick att 2s. 6d. p[er] y[ar]d	00-07-06
Item 4: ells ⅞ of white Corded Sarsinett att 7s. p[er] ell	01-14-01
Item 19: ells ½ of Tabby in remnants att 3s.3d. p[er] ell	03-03-04
Item 23: ells ½ of French Sarsinett att 2s.4d. p[er] ell	<u>02-14-10</u>
	<u>48-07-11½</u>

243

Item 7: y[ar]ds ¼ of flowered Silke att 2s. 6d. p[er] y[ar]d	00-18-01½
Item remnants of silk	00-05-00
Item 13: y[ar]ds of narrow Lace att 1s. 2d. p[er] y[ar]d	00-15-02
Item 10: y[ar]ds ½ of white Swanskin att 14d. p[er] y[ar]d	00-12-03
Item 17: y[ar]ds ¾ German Linnen att 10d. p[er] y[ar]d	00-14-09½
Item 24: y[ar]ds ½ of Bowdy Cheams? att 1s. 8d. p[er] y[ar]d	02-00-10
Item 2: y[ar]ds of Rhoane Canvas att 1s. 6d. p[er] y[ar]d	00-03-00
Item 6: Ells of bagg holland att 3s. 6d. p[er] ell	01-01-00
Item 5: ells & ¼ of Izingham holland att 2s. 6d.	00-13-01½
Item 5: y[ar]ds ½ of Callico att 1s. 4d. p[er] y[ar]d	00-07-04
Item 5: ells & ¼ of holland at 2s. p[er] ell	00-10-06
Item 4: y[ar]ds ¼ of haire shag att 2s. 6d. p[er] y[ar]d	00-10-07½
Item Some remnants of shag att	00-12-00
Item 4: Bodices & 3: stomingers att	00-05-06
Item 22 y[ar]ds of white worsteed Lace att 8d. p[er] y[ar]d	00-14-05
Item 30 y[ar]ds of the same att 4d. p[er] y[ar]d	00-10-00
Item 13 pair of Youths hose att 22d. p[er] paire	01-03-10
Item 10 Groce of Buttons att 1s. 8d. p[er] Groce	00-16-08
Item 5: Groce of Buttons att 3s. 6d. p[er] groce	00-17-06
Item 3: Groce of Buttons att 3s. p[er] Groce	00-09-00
Item 4 Groce of Buttons att 14d. p[er] Groce	00-04-08
Item 6: Groce of Brest Gimp att 8d. p[er] Groce	00-04-00
Item 1: Groce of haire buttons att 2s. 4d.	00-02-04
Item 11: groce of haire Buttons att 1s. 6d. p[er] Groce	00-16-00
Item 6: Groce of haire buttons att 1s. 8d. p[er] Groce	00-10-00
Item 2: Groce & 5 Dozen of frost buttons att 7d. p[er] Groce	00-16-11
Item 1: Groce of frost Buttons att 6s.	00-06-00
Item a parcell of Gold & Silver Buttons att	00-10-00
Item more in Buttons	00-02-00
Item 14 pound of thread att 1s.8d. p[er] pound	01-03-04
Item 4: y[ar]ds of Gold & silver Lace att 16d. p[er] y[ar]d	00-05-04
Item 7 ounces ⅓ of Vouice Silver Lace att 3s.4d. p[er] ounce	01-04-05½
Item 6: oz: ⅛ of Vouice Gold lace att 4s.4d. p[er] oz: [ounce]	01-06-06½
Item 1 oz. of Vouice Gold Button hole thred att 3s.10d. p[er]	00-03-10

Item 1 oz. of Vouice Silver B:tt thred att 4s.10d. p[er] oz:	00-04-10
Item 17: y[ar]ds of Gold & silver lace att 6d. p[er] y[ar]d	00-08-06
Item 11: y[ar]ds of the same att 9d. p[er] y[ar]d	00-08-03
Item remnants of silver lace & Brayde Girdles	00-02-06
Item 15:^li of cutt tobacco att 16d. p[er] li: (pound)	01-00-00
Item halfe a rhaine of paper att	00-03-06
Item 3: Groce & 4 Dozen of pound Galloome att 18s. p[er] Groce	03-00-00
Item 3: Groce & 1 piece of Dozen Galloome att 14s. p[er] Groce	02-05-06
Item remnants of Galloome & Cotton tapes	00-10-00
Item remnants of Ribbin	00-12-00
Item more in remnants of Ribbin	00-15-00
Item 7: pieces of 6d. ferrett att 6s. p[er] piece	02-02-00
Item 2: pieces & 1 dozen of 4d. ferrett att 1s. 8d. p[er] piece	00-11-08
Item 2: Dozen of pound 8d. ferrett at 3s. p[er] dozen	00-06-00
Item 1: piece of figur'd Ribbin att	00-07-00
Item 2: pieces of 12d. Taffaty att 11s. p[er] piece	01-02-00
Item 5: pieces of 6d. Taffaty att 6s. p[er] piece	01-10-00
Item fine thread att	01-00-00
Item in Capps & Cadis	00-08-00
Item 7: pieces of 6d. ferrett att 6s. p[er] piece	02-02-00
Item ¾ pound of Coventry blew thred at 4s. p[er] li.	00-03-00
Item Silk Loop & Laces	00-06-00
Item narrow Breades	00-04-00
Item Jucles tapes Buttons etc.	01-01-06
Item threads & Laces	00-07-00
Item a parcell of Small bookes	01-02-01 ½
Item in Stitching & sowing Silke	00-10-00
Item in thread & Mockadge Ends	01-06-10
Item 6: Dozen of Cards att 14d. p[er] Dozen	00-07-00
Item Six Papers of Tape att 20d. p[er] paper	00-10-00
Item 9: papers of white Tape att 2s. 2d. p[er] paper	00-19-06
Item 5: papers of tape att 18d. p[er] paper	00-07-06
Item 6: papers of tape att 20d. p[er] paper	00-10-00
Item Woollen & Irish hose	01-00-06
Item hooks & eyes	<u>00-02-00</u>
	<u>49-12-01</u> ¾

Item Spectacle Cases	00-01-06
Item Knifes Sheathes Inkhorns & Comb Cases	00-02-04
Item 1 pound & 2: ounces of Cynnamon att 8s. p[er] li. [pound]	00-09-00
Item Druggs & Spice in ye Boxes	00-08-00
Item 3: Dozen of Wickyarne at 6d. p[er] Dozen	00-18-00
Item 17 ^li of hemp at 1s. p[er] li.	00-17-00
Item Copperas & Starch	00-01-03
Item 43 ^li of tobacco att 7d. p[er] li.	01-05-01
Item 4 ^li of Wickyarne att 6d. p[er] li.	00-02-00
Item in twine & Cords	00-00-03
Item 9 ^li & ½ of Roll Tobacco att 7½d. p[er] li.	00-05-11 ¼
Item 12 ^li ½ of Roll Tobacco att 7½d. p[er] li.	00-07-09 ¼
Item 2 ^li of Cutt Tobacco att 16d. p[er] li.	00-02-08
Item a p[ar]cell of Tobacco Pipes att	00-01-04
Item 30 ^li ¼ of Cutt Tobacco att 20d. p[er] li.	02-10-05
Item 5: ^li of White Starch att 3d. p[er] li.	00-01-03
Item 3: Gallons of Vinegar att 10d. p[er] Gallon	00-02-06
Item 3 Boxes with sev[er]all remnants of buttons att	03-00-00
Item a parcell of small Cords a Curry Comb & 2 lanthorns	00-04-06
Item 8: Gallons of English Spiritts att 2s.6d. p[er] Gallon	01-00-00
Item 4: Coverlids att 2s.6d. Each	00-10-00
Item 3: plaine Truckle bed Ruggs att 3s. each	00-09-00
Item 1 woollsett Rugg att	00-07-00
Item 2: Ditto att 8s. each	00-16-00
Item one other Rugg att	00-09-00
Item two Brushes att	00-00-03
Item 12: yards of shagg att 12d. p[er] y[ar]d	00-12-00
Item 9: yards ½ of shagg att 18d. p[er] y[ar]d	00-14-03
Item 7: yards ½ of Kersey att 2s. p[er] y[ar]d	00-15-00
Item 19: y[ar]ds ½ of narrow Ticke att 1s. p[er] y[ar]d	00-19-06
Item 22: y[ar]ds of Ticke att 15d. p[er] y[ar]d	01-07-06
Item 5: yards of Teek att 18d. p[er] y[ar]d	00-07-06
Item 10 y[ar]ds of Teek att 8d. p[er] y[ar]d	00-06-08
Item 6: y[ar]ds ¾ of Canvas att 14d. p[er] y[ar]d	00-07-10 ½
Item 9: ells & ½ of broad Ozenbriggs att 9d. p[er] ell	00-07-01 ½
Item 11 ells & _ Ditto att 8d. p[er] ell	00-07-08
Item 29: ells Ditto att 8½d. p[er] ell	01-00-06 ½
Item 10 ells of broad Dowlas att 22d. p[er] ell	00-18-04

Item 6: y[ar]ds Ditto att 1s. p[er] y[ar]d	00-06-00
Item 6: ells Ditto att 20d. an ell	00-10-00
Item 13: y[ar]ds Ditto att 1s. p[er] y[ar]d	00-13-00
Item a remnant of Strip'd Linnen att 3s.6d.	00-03-06
Item 7: y[ar]ds of Buckram att 7d. p[er] y[ar]d	00-04-01
Item 3 y[ar]ds & ½ Ditto att 10d. p[er] y[ar]d	00-02-11
Item remnants of Linnen & stuffe att	01-12-00
Item 13 Sacks att 2s. each	01-06-00
Item 4: Sacks att 2s.10d. Each	00-11-04
Item Candles boxes & twine att	00-04-00
Item 9: yards of Irish frize att 13d. p[er] y[ar]d	00-09-09
Item 5: ells of Course Canvas att 8d. p[er] ell	00-03-04
Item 39 y[ar]ds of bayes in sev[er]all remn[an]ts att 4d.	00-13-00
Item 7: y[ar]ds of Yellow Cotton att 14d. p[er] y[ar]d	00-08-02
Item 12: y[ar]ds of stuffe att 6d. p[er] y[ar]d	00-06-00
Item 6: y[ar]ds of Cotten in remnants att 12d.	00-06-00
Item 6: powderhornes att	00-01-00
Item a Box of brayed buttons att	00-03-00
Item in Inckles & Cadis	00-03-00
Item 2: Collars of Bandileers	00-03-00
Item 6 pound of white soape att 3d. p[er] pound	00-01-06
Item Apothecaries Druggs	01-13-07
Item 7 li ¼ of Galls att	00-03-08
Item 9 brass skales att	00-18-00
Item Brown Paper & Chalk	00-04-00
Item 12 li ½ of brass weights att	00-07-00
Item a brass Mortar weighing 23 li att 8d. p[er] li.[pound]	00-15-04
Item lead weights weighing 1hundredweight 1 quarter 4 pound att 12d. p[er] hundredweight	<u>00-15-05</u>
	<u>37-06-04</u>
Item 1: great Beam & Scales att	00-08-00
Item 8: nests of boxes	01-00-00
Item 4 great Chests, a Counter, Loose boards & boxes	01-00-00
Item 1: old Iron Mortar & Pestle att	00-03-00
In ye Chandling house	
a Copper furnace	02-10-00
600 li of Tallow at 20s. each hundred	06-00-00
1 Brass Scales & brass pounds	00-03-00

Implem[en]ts belonging to ye Chandling room	03-00-00
8: Dozen of Glass bottles at 22d. p[er] Dozen	00-14-08

In ye Chamber over the Shop

1: bedsteed, 1 paire of Curtains & vallenes, 1: rugg Mattresse & cords	01-00-00
3: Ruggs 2: dust beds; 1 feather bed & bolster	02-06-00
1: standing bedsteed & 1 truckle bedsteed	00-10-00
1: new sack, 6: bottomes? of twine & 3: lanthorns	00-06-00
1: pillion & 1: bag of hops	00-10-00

In ye the Great Chamber

2: Ruggs, 1: feather bed & bolster, 3 pillows & one Suite of Curtains & vallens	03-10-00
6: Chairs, a Closestool & pan	02-05-00
1: large Chest 1 table 1 Looking Glass 1: Case of Drawers & 1: trunck	02-06-00
1: Grate tongs & Slice Andirons window Curtains & Curtain Rods	00-12-00

In ye Little Chamber 1: bed 1: boulster 1: Pillow 1: Rugg 1: Suite of Curtains & vallens 3 Chaires & 1: chest	03-05-00
1: Dozen of Diaper Napkins & two table Clothes	00-13-00
1: paire of holland sheets & 21 other sheets	02-05-00
2: holland Pillowbers 10 flaxen & other Pillowbers	00-12-00
1: Dozen of table Clothes & 2 Dozen of Napkins	01-02-00

In ye Parlo 1: Grate 1: paire large brass andirons 2: small tables 6: chaires 1: Looking Glass, 1: hanging shelf 2: Joint Stooles a p[ar]cell of old bookes & 1: cradle etc.	03-00-00

In ye Kitchin & Buttery

21: pewter plates 13 platters 1: Cheese plate, 12: porring[ers] 4 tankards 4: Candlesticks 2: Tin Coffins 2: dripping panns 2: Covers? 3: brass kettles 2: brass potts & 1: brass skillett	05-00-00
1: still 1: brass Candlestick 1: Dog wheel & Spindle 1: Grate, andirons, wickyarne 3 tables 4 spitts Spoons tankards etc. in ye kitchen	01-10-00

In ye stable

Brewing vessells old Dry Casks, boxes & pack sadle old Cradle & small Casks	01-00-00
1: Iron Pott & 1: Iron marment	00-09-00
1: Brandiron	00-02-00
2: Piggs	00-16-00
14: Boards	00-09-04
Pailes & wooden Vessells	00-03-00
Strong water measures	00-04-00
A parcell of Latts	00-14-00
2: smoothing Irons 1: warming pan & 1: frying pan	00-08-00
24^li of Gunpowder att 1s. p[er] li.	01-04-00
1: Gun or fowling piece	00-06-00
6^li. of glue att 4d. p[er] li.	00-02-00
Boards, benches 1 trind w[i]th old Salt baskettes	01-00-00
	52-08-00
Item Earthenware & Glasses att	00-05-00
Debts Due to ye Deced[en]t James Harries att ye time of his death and received by Mary Harris his relict & executrix Since	89-15-11
Book Debts Due to ye said Decead[en]t att his Decease still Due & unpayed	100-01-10
Sume totall is	446-07-00 ½
Appraisers Names Chas. Morgan Tho: Jones	

January the 18th Anno D[omi]ni 1692   This paper writing was this day produced unto Thomas Maddocks, gent[leman], at the time of his examination in the said cause by virtue of a comission for examincon of witnessess then executed by us   Will. Proger   Mordecai Jones   Will. Jenkins

[National Library of Wales Document Reference: LL/ 1692/ 185]

Appendix 2

An Inventory of all & Singular ye Goods, Chattles and Creditts of Jennet John Late of ye p[ar]ish of Lancarvan, in ye County of Glamorgan & Diocess of Landaffe, dec[eas]ed Made, valued, & Apprais'd the 18th of June An[no] Dom[ini] 1733 By ye Appraisers hereunto Subscribed as follows

	£ - s - d
Imp[rimi]s Her Wearing apparel apprais'd to	3 -10- 0
It[em] Twelve Ewes and Lambs at 8^s 6^d p[e]r Couple	5 - 2 - 0
It[em] six dry sheep at 6^s p[e]r	1 -16- 0
It[em] Two Oxen	6 - 0 - 0
It[em] Two Heifers	2 -10- 0
It[em] Four Cows	8 - 0 - 0
It[em] Three Calves	1 -10- 0
It[em] One Mare & Colt	2 -10- 0
It[em] Two feather Beds w[i]th their appurten[an]ces	1 -10- 0
It[em] Brass & Pewter	1 - 1 - 0
It[em] one Table, 4 stooles, 1 Cubboard, & 1 Bedstead	0 -15- 0
It[em] One Chest & 1 Cage 5^s, one Bakestone, & Brandier 1^s	0 - 6 - 0
It[em] one Iron Pot, pot Hook, shovel & Tongs	0 - 2 - 6
It[em] one fire Grate 1^s, Lumber stuffe 1^s	0 - 2 - 0
It[em] Implements of Husbandry	3 - 0 - 0
It[em] standing Wheat	8 - 0 - 0
It[em] standing Oats £2, Pease standing 10^s	2 -10 - 0
It[em] one small Pig	0 - 6 - 0
	Tot[al] 48-13- 6

Sign'd by us Thomas Sweet sign[um] James A [his mark] John
Exhibited at Llandaff, 21st June, 1733, by William Claxon, brother & administrator.

An acc[oun]t of Jennet John's Debts w[he]n Deceas'd

	£ - s - d
P[ai]d ye Rent Due	11- 5 - 6
P[ai]d Two Labourers for work	0 - 3 - 0

P[ai]d Anne Meirick for attending her w[he]n sick	0 - 8 - 0
P[ai]d Griffith John for mending of shoes	0 - 0 -11
P[ai]d David Penry for corn & mault	0 -10- 0
P[ai]d Thos Sweet for mault & Drink	0 - 5 - 2
P[ai]d Robt Thos of Lanvithin	0 - 13- 8
P[ai]d towards ye Rates	0 - 1 - 0
P[ai]d ye Constable Rate	0 - 0 - 7½
P[ai]d ye Taylors	0 - 3 - 6
P[ai]d James John for work	0 - 1 - 0
P[ai]d ye Window Tax	0 - 1 - 0
P[ai]d Joseph Gabriel for work	0 - 2 - 1
P[ai]d for spinning of flanen 1s 6d also Weaving 2s	0 - 3 - 6
P[ai]d for Candles	0 - 0 - 9
P[ai]d Mary Meirick	0 - 1 - 6
P[ai]d ye funeral Expences	3 - 0 - 0
Tot[al]	17- 8 - 4½

Administration Bond: Jennet John: 21st June, 1733

In the Consistory Court of Llandaff, 21st June, 1733. administration of the goods etc. of Jennet John, deceased, was granted to her brother, William Claxon of Llancarvan, yeoman, 'to the use & during the minority of Mary John, Jennet John, William John and David John, the naturall & lawfull children of the deceased.' William Claxon and Rees Powell of Llantwit Major, gentleman, were sworn by the Court in the sum of £100 for William Claxon to make and exhibit a true inventory of the goods etc. of his late sister at or before the 21st September next, to administer according to law, and to make a true account of his administration at or before the 21st June, 1734. Both boundens signed the administration bond.

[National Library of Wales Reference Number LL/1733/ 57]

****

Appendix 3

Information from the Inventories relating to the seven major categories of wealth – Apparel [App], Household Goods (Hse), Farm Crops/Livestock/Equipment [L/C], Trade Goods [trade]; Debt [debt]; and Ready Money & Leases [RM/Leases] – converted into money terms and as a percentage of total wealth, and recorded in tabular form, and in the order the documents appear in the test.

Name	App	Hse	L/C	trade	debt	RM/Leases
Village Shopkeepers						
D.Lewis/St. Athan	30/-	£6		£31		
1642/£37	4%	16%		83%		
T.Mawrice/Bonvilston	30/-	£6-10-8	£9-2-0	£5	5-5-0	
1673/£27-5-8	7%	23%	33%	18%	19%	
W.Hart/StAndrews	£2	£25-6-8	£28-4-0	£83-6-1¼	£79-12-7	
1696/£220-01-04½	1%	11%	13%	38%	37%	
J.Lewis/Llanblethain	£1			£8-7-10	£11-17-9	
1696/£22-4-7	4.5%			38%	57%	
M.Richards/Merthyr Dyfan	£3	£6-15-0		£15		
1708/£24.15.0	12%	28%		60%		
J.Leckey/Llantwit	£1	£16	30/-	£74.18.11	£95.19.8	
1708/£202-13-07	½%	8%	0.75%	37%	48%	
J.Thomas/Laleston	£2	£10.8.11	£2	£139.10.4½	£32.2.11	£10RM
1710/£193-02-02½	1%	5%	1%	70%	16%	5%
Pedlars						
R.Lewis/Llandaff	£1	£4-14-2	£2-16-8	£5		£0-4-9
1684/£15-1-10	7%	31%	19%	33%		7%
D.Griffiths/Colwinston	10/-	£1-6-8	£3	£13	£0-5-4	
1686/£18-3-0	3%	7%	16%	67%	1%	
General/Provision Stores in Towns						
E.Lambert/Cardiff	£10			£40		
1685/£50-00-00	20%			80%		
H.Hammonds/Cardiff	£4	c.£45?	£6	£101-19-8	£240.2.4	30/-RM ¼%
1700/£578-14-03	<1%	c.8%	1%	17.5%	41%	£180L 31%
T.Edward/Cardiff	£1	£10.8.3	£3.10.0	£23.16.0	£5	£1 RM
1704/£48-03-06	2%	20%	7%	50%	10%	2%
A.Wells/Cardiff	£2	£32-0-6		£17-16-0		
1705/£49-06-06	4%	65%		30%		
W.Hedges/Cardiff	£1	£10-17-6		£3		£50 RM
1708/£64-17-06	1½	17%		5%		76%

Appendix 3

Name	App	Hse	L/C	trade	debt	RM/Leases
R.John//Cowbridge	£1	£17.10.0	£45	£70	£132.10.8	
1717/£286-15-0	<0.5 %	6.5%	15%	24%	46%	
W.Foord/Cardiff	10/-	£8-2-9	2/-	£12-16-5		£1-5-0 RM
1717/£25-4-0	2%	32%		51%		5%
M.Lewis/Cardiff	10/-	£9-18-1	£7-2-0	£15-12-9	£3	
1720/£35-15-10	1.5%	28%	20%	44%	9%	
F.Brewer/Cardiff	30/-	£27.5.8	£23.7.1	£17.3.6	£30	
1740/£102-08-02 ½	1.5 %	27%	23%	17.5%	30%	
T.Young/Cardiff	£4.0.6	£15.14.0		£86.14.2		
1760/£106-08-08	4%	15%		81%		

General/Provision Stores in Towns

J.Howells/Cardiff	..	£12-0-6		£10-6-10		
1851/£22-7-4		54%		46%		

Hardware Trades: Shopkeepers

T.Richard/Cowbridge	£1	£3-10-0	£10	£4		
1699/£18	5.5%	19%	55%	22%		
K.Bassett/Cowbridge	£1	£16.5.0		£27.5.5	£134.2.8	
1707/£174-16-10	<1%	9%		15%	75%	
J.Watkin/Cardiff	..	£4-17-0	£5-4-9			
1763/£10-1-9		46%	54%			

Hardware Trades: Chandler

M.Jenkins/Cardiff	42/-	£17.16.0	£11.16.0	£34	£92.6.1	£48RM
1737/216-09-04	1%	7%	5%	13%	44%	23%

Hardware Trades: Blacksmiths

J.Thomas/Cowbridge	10/-	£3-8-2		£2-10-0		
1685/£6-8-2	8%	53%		38%		
J.P.Harris/Cardiff	30/-	£11.7.0		£63.14.0		£280.12.6
1856/£361-03-06	1%	4%		18%		77% RM

Fabric Trades: Weavers

J. Alexander/Llancarvan	20/-	50/-	4/6	37/-	£32.10.0	
1633/£37.11.6	2.6%	6.6%	0.6%	4.5%	86.6%	
ReesJ.Hopkins/Llanishen	10/-	£2-10-0	£16	£1		
1652/£19	2.5%	13%	84%	5%		
M.Edmund/Whitchurch	£1	£6-16-0	£21-15	£2	£14	
1689/£46-01-00	2%	15%	47%	4%	30%	
J.Tucker/St.Andrews	15/-	£4-3-4	£14-8-0	25/-	£2-18-0	
1691/£23-10-2	3%	16%	16%	5%	12%	
D.William/Llanblethian	30/-	£5-2-5		£6-10-0		
1702/£13-2-6	11%	40%		49%		

Fabric Trades: Tucker

Jas Richards/Llanblethian	£1	£10-0-6	£6-12-0	£1-16-6		
1724/£19-9-0	5%	51%	34%	9%		

Fabric Trades: Tailor

R. Williams/Llancarvan	50/-	£9.9.0	£10.13.4		£56.7.0	
165/£78-19-04	3%	12%	13%		72%	

Fabric Trades: Mercers

H.Hoare 1684	£5	£42-15-0		£57-15-0	£10	£5
1684/£122-10-0	4%	35%		47.5%	8%	4%

Name	App	Hse	L/C	trade	debt	RM/Leases
L.Sheares/Cardiff	£7	£63-17-2		£515-13-9	£300	£31RM 3.5%
1687/£926-16-09	<1%	7%		56%	32%	£20L 2%
W.Richard/Cardiff	£5	£99-09-0	£5-10-0	£450-8-6	£800	
1694/£1360-0-0	<0.5%	7.5%	<0.5%	33%	59%	
J.Hoar/Cardiff	£2	£37-16-0		£171-13-1	£15	£66RM
1708/£298-08-11	<1%	12%		57%	5%	22%
W.Hiley/Cardiff	£4	£50.15.11		£82.1.5		£2.10.5RM
1723/£136-9-6	3%	36%		60%		2%
F.Hiley/Cardiff	£2	£42.11.6		£64.7.7	£22B	
1724/£133-14-05	1.5%	32%		49%	17%	
J.Stidder/Cowbridge	£2	£31-7-4	£33-10-0	£425-17-6	£238-13	£80RM 10%
1737/£826-12-04	0.25%	4%	4%	51%	28%	£73 L 9%

Fabric Trades: Mercers

Name	App	Hse	L/C	trade	debt	RM/Leases
J.Vallence/Cowbridge	..	£72-18-10	£46-5-0	£860-13-11	£479	£188.17.6RM
1750/£1584-13-11 ½		5%	3%	54%	30%	12%

Fabric Trades: Feltmakers

Name	App	Hse	L/C	trade	debt	RM/Leases
G.Evans/Cardiff	£1	£5-15-0	5/-	£4		
1683/£11	9%	52%	2%	36%		
E.Sweete/Cardiff	£7	£45.10.0	90/-	£50.8.4		£14 RM
1686/£121-08-04	6%	37%	4%	41%		11%
W.Lewis/Cardiff	50/-	£11.11.7	1.5.0	£14.5.11½	£229	
1731/£255-09-02 ½	1%	5%	0.5%	6%	90%	

Fabric Trades: Hosiery: Stocking Knitters

Name	App	Hse	L/C	trade	debt	RM/Leases
Ann Howell/Peterston	£1	£2-5-0		£0-2-0	£9-15-0	
1715/£13-2-6	7%	19%		<1%	74%	
Mary Miles/Bonvilston	7/-	£2		£-0-6-0		
1725/£2-13-0	14%	75%		11%		

Fabric Trades: Hosiery: Shopkeepers

Name	App	Hse	L/C	trade	debt	RM/Leases
M.Evans/Cardiff	£2	£5-15-6		£9-18-0		
1665/£17-13-0	12%	30%		60%		
J.Hipwell/Cardiff	£4-6-0	£16-1-6		£65-2-0		
1856/£85-5-0	5%	18%		77%		

Fabric Trades: Hosiery: Wholesalers

Name	App	Hse	L/C	trade	debt	RM/Leases
J.Jenkins/Cardiff	£7	£20.14.0	£11	£100	£217.10.0	£120RM
1684/£478-4-0	1.5%	4.5%	2.5%	21%	45%	25%
T.Jones/Cardiff	£10	£120-10-0	£195-3-0	£150		£50L
1686/£526-3-0	2%	23%	37%	29%		10%

Leather Trades: Tanners

Name	App	Hse	L/C	trade	debt	RM/Leases
W.David/Cowbridge	£2	£4-9-6		£2-10-0	£1	
1690/£28-0-2	7%	16%		74%	3%	
Cradock Nowell/C'diff	..	£140-10-0	£20	£320	£150	£280 L
1709/£910-10-0		15%	2%	35%	16%	31%
T.Holiday/Cardiff	25/-	£2-17-0	£1-15-2	£0-2-0	£1-10-0	
1729/£7-5-0	175	40%	24%	1.5%	21%	

Leather Trades: Boot & Shoe Makers [Cordwainers/Corvisors]

Name	App	Hse	L/C	trade	debt	RM/Leases
H.Spencer/Llandaff	£2	£16-14-8	8/-	£12		
1643/£30-7-8	6%	57%	1%	36%		
E.Matthew/Cowbridge	£5	£8-3-4	£37.10	£6-10-0		
1667/£62-13-04	8%	13%	58%	10%		

Appendix 3

Name	App	Hse	L/C	trade	debt	RM/Leases
R.Thomas/ Kenfig	8/8	£0-13-4		£6-9-10	£2-10-0	
1684/£10-19-3	3.5%	6%		62%	23%	
W.Rees/Pile & Kenfig	10/-	£1-10-0	£4-5-0	£1-18-09		
1690/£8-3-6	6%	18%	53%	235		
J.Griffiths/St.Andrews	15/-	£1-5-6	£2	2/-		
1731/£4-2-6	18%	30%	47%	2.5%		
Leather Trades: Sadlers						
D.Griffiths/Colwinston	£1	£1	£11-3-6	£5-13-9		
1719/£18-17-3	5%	5%	59%	30%		
T.Glascot/Cardiff	10/-	£10-5-1	a sow	£6-3-6	£2-10-0	
1732/£19-8-7	2.5%	52%		31%	11%	
Leather Trades: Sadlers						
N.Young/Cowbridge	..	£28-2-0		£81-5-4	£339	£250
1842/£698/16-05		4%		12%	48%	36%
Fabric Trades: Glovers						
S.William/Cowbridge	£3	£13-16-8	£1-13-4	£52-17-11		
1668/£71-01-11	4%	19%	2.5%	74%		
L.Gronow/Cowbridge	£3	£10-10-0	£19	£27/7/1		
1671/£69-00-00	4½	15%	28%	40/10/1½		
J. Morgan/Llantwit	£1	£6.16.8	£4.19.4	£4.13.4		
1681/£17-9-4	5.7%	39%	28.5%	26.5%		
A.Yeomans/Cardiff	£10	£61.10.0		£20		
1686/£100-10-0? 91.10.0	11%	66%		22%		
R.Llewellin/St.Andrews	6/8	16/8	18/8	5/-		
1699/£2-7-0	14%	36%	40%	11%		
A.Yeomans/Cardiff	£3	£60.7.9		£107.18.11	£63.5.4	
1719/£234-04-00	1.5%	26%		46%	27%	
Wood Trades: Carpenters						
T.Smyth/Cardiff	..	30/-&36/-		£6-19-6		
1694/£9-15-6		16%&18%		68%		
T.Powel/Cardiff	£1	£19-17-10	12/-	30/-		
1732/£22-9-10	1.5%	88%	3%	7%		
E.Evans/Cardiff	21/-	£16-6-8		£51-12-0	£2	
1751/£71-14-08	1.5%	23%		70%	3%	
T.David/Llandaff/Ely	£8	£20	£31.14.0	£35	29.0.7	£295-0-7RM
1850/£429-16-00	2%	5%	7.5%	8.5%	7%	67%
J.John/Dinas Powys	£1	£19-17-0	£18	£26-1-0		
1857/£65	1.5%	30%	28%	40%		
Wood Trades: Cooper						
J.Hammans/Cardiff	£2	£28-6-4	£3-3-0	£2-10-0		
1684/£38-12-2	5%	79%	8%	6%		
Wood Trades: Sawyer						
W.Owen/Llandaff	£1	£9-10-0		£9-15-0	£67-19-0	
1712/£89-11-00	1%	11%		11%	75%	
Wood Trades: Ship Builder						
T.Jenkins/Cardiff	..	£27-5-7		£48-8-9		
1846/£75-14-04		37%		65%		

255

Name	App	Hse	L/C	trade	debt	RM/Leases
Wood Trades etc.: Builder						
E.Jones/Cardiff	..	£17-19-6		£710		
1854/£729-19-06		2.5%		97%		
Farmers with Other Commercial Interests						
R.John/St.George-S-Ely	£1	£11	£53-7-6	£10	£17-19-8	
1674/£93-12-02	1%	11%	56%	10%	18%	
W.Freame/Cowbridge	£5	£47.15.0	£34	£12		£40L
1696/£151-15-0	3%	32%	22%	8%		26%
R.Bawdrey/Cardiff	£5	£25-19-0	£126.8.0	£90-10-0	£239-19-2	£4RM <1%
1705/£693-09-07 ½	<1%	4%	18%	13%	34%	£150L 21%
E.Rees/Llandaff/Ely	£1	£4.16.6	£69.4.6	£14		£20L
1720/£109-01-0	1%	4.5%	64%	13%		19%
Farmers with Other Commercial Interests						
T.Gronow/St.Andrews	£2	£5	£75.19.10	£40	£2	£65L
1721/£182-9-10	1%	3%	42%	22%	1%	36%
M.Howell/Whitchurch	£2	12/-	£28-7-6	£6		
1722/£36-19-6	5%	1.6%	77%	16%		
E.Wattkins/Llanishen	£1	£18-2-2	£45-2-8	£8-18-0	£1-4-0	
1729/76-19-10	1.3%	24%	65%	9%	2%	
W. Lee/Cadoxton	£5	£25.5.6	£36.1.0	£9.13.6	£33.7.0	£64L
1779/£173-07-06	3%	5%	21%	5.5%	19%	37%
Gardener						
W.Jones/Cardiff	30/-	£7-17-11		£26-2-9		
1753/£35-10-8	4%	22%		73%		
Salters						
J.Wollrin/Cardiff	£30	£256-3-0	£368	£364	£150	
1673/£1117-03-0	3%	23%	32%	32%	13%	
J.Stanmore/Cardiff	£5	£72		£105	£60	£50RM 15%
1682. £325-10-00	1.5%	22%		35%	19%	£32L 10%
R.Davies/Cardiff	50/-	£1-16-0		£11-9-0		
1686/£16-15-0	15%	12%		69%		
M.Murton/Cardiff	£1	£7-15-0	£1	£5		
1699/£14-15-0	7%	53%	7%	35%		
Gentlemen with Commercial Interests						
H.Hill/St.Athan	£50	£75	£49	£100	£500	£180RM 15%
1666/£1135-0-0	5%	7%	5%	9%	44%	£180L 15%
R.Lewis/Llandaff	£1-6-8	£2-4-6		£5-16-3		
1684/£9-7-5	14%	23%		61%		
Gentleman/Parson with a Book-binder's Press						
R.Jenkins/Llanishen	£6	£1-5-0		£0-2-6	£15-5-4	
1698/£25-12-10	26%	5%		0.5%	64%	
Mariners						
T.Spencer/Penmark	£3	£74.16.6	£133.0.6	£110.6.0	£93.17.6	
1681/£381-17-00	1%	20%	35%	29%	24%	
J.Brewer/Cardiff	£1	£18.15.0		£80	£1	£60L
1685/£161-02-10	<1%	11%		50%	<1%	37%
R.David/Cardiff	£2	£5.5.0		£103.10.0		
1693/£110-15-0	2%	5%		93%		

Appendix 3

Name	App	Hse	L/C	trade	debt	RM/Leases
N.Stidman/Cardiff	£2	£7.18.0		£40	£8	
1695/£58-00-00	4%	4%		68%	14%	
J.Greenfield/Cardiff	£10	£50.12.0	£5-5-0		£4412	£3RM
1736/£4525	0.2%	1%	0.1%		98.7%	<0.1%
R.Priest/Cardiff	£8	£75.4.7		£190	£277	£50RM
1742/£610-05-07	1%	12%		31%	45%	8%
J.Williams/Cardiff	£5	£12.14.6		£15	owes	£48.6.0RM
1847/£170-14-06	5%	13%		15%	£70+	Cotts.£90
Innkeepers						
R.Sheares/Cardiff	£20	£14.16.8	£71	£289.12.0	£35	To sea £8
1662/£479-01-08	4%		16%	59%	7%	<2%
R.Hawkins/Cardiff	£11		£15-10-0	£65-3-4	£703	£16L
1673/£196-08-04	5%		7%	53%	35%	8%
Innkeepers						
W.James/Llandaff	£3	£49.10.0	£118.5.0	£37.13.0	£56.5.3	
1685/£265-03-03	1%	18%	45%	14%	21%	
W.Robotham/Cardiff	£5		£4	£125		
1686/£129-10-0	4%		3%	95%		
R.Hodds/Llandaff	£3	£20.18.8	£4.12.0	£56.13.6	£189.10.0	
1687/£287-07-00	1%	7%	2%	20%	66%	
K.Hammond/Cowbridge	£3	£80-15-7		£124.16.11	£366	£236.7.6RM
1720/£883-17-10 ½	0.3%	9%		14%	41%	26%
H.Williams/Cardiff	£3	£31.2.0		£36.14.2	£328+	£41+RM 9%
1735/£482-05-10	<1%	5%		7%	68%	£37L 7%
C.Powell/Cardiff	£6	£4-17-0		£78-18-6		£5 L
1839/£95-16-08	6%	5%		80%		5%
J.Morgan/Cardiff	£2		£37.17.0	£40		
1845/£80-05-10	2.5%		47%	50%		
J.Nisbett/Cardiff	50/-	£33-16-8		£43-19-8	£183-16-9	
1846/£82-16-4	3%	40%		53%	[he owes]	

Appendix 1: J. Harries, Mercer of Usk, Monmouthshire

J.Harries/Usk	—	£44.6.2		£209.4.1¼	£189-17.9	
1692/£446-07-00 ½		10%		47%	42.5%	

Appendix 2: Jennet John, widow, Llancarvan

J.John/Llancarvan	3-10-0	£3-16-6	£41-4-0		£17-8-4½	
1733/£48-13-6	7%	8%	85%		she owed	

Appendix 4

A Chart Linking Value of Clothes to Overall Value of Estate for 101 Persons Named in the Documents

In the inventories in this book, a value for clothing is given for 101 individuals. These valuations have been placed in 13 'clothing-value-bands,' the lowest being a '0-£1,' band, and the highest a '£50' band. The 'clothing-value-bands' appear in the table under the heading 'Value of Clothes in £.' The 101 persons have also been placed in 11 'Estate Value Groupings,' based, obviously, on the total value of each testator's estate. The lowest grouping includes all those with total estate valued between '0 and £10,' and the highest the single individual with estate valued at over £2,000. As can be seen from the table, for those persons with clothing valued at £1 or less, 5 had total estate of £10 or less; 12 had estate valued at between £10+ and £20; 6 had estate of between £20+ and £40; 7 had estate of between £40+ and £100; 3 had estate valued at between £100+ and £200; and 2 had total estate of between £200+ and £300. Obviously, different value-groupings for both clothes and total estate could have been selected. The groupings are merely an aid to comparison. In chart form, the groupings highlight features of the information that might otherwise be less clear.

Value of Clothes in £	0-£10	£10+ -£20	£20+ -£40	£40+ £100	£100+ £200	£200+ £300	£300+ £500	£500+ £700	£700+ £1000	£1000+ £2000	£2000+
0-£1	5	12	6	7	3	2					
£1+-£2	2	2	7	4	5	2	1		1		
£2+-£3		1	1	4		5	2		1		
£3+-£4					1			1			
£4+-£5				2	6		1	1		1	
£5+-£6			1	1							
£6+-£7					1		1		1		
£7+-£8							1	1			
£8+-£9											
£9+-£10				1	1			1			1
£10+-£11						1					
£20							1				
£30										1	
£50										1	

Appendix 4

A Chart Linking Value of Household Goods to Overall Value of Estate for 101 Persons Named in the Documents

In this chart the Estate Value Groupings are as in the previous chart. The groupings recorded under 'Value of Hse'ld Goods,' reflect the larger amounts of wealth 'locked up' in household goods rather than clothing.

	\multicolumn{10}{c}{Estate Value Groupings}
Value of H'se'ld Goods	0 £10	£10+ -£20	£20+ -£40	£40+ £100	£100+ £200	£200+ £300	£300+ £500	£500+ £700	£700 £1000	£1000+ £2000	£2000+
£0-£5	9	8	5	2	2						
£5+ -£10		4	6	5	1						
£10+ -£15		2	1	5	2	1	2				
£15+ -£20			2	3	3	3			1		
£20+ -£30			1	1	2	2	2	2			
£30+ -£40				2		1	1		1		
£40+ - £50				4	1		1				
£50+ -£60				1							1
£60+ -£70				1	1			1			
£70+ - £80						2	1		2		
£80+ -£90								1			
£120.10.0							1				
£140.10.0								1			
£204.18.0									1		

****

259

A Chart Recording the Relationship Between Debt and the Wealth of 108 Persons Placed in Eleven Wealth or 'Estate Value Groupings'

Estate Value Groupings	Number Indivs. in Group	Number Owed Money	Total Value of Estate of all Indivs.	Amount Owed In £	Amount Owed as %	Total Value of Trading Goods [*1]
0-£10	8	1	£50.2.1	£1.10.0	3%	£26.17.5
£10-£20	15	5	£252.7.6	£19.0.4	7.5%	£141.17.2
£20-£40	16	7	£468.1.11	£71.16.1	15.3%	£213.0.1
£40-£100	20	8	£1414.18.11	£172.9.8	12.2%	£824.3.8
£100-£200	18	10	£2576.12.3	£288.12.7 – £348.12.7[*2]	11.2% - 13.5%	£1240.15.0
£200-£300	9	9	£2244.11.8	£953.10.4	42.5%	£860.18.6
£300-£500	7	6	£2937.8.0	£763.10.11½	26%	£999.0.8
£500-£700	5	4	£3107.8.10½	£1096.13.0½	35.3%	£941.6.0
£700-£1000	5	4	£4307.16.5½	£1054.13.0	24.5%	£2149.18.2
£1000-£2000	4	4	£5196.14.1½	£2029.9.1	39%	£2243.17.5
£2000+	1	1	£4525.0.0	£4412.0.0	97.5%	£5.5.0

[*1] Shop/Trade Goods Owned + Any Farm Goods Owned
[*2] One Person had 'ready money and debts due' valued at £60. So Exact Total not possible.

****

A Chart Recording Estate Value, Debt in £-s-d, Debt as a Percentage of Estate Value, and the amounts of Sperate or Desperate for Eight of the Nine Persons in the £200-£300 'Estate Value Group

Name/Parish/Occupation of 8 Individuals in £200-£300 Estate Value Group

	W.James Llandaff Innk'per/ maltster	R.Hodds Llandaff Innk'per	W.Hart St.And'ws Shopk'r	J.Hoar Cardiff Shopk'r	J.Leckey Llantwit M. Shopk'r	A.Yeomans Cardiff Shopk'per	W.Lewis Cardiff Feltm'kr	M.Jenkins Cardif Chandler
Est. Value	£265-3-3	£287-7-0	£220-1-4½	£298-9-11	£202-13-7	£234-4-0	£255-9-2½	£216-9-4
Debt Owed In £ & in £ & as % of Estate	£56-5-3 21%	£189-10-0 66%	£79-12-7 37%	£15 5%	£95-19-8 48%	£63-5-4 27%	£229 90%	£92-6-10 44%
Sperate	?	nil	£40-5-0	?	?	£45-8-2	?	£73-6-10
Desperate	?	£189-10-0	£39-7-7	?	?	£17-7-2	?	£19

Glossary

Source: *The Oxford English Dictionary*

allom/alum   mineral salt used in dyeing, tawing skins & medicine
andiers; andirons; andiarns   a pair of metallic supports for wood or cooking pots in an open fireplace
appurtenances   an accessory; a right belonging to a property
arras   a fabric usually woven with coloured, figured scenes; especially a hanging of such material for the wall of a room; tapestry
auger   a large, generally T-handled tool usually for boring wood
bandileers   a broad band usually of leather worn over the shoulder & passing under the arm with loops for holding ammunition
bazil   sheepskins tanned in bark; distinguished from roan, which is tanned in sumach; an inferior leather that tears like paper;
bellmetal   alloy of copper and tin – containing more tin than in bronze
bengall   piece goods exported from Bengal to England in the 17th C.
bitle   obsolete form of beetle
bolster   a double-length pillow
bows   unshaped wooden piece passing upwards through a yoke & retained by pins; ox-bow
brandiron; brandierns   a brand iron
brimstone   the former common name for sulphur
broaches   a metallic tool with file-teeth for dressing/enlarging holes; a narrow pointed chisel for dressing stone; a boring tool for sampling casks; a spit
buckthorn/'syrop of buckthorn'   shrub, the berries of which yield sap-green & other pigments; formerly used as a powerful cathartic
buffet   low stool; a footstool; a side-board or side-table
bulk-harpes   [see Rice Lewis: 1684: – '3 new bulk harpes [value] 15/-']; bulk – to pile in heaps, as fish for salting; the pile in which fish are laid for salting; harp – a sieve or screen used in sifting; [read inventory to aid possible interpretation of these definitions]
bushels   a measure of capacity used for corn, containing 4 pecks or 8 gallons; a great variety of local values, e.g. Welsh Bushel, Winchester bushel; frequently, no longer a measure but a weight in pounds (lbs) of flour or grain – 30, 40, 45, 50, 56, 70, 75, 80, 90, 93, or 220 lbs. depending on locality
burdett   a cotton fabric
butt   [and wheels] a farm cart
buttry/buttrie   place where bread, ale, butter etc. were kept
cadis   a coarse serge-like fabric; a narrow ribbon-like/tape-like worsted fabric for bindings, garters, etc.; worsted yarn, erewel; lint, floss, cotton wool used for wadding

callimancoe a woollen stuff of Flanders, glossy on the surface and woven with a satin twill & chequered in the warp so that the checks are seen on the one side only - much used in 18th C.

camlet a fine closely-woven, nearly waterproof fabric, made of mixed wool and silk, once much used for cloaks

cantaloon a woollen stuff manufactured in the West of England in the 18th C.; [in Defore's 'Tour of England:' 'western goods: shalloons, cantaloons, Devonshire kersies etc;' 'in Bristol and many towns on that side; druggets, cantaloons & other stuffs']

cantharides Spanish fly: Cantharis vesicatoria: a bettle found in the Mediterranean & S. Russia, dried and applied externally in quantity as a blister, or intenally, as an irritant, diuretic or aphrodisiac

cardes instrument with iron teeth, used in pairs, to part, comb out, and set in order the fibres of wool, hemp etc., one of the cards being held in the hand, and the other fixed to a 'stock' or support

carpet fabric cover for a table or other furniture

carsey; see kersey

casters a cruet for condiments such as a pepper-caster; also, a stand for holding cruets; any vessel/bottle for dispersing powders, perfumes, liquids

chafara dish; chaffron dish, chaffing dish a vessel to hold burning charcoal or other fuel, for heating anything placed on it; a portable oven

chattle any article of personal property – money, capital, livestock, a bond, bill, or promissory note, a leasehold estate; every kind of property which is not freehold;

chattel lease a lease held for a specific number of years

cheeks & bars metal pieces making up a grate

cheyney fabric of worsted or woollen stuff in which different arrangements of colours are given to the threads of the warp in order to produce a pattern

civet [boxes] a yellowish or brownish unctuous substance having a strong musky smell, obtained from sacs or glands in the anal pouch of several animals of the civet genus; used in perfumery

close stool a commode

cogloft related to: 'to connect timbers by means of a cog'

copperas a green crystalline astringent (ferrous sulphate) used for dyeing;

cords bed-cords; ropes stretched across the frame of a bed to provide a platform on which the bed clothes and bed user lay

citterne (cithern) a lute-like musical instrument with wire strings

coffer box for valuables

coffin a pie dish or mould

cordwainer, corviser, cordiner cordviner a shoemaker; a worker in cordovan leather

costrel a large bottle with an ear or ears by which it could be suspended from the waist; a small wooden keg; a vessel for holding or carrying wine

crane an iron arm swinging horizontally attached to the back or side of a fireplace used for suspending pots or kettles over a fire

crewels a thin worsted yarn of two threads used for tapestry & embroidery, or for making fringes, laces, vestments & hosiery; the balls or bobbins on which yarn is wound up for use;

crowpers [see D. Griffiths: 1719: saddler] obsolete form of crupper; a leather strap buckled to the back of a saddle & passing under the horse's tail, to prevent the saddle from slipping forward

cubb [see H.Hammonds: 'one cubb & stilling [value] 12/-'] a tall, pen or shed for cattle; a coop or hutch; a chest/ bin, or other reseptacle

cypres hood cypress – a light transparent material resembling cobwebs, made of lawn or crape and when black much used in mourning; cypress hood – a piece of cypress used as a kerchief for the neck or head, or as a band for a hat – in sign of mourning

desperate debts non-recoverable debts

diaper a fine figured linen cloth woven with ornamental devices – scroll work, lattice work, leaf or flower designs

dicker ten hides or skins

dimity a stout cotton fabric with raised stripes, crimps, ridges etc. used for covering furniture, sometimes printed in colours

docks a piece of leather harness covering the clipped tail of a horse

dornix; dornick; cloths manufactured at the Flemish town of Doornick, Flanders, especially damask-linen, hangings & carpet; linsey-woolsey;

dowlas a strong unbleached linen cloth said to have been first made at Doullens, France; in 18th C. mainly manufactured in S. Scotland and Yorkshire

druggett a coarse woollen felted or woven fabric often printed on one side & used usually for rugs and table covers

dutty from dhoti – a loin-cloth; so presumably, material of this kind

ferritt/ferrett narrow worsted or cotton ribbon for binding; earlier, ribbon made of silk

fflitch/flicke the side of an animal salted and cured

fowling piece a light smooth bore shotgun for bird shooting

frise obsolete form of frieze; to cover with a nap – on cotton or leather

fustian a stout cloth made of cotton and flax

fustick the wood of a S.American or West Indian tree used as a yellow dye

galloome a closely woven worsted lace used for binding

gauls oak gauls used in the manufacture of ink & tannins; used in dyeing and medicine

gobbards [a pair of] a spit

gridiron a small platform with short supporting 'feet' and a long handle, upon which meat was cooked over a fire

gunne a pot

hampiers containers for carrying articles – on pack animals

heampe (see 'his steele heampe' R. Thomas: cordwainer: 1684; also Thos. Richards, 1699; 'his shop wares being leather nailes & hemp [valued at] £10'

hogshead a large cask or barrel esp. one containing from 100 to 140 gallons; a large measure of liquid esp. one of 63 wine gallons (52½ imperial gallons); [a London hogshead of beer measured 54 gallons; a London hogshead of ale was 48 gallons; elsewhere in England a hogshead was 51 gallons; see too 'oxetts'

holland   a fine linen (originally manufactured in Holland)
inckle   linen tape
indigo   [see J. Thomas: shopkeeper: 1710 – 'a small quantity of indigo & gauls, verdigrass & white copperas, senna, salt peter, a little madarn & fustick att 4/6']; a blue plant extract used in dyeing
jack   a jug or tankard; a contrivance for turning a spit
kenting/kentins   a type of fine linen cloth
kersey   a kind of woollen cloth, usually coarse and ribbed, woven from wool of long staple (probably originating in the town of Kersy in Suffolk) used esp. for hose
kilderkin   a small barrel, ½ or a ¼ the size of a common barrel; a measure of 18 gallons, or two firkins
kipes   [see H.William: innkeeper/maltster: 1735: – 'a small hand mill & 2 kipes']; a basket used as a measure; osier basket used for catching fish
lees   [see R. Hodds: innkeeper: 1686: – 'a remnant of lees']; the dregs (of wine)
linsey-woolsey   coarse cloth made of linen and wool or cotton and wool; neither one thing or the other
livery cupboard   a bread and cheese cupboard
logwood   the heartwood of a Central American tree, very hard, and of a brown or reddish brown colour used in dyeing wool, silk, cotton, leather, esp. for the production of blacks; [see J. Thomas: shopkeeper: 1710]
lymbick   [see A. Wells: 1708: – 'one small boyler & a lymbick & pott & iron marmett [value] 15/6'
oxetts   see hogsheads
lyncie   see linsey perhaps
Manchester ware   Manchester became the centre for cotton manufacture & an emporium for all kinds of textile fabric; hence, Manchester ware   [see J. Thomas: shopkeeper: 1710 – 'old decay'd remnants of Manchester ware as buttons, thred, moehaire inkle, tape etc.[valued at] 10/-;'
mannes   flasks [see J. Thomas: shopkeeper: 1710 – '5 mannes or flasks att 5d]
marlin   marlin twine
mashing tub   in brewing; tub in which mault is mixed with warm water to form wort
mault   grain, especially barley, softened by steeping in water & allowed to sprout (green mault), then dried in a kiln; the sprouting develops the enzyme diastase which is capable of saccharifying the starch of the mault and of raw grain mixed with it, hence the importance of mault in brewing and distilling
mockadge   an imitation or counterfeit
mushing   fabric or garment stamped with nicks & notches for ornament
nankeen   kind of cotton cloth (originally made at Nanking from a yellow variety of cotton) later manufactured extensively from ordinary cotton & dyed
neaters   'one smoothing iron & neaters' 2/6 [J. Thomas: Laleston: 1710] not found in O.E.D.
noggin   a small mug or cup
padd   a cushion used as a saddle without a tree or frame
paddisway   a kind of silk; obsolete form of 'paduasoy'

pennystone   a flat stone used as a quoit; a game of quoits
plush   a textile fabric with a nap or shag on one side, longer and softer than velvet, made of silk, cotton or wool etc, or a combination of these; plush breeches – such as worn by footmen
poise   a measure or standard weight of wool
posnett   a small metal pot or vessel for boiling, having a handle and three feet
porringer   small basin
pottox   [see J. Brewer: mariner: 1685: – 'tormentors & a pottox' [in iron goods]
powatum   [see W. Hiley: mercer: 1723 'one glass of powatum & the glass']
press bed   a bed built into a recess that may be folded or turned up so as to resemble a press or closet
press (cupboard)   large cupboard for keeping clothes and linen
quartans   the fourth part of some other measure
reding   'redding twine' – twine coloured with red ochre
relict   widow
renlet; runlet   a cask of varying capacity [large: 12/18 gallons; small: 3/4 gallons; even 1 pint/1 quart]; the quantity of liquor contained therein
sackcloth   coarse textile fabric used for making sacks etc.
sacke   in 17th C, any of various white wines imported from the south
saddle trees   wooden framework forming the foundation of a saddle
saltery   salt works
sanders/sanders   sandalwood
sarsenet/sarsinett   a thin silk fabric used for linings etc.
sconce/skonce   in a candlestick, the circular socket in which the candle is inserted, esp. when having a brim
screntore; screentore   a screen
shagg   coarse, rough wool hair
shaggreens   untanned leather prepared from the skin of horses etc. and covered with small round granulations made by pressing seeds into the grain or hair side of the skin when moist, and when dry scraping off the roughness; soaking causes the compressed or indented portions to swell up into relief; dyed very bright colours esp. green
shalloon   a thin, loosely-woven, twilled worsted stuff (first made at Chalons, France)
shams   a removable ornamental covering esp. which gives a finish to any article or makes it imitate something
skillet   a metal vessel with a handle used for culinary purposes; a metal kettle or pot with three or four legs
slice/slich   a fire iron with a broad flat end for stirring a fire or cleaning out ashes
slip   young pigs
snuffers   instrument for cropping & holding the snuff (the charred part) of a candle wick
snaffles   a simple bridle
sperate debts   hopeful debts
spinet   a stringed musical instrument resembling a harpsichord, but smaller, sounded by means of leather or quill plectons

spitt a slender, pointed rod, usually of iron, for holding meat whilst being roasted on a fire

standard a large drinking cup or goblet; a standing cup

standish a stand or case for writing materials

steanes a vessel of clay or stone

steeling/stilling [see H. Hammonds: shopkeeper: 1700: 'one stilling & 2 half barrels [value] 3/6;' also, H. Williams: innkeeper: 1735: '2 stillings & a costrel'] a stand for a cask

stomacher an ornamental covering for the front of the upper body, formerly worn by both men and women

stuffe basic fabric of any kind

tabby a thick, strong kind of taffeta silk

taffaty term applied to various kinds of silk or linen goods from 16th century onwards; a fine, smooth silk fabric of even texture and having a lustre

tamarind/tamarine a tropical tree having hard, yellowish wood; with leaves and flowers, used as mordants in dyeing; seeds used to make a cooling, laxative drink

tammy woollen, or woollen/cotton cloth, often highly glazed, used for the making of curtains, sieves and strainers

tearse obsolete form of tierce; one third part; old measure of capacity – $\frac{1}{3}$ of a pipe; 42 gallons old wine measure; a cask holding this quantity of wine

teek leaves of East Indian tree yielding a red dye

tent [see R. Hodds: innkeeper: 1686: – 'a remnant of tent'

tester a canopy over a bed supported by the bedposts

thrum finished with fringes/thrums

tick/ticke/ticking/ticken the cover or case for a bed or mattress containing the filling

tormentors a long iron meat fork; a farm machine resembling a harrow but running on wheels for breaking down soil;

treen wooden

trencher a wooden plate or platter on which to carve or serve food

tresses the pair of ropes or chains (later leather) by which a draught animal is connected to a splinter-bar or swingletree

truckle bed a low bed on wheels that could be pushed under another bed

trendle a large oval shallow tub used for a variety of purposes – for butter, milk, whey; for cooling beer, mixing dough, curing bacon; the tub in which pig is scalded

trumpery worthless finery; trifles

tundish wooden shallow vessel with tube at bottom fitting into the bung-hole of a cask or tun; a kind of funnel used in brewing

tunn a cask

tunnel nets a moveable net in which ducks are caught at the end of a decoy pipe

vallions, valence short curtain hanging around the frame or canopy of a bedstead

verdigrass a green or greenish blue poisonous pigment used in dyeing

victualler   an innkeeper
virginals   (a pair of) a square legless spinet – 16th/17th C.
waine   a large, open, four wheeled farm wagon
wainscotte   a fine grade of oak imported for woodwork; oaken board; a wooden, panelled lining for an interior wall
witch   a small chest or coffer; a cone of paper placed in lard & other fat used as a taper